The Healthy Organization

Organizations can no longer afford to waste 'people talent' if they are to remain competitive into the next century. This is the message Susan Newell aims to instil in the reader of *The Healthy Organization*, which explores the issues relating to quality, flexibility and responsibility in organizations.

To be successful, businesses need to promote the positive well-being of individuals, groups and societies. This book introduces some of the most important psychological theories, concepts and methodologies when considering what is meant by a 'healthy' organization. Divided into three parts – the impact of organizations on individual employees, the negative impact on groups which suffer from unfair discrimination within organizations and the impact organizations have on the wider community – the book offers solutions to the dilemmas managers face when they attempt to improve their organization's 'health'. This includes advice on how to promote Equal Opportunities, how to cope with and remove sources of stress, how to improve an organization's ecological image and how to make the workforce feel more valued.

Instructive and introductory, this book will help managers implement a policy of good human relations, whilst at the same time making their company's success more likely.

Susan Newell is Lecturer at Warwick Business School with the Industrial Relations and Organizational Behaviour Group.

ESSENTIAL BUSINESS PSYCHOLOGY
Series editor: Clive Fletcher

This series interprets and examines people's work behaviour from the perspective of occupational psychology. Each title focuses on a central issue in management, emphasizing the role of the individual's workplace experience.

Other books in the series:

Business Leadership
Viv Shackleton

Impression Management in Organizations
Paul Rosenfeld, Robert A. Giacalone and Catherine A. Riordan

Forthcoming:

The Psychology of Personnel Selection
Dominic Cooper and Ivan T. Robertson

The Healthy Organization

Fairness, Ethics and Effective Management

Susan Newell

London and New York

First published 1995
by Routledge
11 New Fetter Lane, London EC4P 4EE

Simultaneously published in the USA and Canada
by Routledge
29 West 35th Street, New York, NY 10001

© 1995 Susan Newell

Typeset in Times by Solidus (Bristol) Limited

Printed and bound in Great Britain by
Biddles Ltd, Guildford and King's Lynn

British Library Cataloguing in Publication Data
A catalogue record for this book is available from the British Library

Library of Congress Cataloguing in Publication Data
Newell, Susan.
        The healthy organization: fairness, ethics and effective
management/Susan Newell.
                p.   cm. – (Essential business psychology)
        ISBN 0-415-12677-0. – ISBN 0-415-10327-4 (pbk)
        1. Employee motivation. 2. Employee morale. 3. Diversity in the
work place. 4. Fairness. 5. Quality of work life.
6. Organizational effectiveness. I. Title. II. Series.
HF5549.5.M63N465 1995
658.3–dc20   94-43132
                                                                            CIP

ISBN 0-415-12677-0
ISBN 0-415-10327-4 (pbk)

Contents

List of figures vi
Series editor's preface vii
Introduction: the importance of *people* for organizational
    success 1

Part I The organization and the individual employee

1 The individual and the work experience 17
2 Stress at work 37
3 Helping individuals to cope with stress 55
4 Increasing individual resilience to stress 68
5 Work, positive health and improved performance 90

Part II The organization and minority groups

6 Discrimination at work: the intolerance of diversity 119
7 The promotion of Equal Opportunities in employment:
    managing diversity 144

Part III The organization and society

8 Business ethics: the impact of the organization on
    the wider community 165
9 Individual decisions and ethical behaviour 178

    Conclusion 192
    References 196
    Index 208

Figures

1 Job factors associated with stress 42
2 The psychometric approach: matching a square peg
to a square hole 80
3 The exchange approach: negotiating job and individual fit 81
4 A two-dimensional view of affective well-being 92
5 Contribution of environmental factors to mental health 109

Series editor's preface

The rapid, far-reaching, and continuing changes of recent years have brought about a situation where understanding the psychology of individuals and teams is of prime importance in work settings. Organizational structures have shifted radically to the point where individual managers and professionals have far greater autonomy, responsibility, and accountability. Organizations seek to reduce central control and to 'empower' individual employees. Those employees combine in teams that are frequently cross-functional and project-based rather than hierarchical in their construction. The traditional notion of careers is changing; increasingly, the expectation is that an individual's career is less likely to be within a single organization, which has implications for how organizations will command loyalty and commitment in the future. The full impact of the information technology revolution is finally being felt, with all the consequences this has for the nature of work and the reactions of those doing it.

The capacity of people to cope with the scale and speed of these changes has become a major issue, and the literature on work stress bears testimony to this. The belief in the importance of individuals' cognitive abilities and personality make-up in determining what they achieve and how they can contribute to team work has been demonstrated in the explosive growth in organizations' use of psychometric tests and related procedures. Perhaps more than ever before, analysing and understanding the experience of work from a psychological perspective is necessary to achieve the twin goals of effective performance and quality of working life. Unfortunately, it is the latter of these that all too often seems to be overlooked in the concern to create competitive, performance-driven, or customer-focused cultures within companies.

It is no coincidence that the rise in the study of business ethics and increasing concern over issues of fairness paralleled many of the organizational changes of the 1980s and 1990s. Ultimately, an imbalance between the aims and needs of the employees and the aims and needs of the organization is self-defeating. One of the widely recognized needs for the years ahead is for a greater emphasis on innovation rather than on simply reacting to pressures, yet psychological research and theory indicate that innovation is much more likely to take place where individuals feel secure enough to take the risks involved, and where organizational reward systems encourage experimentation and exploration – which they have signally failed to do in the last decade. Seeking to help organizations realize the potential of their workforce in a mutually enhancing way is the business challenge psychology has to meet.

The aim of the *Essential Business Psychology* series is to interpret and explain people's work behaviour in the context of a continually evolving pattern of change, and to do so from the perspective of occupational and organizational psychology. The books draw together academic research and practitioner experience, relying on empirical studies, practical examples, and case studies to communicate their ideas. Hopefully, the reader will find that they provide a succinct summary of accumulated knowledge and how it can be applied. The themes of some of the books cover traditional areas of occupational psychology, while others will focus on topics that cut across some of these boundaries, tackling subjects that are of growing interest and prominence. The intended readership of the series is quite broad; whilst they are most directly relevant for practitioners, consultants, and students in HR and occupational psychology, much of what they deal with is increasingly the concern of managers and students of management more generally. Although the books share common aim and series heading, they have not been forced into a rigid stylistic format. In keeping with the times, the authors have had a good deal of autonomy in deciding how to organize and present their work. I think all of them have done an excellent job; I hope you think so too.

Clive Fletcher

Introduction

The importance of people for organizational success

INTRODUCTION

Psychology involves the scientific study of human behaviour and mental processes. The aim of psychology is to promote a better understanding of why people think and act as they do. Such understanding can then be used to promote change. Psychology is therefore crucial to understanding organizations as it is the people who work within an organization that determine how successful the enterprise is, whether this is a voluntary organization or a commercial one. Indeed, it may well be that the people element is more important in the 1990s than it has been previously. Compared to even twenty years ago the pace of change is considerably greater. The internationalization of markets means that competitive pressures in most industries are much greater. To remain competitive within these dynamic environments depends on the skills and abilities of the organizational employees. Yet in many organizations the skills of employees, especially those at the lower levels of the organizational hierarchy, remain untapped and wasted. At the same time, those at the top of the organization are overloaded with work. The argument presented in this book is that organizations can no longer afford to waste people talent if they are to remain competitive into the next century.

ORGANIZATIONS IN THE 1990s

Organizations in the 1990s exist in a fiercely competitive global economy and will only survive if they can satisfy their customers. Bolwijn and Kumpe (1990) argue that the determinants of customer satisfaction have changed over time. In the past the most important product or service feature was price. If you could undercut your competitor's price then customers would buy your product/service. However, they argue that since the 1970s other features have been added to the list of determinants of market competitiveness, namely quality, flexibility and innovation. Products and services must be of high quality, must cater for a particular market niche, rather than a mass market, and must have innovative features which make the product/service stand out from the competition. It is also possible to offer a fourth criteria for success which is becoming increasingly important: that of the social and moral responsibility of the organization. Organizations that appear to disregard the human rights of both their own employees and/or the wider community are likely to be penalized by a failure to attract and recruit good staff, and by customers boycotting their products or services.

The traditional way of increasing competitiveness was to reduce costs and this was achieved by reducing overheads. This was typically translated into reducing the number of employees involved in producing and delivering the product or service. Staff reductions have been achieved by mechanization, with machines developed which can substitute or amplify the abilities of the human body (Braverman, 1974). The irony is that this has often been done at the expense of quality, flexibility and innovation, and with a disregard for the impact on employees or the wider community. Quality, flexibility, innovation and organizational responsibility are only going to be achieved through the dedication and co-operation of people.

Quality

The quality of service, whether in a hospital, factory, shop, restaurant or airline, is heavily reliant on the relationship between provider and recipient. My experience of doing the weekly shopping is likely to be very different if I am offered help in packing my shopping by a friendly, helpful sales assistant compared to being offered no help and being served by a surly checkout attendant. Given that I have a choice of where to shop, and with the current competitive market this is true for most services and products, I will choose to return to the shop where the service quality is superior. Thus, my custom is determined by the quality of the service provided. The issue for firms is therefore to motivate front-line employees to care about the quality of their service or product. The problem is that many organizations try to do this within a framework in which it is very clear to those who are being asked to 'care', that their employers do not care at all for them. They are asked to do routine, repetitive, dead-end jobs, earning wages often barely above the poverty line, they are expected to obey orders which they have had no involvement in setting and realize that they will be dismissed if it no longer suits the company to keep them on. It is not surprising that in this situation the sales assistant is going to respond with a negative attitude. After all, if I do complain about the quality of service at the checkout, the sales assistant is probably powerless to do anything about it at least in terms of helping me to pack. To break this cycle individuals need to be given opportunities to develop their skills and then empowered to put these skills to use.

However, in many organizations, rather than empowering workers in such situations, the emphasis is on increasing control. For example, Schlesinger and Heskett (1991) found that in these situations of low opportunity and power a destructive cycle is set in motion. Management decide that there is no point investing in training for people who will leave and who show no commitment to the company, so the decision is made to take even more skill out of the job, which in turn is used as a justification for reducing wages. Computers are used to replace some staff and to monitor closely those that are left because it is assumed that they cannot be trusted to work without close control. However, the research by Schlesinger and Heskett indicated that this cycle evokes performances from sales staff which lose customers, something which no firm can afford in a competitive market.

Flexibility

In terms of the need to be flexible, the argument is that the increased affluence of customers means that they are more demanding. They will not be satisfied by a standard product but rather want to feel that their particular requirements are catered for. This leads to the recognition that mass marketing strategies need to give way to a focus on market niches. It also makes it clear that understanding customers, and responding to their perceived needs and the changes in those needs, is a vital requirement for organizational success. The products and services that are offered by firms need to be constantly changed to meet the ever-increasing aspirations of customers. Moreover, the speed of change is crucial. An organization that waits for its competitors to change before doing so itself can pay a heavy cost in lost market share.

Many organizations respond to this demand for flexibility by introducing teamwork. The idea is that multi-disciplinary teams of workers can work together so that they can respond quickly to changes in product design and output requirements. However, successful group work can only be achieved if effort is put into building those teams, and modifying organizational structures and processes to accommodate them. In many organizations, teams have not been successful because they have been created, on paper, but with no effort to respond to the requirements of 'real' teamwork. Hackman (1990), for example, identifies a number of 'trip wires' that organizations stumble over in designing and leading teams. They may, for example, create a team but give it no authority to actually make decisions and act on these. Everything must be overseen by the manager who dictates what the team must do and how. Another trip wire he identifies is the creation of teams without the organizational supports in place – e.g. not changing reward systems which continue to be based on individual performance rather than team performance. To be effective, therefore, organizations need to devolve power and responsibility down to the team level and provide training and development in team skills.

Innovation

Finally, Bolwijn and Kumpe (1990) argue, in the 1990s there is a market demand to be innovative, not simply to respond to customer demands, but to some extent to create customer demands by inventing and developing new products and services that were previously not conceived of. Probably the best documented example of this was the development of the Sony Walkman. Innovation depends on individual employees being aware of the latest developments in other areas and seeing their application in their own firm. The individual must then have the power and authority within his own firm to persuade others that the idea is a good one and will lead to some competitive advantage. Innovation will therefore only occur if individual employees are willing and able to seek out new ideas, and have influence within their organizations to ensure ideas are turned into new products, services or processes (Rogers, 1962). This will not be achieved where individuals feel they are being exploited by organizations and are viewed as expendable commodities.

Social and moral responsibility

In this book it is argued that there is a new competitive contingency which organizations need to respond to – being perceived by the wider public as acting responsibly both towards their own employees and towards the wider public. Organizations that gain a reputation for treating employees badly will find it very difficult to recruit high calibre personnel. Even in a recession there remains a shortage of people with certain types of skills and experience. People who possess such skills and experience will therefore avoid employers who gain a reputation for poor human relations. Interestingly, the recognition that organizations cannot afford to get such a reputation has been exploited by employees to encourage an improvement in human relations in their work organizations. In the USA there are examples of the names and misdeeds of managers who have acted improperly being posted on billboards so that all can see them!

Furthermore, the general public are becoming increasingly concerned about the fact that some organizations appear to be totally oblivious to their impact on the wider community. Thus, organizations have, in the past, ignored the fact that they have polluted our air and water, have failed to take the necessary precautions to ensure the public safety, or have blatantly deceived the public in their advertising campaigns. However, it is increasingly clear that the public are no longer willing to tolerate such action. Law suits against companies for negligence are brought on a much larger scale than ever before, hence the proliferation of company lawyers as *the* profession within organizations. Furthermore, it is clear that the public can be influenced in their buying patterns by perceived organizational immorality, boycotting products and services that are seen to be based on unethical business behaviour. Organizations, therefore, need to think much more seriously about the social morality of what they do. Decisions that are made at all levels of the organization need to be informed by ethical principles. This will only occur if employees within the organization feel that they themselves are treated according to such principles. If they believe their well-being is disregarded by those in positions of power, they are hardly likely to expect ethical concerns to be important in the decisions which they make as representatives of the organization.

The point about all of this is that ensuring quality, flexibility, innovation and responsibility depends on having employees who are competent, i.e. who have been developed so that they have the necessary skills; who are given the opportunity to express that competence, i.e. are empowered to make decisions, and use their skills and knowledge; and who are willing, i.e. have the commitment, to ensure that the products or services which they are involved with are of a high quality, can respond to changes in customer demands, contain innovative features and will have no negative impact on the wider community. However, in the past, the dominant thrust has been to reduce worker skills and make decisions for workers. In response, it is hardly surprising that workers show little commitment to the organization.

There is, therefore, a contradiction in much current organizational practice. On the one hand, success is seen to depend on people actually fully developing and using their skills and abilities to work towards organizational success. Hence the current fashion for organizations to include in their mission statement a sentence such as 'people are our greatest asset'. Unfortunately, in many organizations these are little more than empty words. Thus, on the other hand, people are put in jobs which are stressful, and whole groups are discriminated against and not empowered to use their potential to make a full contribution to the organization. Ability and potential are stifled by stress and prejudice. To redress this underutilization of organizational talent is vital for success in international markets.

TAPPING PEOPLE POTENTIAL

At present, in many organizations there remains a clear divide between employees at the top and bottom of organizational hierarchies, even though the hierarchies themselves may have dramatically shortened. On the one hand, those at the bottom of the hierarchy are denied any responsibility in work. They work on routine jobs which demand little in the way of skill or knowledge. In such jobs there tends to be a high concentration of certain people – women, ethnic minority members, and those from other nationalities and cultures. In other words, anyone who is not white, male and

British, because the structures and procedures of organizations have been developed based on this very homogeneous group, and anyone who does not 'fit' will find it more difficult to achieve success within the organization and so suffer discrimination. Yet this is an enormous waste of talent, as well as being morally irresponsible.

On the other hand, those at the top of the organization, those in positions of power, also suffer. They tend to be overloaded with work because all decisions are passed up the hierarchy to them. Thus, they often have to work extremely long hours to ensure that the work gets done. In consequence, family life tends to suffer as they have so little time to spend with their family or indeed on other leisure pursuits. The resulting stress, in the long term, takes its toll on the ability to cope with such high levels of responsibility.

The clear solution to this is to pass some of the responsibility and workload from those at the top to those at the bottom: to reduce 'waste of talent' stress – the underutilization of the skills and potential of those at the bottom of the organizational hierarchy – by reducing 'overload' stress – the responsibility overload of those at the top of the organizational hierarchy. Unfortunately, in practice, many organizations find this difficult to achieve because the changes that would be necessary pose dilemmas for those in power who would have to make the decision to pass some of their authority down the hierarchy (Zuboff, 1986). Thus, managers' authority has traditionally been based on restricting access and understanding of information and knowledge to themselves so that only they are able to make decisions. If this information and responsibility were no longer the sole prerogative of management then it would be seen to threaten their traditional authority. What is needed is a revaluation of the managerial role. Management needs to be seen not as about controlling workers but as about providing learning experiences for workers so that they can develop the skills necessary to take on the new responsibilities.

To get the best out of people depends on more than reducing the amount of stress in jobs and removing the direct sources of discrimination. Real organizational growth can only occur when people are encouraged to grow and develop as well. To take an analogy with physical health, if I am not sick, it does not necessarily imply that I am very healthy. I may smoke, eat lots of fatty food and do no exercise. Likewise, in an organizational setting, I may not feel stressed because I have learnt how to cope with stress, and I may not suffer because of blatant sex discrimination. However, this does not mean that I am given the full opportunity to use my talents within the organization. My job may offer no scope for development and I may not feel confident enough to try for promotion because there are no role models that I can look to for support. In other words, the organization that is going to make full use of my talents has to do more than remove the sources of stress and discrimination. Removing these is necessary but it is also important to provide the organizational environment in which people can develop positively. Only in those organizations which achieve this will there be the ability to be competitive if this means being concerned with quality, flexibility, innovation and responsibility.

It is these themes which form the focus of this book. To survive, organizations need to reduce their negative impact on individuals, groups and society. To be successful, organizations need to promote the positive well-being of individuals, groups and society.

GOOD AND BAD EMPLOYERS

Ever since the Industrial Revolution, when people first came together to work in large factories and offices, there have been examples of managers and owners who have been concerned with the well-being of employees. This concern was based on both a moral and economic foundation. Moral, because many of the early managers and owners simply believed that the excessive exploitation of workers was unreasonable. Economic, because it was believed that treating workers more humanely would actually increase productivity. Owners who had such concerns introduced various innovations into the organization of work, and the general treatment of employees and their families. The aim was to improve the well-being of workers and their families. Examples will be discussed in Chapter 1.

Thus, there have always been 'good' employers who have been considerate of the needs of workers for a healthy work environment and satisfying work. The first employers that worked to create more congenial work environments were accused of paternalism. Employees were *given* certain benefits which these benevolent employers believed would be good for them, such as sick pay, annual leave, better housing. What distinguishes these early attempts to be a 'healthy' organization from more contemporary examples is the element of choice. 'Good' employers in the 1990s recognize that work has a significant impact on employees which can be positive or negative. They attempt, through their human resource management policies, to maximize the positive and minimize the negative impacts. But 'good' employers in the 1990s attempt to achieve this through a flexible approach as they also recognize that individual employees are very different. They do not try to impose their own solutions on employees. Rather, they empower individuals to find their own solutions. In this way organizations are able to 'manage diversity'.

In a sense, this recognition that employees are different, with the consequent need to be flexible, is a reflection of the fact that employees are more varied in the 1990s than they were in the earlier period. The traditional white, male employee who is the family breadwinner is no longer the typical employee. Women, ethnic minority members and other culturally diverse groups will also constitute a significant proportion of most organizations in the 1990s, and the idea of a 'breadwinner wage' is increasingly irrelevant as family structures become more diffuse. Thus, there is a need to give employees scope and freedom to choose work lifestyles and benefits which suit their unique circumstances. For certain individuals working flexi-time will be very important, in order to fit in family commitments. For older workers, nearing retirement age, there might be a desire to reduce the hours of work so that they can get used to increased leisure time. Employees can also have choice in how they make up their compensation package; some may choose to contribute a large proportion to a pension scheme, others may prefer a company car.

Unfortunately, while there have always been 'good' employers, it is also true to say that there have always been, and remain, a large number of 'bad' employers. 'Bad' employers control 'unhealthy' organizations that have not adopted the policies, procedures and structures which give recognition to individual employee needs and remove sources of discrimination, nor do they have cultures which promote moral and social responsibility considerations. Instead, in such organizations, employees work in environments which do not promote physical and psychological well-being and work in jobs which induce stress. The structures and procedures in such organizations were set up to cater for the white male and so discriminate against other groups, such as women and ethnic minority members who, in consequence, remain vertically and horizontally segregated. Furthermore, decisions that are made within these organizations will not take full account of the implications for individuals and groups within the wider community.

At the same time, the common assumption of the 1990s is that people are the most important resource of an organization. It is people that make the difference between success and failure. Success can only be achieved if people are given the opportunity to develop their full potential and so make their optimal contribution to the organization. In this book we consider the many ways in which employees are prevented from making their full contribution and the consequences of this for the individual employee, the group, the wider community and the organization itself. We will also look at how organizations can become more 'healthy', with the consequent benefits to employees, the community and the organization.

STRUCTURE OF THIS BOOK

Psychology has an important role to play both in helping to examine the impact of work organizations on the individual and community and, through improving our understanding, in promoting organizational change. However, there is a lot of potentially relevant material in this sphere. Being an introductory text, this book cannot cover all the relevant areas, nor can it consider the areas it does cover in a great deal of depth. Rather, the aim of this book is to introduce the reader to some of the most pertinent topics in this sphere of psychology and work. This inevitably involves selective attention to the material available. But the major consideration in this process has been to introduce some of the most important psychological theories, concepts and methodologies, and consider how these can help us in understanding what is meant by the 'healthy organization'. In the text, gender terms (e.g., his, her, she) have been used interchangeably to reflect the fact that reference is being made to either sex.

Following this introduction, the book is divided into three parts. Part I deals with the impact of the organization on individual employees. Part II considers the organizational impact on groups which suffer from unfair discrimination. Part III deals with the impact of the organization on the wider community. In each part, there is a consideration of what the impact actually is, a review of organizational initiatives which have sought to moderate the negative impact and a discussion of the benefits of going beyond the mere reduction of the negative effects to the promotion of positive health and well-being.

Part I: The organization and the individual employee

The five chapters in Part I deal with the impact of the organization on the individual employee. Where the impact is negative and the individual becomes stressed he will be less able to fulfil his potential. Thus, from the negative perspective we can consider the causes of stress at work on individual employees and look at how this stress can be reduced. However, as seen above, to reduce stress will not automatically promote good health. Thus, from a positive perspective we can look at how to promote physical and mental health within the organization so that individuals can grow and develop.

Chapter 1 explores the general experience of work for individuals. Chapter 2 focuses on negative mental health by looking at some of the literature on work stress. Questions about the nature of stress and how it is manifested are considered, as well as how the work environment can be a major cause of stress. The next two chapters deal with how organizations can reduce stress. In Chapter 3 we look at initiatives which focus on helping the individual cope with stress that has already developed from working in a pressurized organizational environment, for example through relaxation training. In Chapter 4 we look at initiatives aimed at helping individuals to develop greater resilience to sources of stress so that they will be better able to cope with potentially threatening situations. Finally, in Chapter 5 we look at ways of going beyond merely reducing stress to ways of promoting positive health within the work environment. Here the aim is not only actually to try to reduce the causes of stress in the work environment but, at the same time, to promote positive health. It is only by actually removing the sources of stress and building healthy environments that real individual potential can be tapped. The measures considered in the two previous chapters simply deal with the symptoms and not the causes of poor mental health and stress.

Part II: The organization and minority groups

The first part of the book deals with the impact of work at the individual level. The two chapters in Part II consider how specific groups are adversely affected in work because of discriminatory attitudes and practices which put them at an unfair disadvantage. While there are several groups which suffer from discriminatory processes, I have chosen to consider two in some detail. Chapter 6 looks at discrimination against women and discrimination against racial minorities. An overview is given of the position of the group (women or racial minorities) in employment and the legislation that has been passed to try to prevent unfair discrimination taking place. This provides a context for considering why these groups suffer from discrimination and the consequences for both the individuals themselves and the organization. The second chapter in Part II deals with how to promote equal opportunities and hence provide an organizational climate in which the management of diversity is able to flourish. Chapter 7 argues that to really achieve this requires a commitment from all organizational members which goes well beyond compliance with the Equal Opportunities legislation. To conform to the law will not automatically lead to the opening up of opportunities for groups previously discriminated against. Individual members of such groups are likely to remain an underutilized resource unless positive action is taken by the organization to manage a diverse workforce at all levels in the hierarchy. This requires active consideration of structures, processes and attitudes at all levels.

Part III: The organization and society

Finally, in Part III (Chapters 8 and 9) there is a consideration of the impact of work on the wider community. Organizations do not exist as islands, unaffected by and unaffecting the communities and societies in which they operate. Rather, they have an enormous impact. This is both positive and negative. Work organizations bring jobs to a community and as such can lead to the prosperity of an area. However, a decision by an established company to relocate to a greenfield site can have a dramatic negative impact, leading in extreme cases to the 'death' of a community as evidenced in some of the former Welsh mining communities. Similarly, the products and services offered by work organizations can lead (and have led) to a much improved quality of life. But organizations can also make products that kill or maim, as evidenced by the thalidomide drug. Also, today there is much concern about the environmental impact of work organizations. In the past firms have typically been unconcerned about how they have polluted the water and air around them. Now they are being urged to 'clean up'.

All of these issues about the impact of the organization on the wider society raise complex questions. For example, is it fair to expect chemical companies in the UK to 'clean up' when firms in other countries are not doing so and so do not have to carry the extra costs of being 'environmentally friendly'? Such dilemmas have led to a growing interest in the subject of business ethics which is considered in Chapters 8 and 9. Chapter 8 focuses on what is meant by business ethics from a macro-perspective and analyses how it is important in the 1990s. Chapter 9 considers business ethics from a micro-perspective, examining why individual employees engage in immoral and socially irresponsible behaviour within their employment when they would not dream of such behaviour in their private life. The chapter ends by considering how organizations can promote greater levels of social and moral responsibility.

Altogether, this book provides an introduction to an important area of work psychology. Its focus is on how the 'healthy' organization can promote the health of both employees and the wider community, while at the same time making its own success more likely. Conversely, the 'unhealthy' organization can have a very damaging impact on employees and the community, as well as being self-destructive.

Part I
The organization and the individual employee

1 *The individual and the work experience*

INTRODUCTION

Since the Industrial Revolution there has been a clear and narrow conceptualization of the meaning of 'work'. Following the Industrial Revolution work became physically separated from home so that people went 'to work' and 'returned home' at the end of the working day. Going 'to work' continues to be the dominant pattern for adults in our society today even though there are certain groups who do not conform to this pattern. Some women and men may spend some time 'working' within the home caring for children and elderly relatives. Women and men may spend time between jobs if made redundant or if they leave their job for some other reason. Both males and females, once they reach retirement age, may no longer go out to work. It is nevertheless the case that most people will go out to work at some point in their life. Thus, while 'work' clearly takes place in the home, in everyday speech the term is usually restricted to mean activity which takes place outside the home in some kind of employment. When a person cooks a meal for the family in the home this is not seen as proper 'work'. But if the same person cooked a similar meal as a chef in a restaurant, this would be considered 'work'.

Work has become synonymous with employment, which typically takes place in some form of organization which is physically and temporally separated from home. This kind of work is seen as socially valuable, while work done in the home is undervalued. A good example of this can be observed on chat shows when the host asks the competitor, 'what do you do?'. The typical response is to give a job title such as nurse, fireman or nursery teacher. If a person works at home the reply will typically be something like, 'Oh, I don't do anything, I'm just a housewife', and this despite perhaps having three pre-school children to look after at home. On a recent chat show a woman, who clearly wanted to question the common degradation of housework, described herself as a 'domestic engineer'. However, the need to construct a new word for work in the home only emphasizes the common devaluation of 'housework'.

The important point to recognize is that this is a social construction of the meaning of work. It is a reflection of the work ethic which prevails in our society. The work ethic assumes that it is the duty and right of everyone to work (i.e. to be given the opportunity to be employed). This conception of work is very much a product of our western culture in the twentieth century. In Roman times, for example, it was considered virtuous not to work, except perhaps on intellectual tasks. Furthermore, our current conception of work is likely to change. Indeed, back in the 1970s there was a lot of talk about the coming of a new 'leisure age' and there were documentaries made about how we would all be spending much more of our time outside employment in various kinds of intellectually stimulating leisure pursuits by the 1990s. Clearly, this has not happened and those who have been unable to find work in the 1990s recession are not seen as reaping the benefits of a new leisure age. Thus, people continue to spend large chunks of their time going 'to work' in some form of employing organization. This book is about the impact of this experience on the individuals thus employed and about the wider impact of work organizations on the communities in which they exist.

EMPLOYMENT IN THE NINETEENTH CENTURY

At the beginning of the Industrial Revolution, when people first started to work in large factories and down the coal mines, the conditions for many were terrible. Employees, including small children, had to work excessively long hours (fifteen to sixteen hours a day was common and for seven days a week) in dirty, dangerous, cold (or hot) conditions, as graphically related in some of the literature from that period, for example by Charles Dickens. Employees were seen as a commodity to be exploited to the full, until they were so sick that they could no longer produce the required output.

When this happened, there was no National Health Service, and the person and any dependent family had to rely on relatives and friends or charity. Most employers saw nothing wrong with this human exploitation. It was seen as acceptable because it conformed to the 'natural laws of nature', in that only the fittest could survive such a lifestyle.

There were, however, a minority of more humanitarian employers and campaigners who believed that this gross exploitation was morally wrong, just as there had been those who campaigned against slavery on moral grounds. Several influential Quaker families who ran large businesses were key players in this bid to improve the lot of the ordinary worker. Companies such as Cadbury and Rowntree (confectionery), and Lever Brothers (soap), were leading examples in the UK, doing much to improve the conditions of their workers and the workers' families during the later part of the nineteenth century. They provided subsidized housing in small villages which they created around the factory (Cadbury's Bournville and Lever Brothers' Port Sunlight) and set up progressive unemployment benefit and sick pay schemes. These companies were also among the most successful companies in the UK and this influenced other employers to follow their example. Unfortunately, because many of these other schemes were not motivated from the same kind of moral obligation, the welfare provision was often used as a cheap substitute for higher wages and to 'encourage' (blackmail) employees not to join trade unions.

Nevertheless, many of these early schemes were aimed at improving the physical environment of work and at ameliorating hardship among employees. While today such provision may be considered as paternalism, the motives at the time, at least for some, stemmed from a genuine concern to improve the physical and mental well-being of employees. They were thus driven from a moral and humanitarian perspective. Later, in the early part of the twentieth century, it became apparent that to treat people more humanely actually made economic sense as well. While the credit for this idea is generally given to the research undertaken at the General Electric Company in the USA (the Hawthorne studies), in fact, researchers in the UK had earlier discovered this fact. And the still earlier work of F.W. Taylor illustrated the importance of rest pauses. We will briefly consider some of this early research in this chapter, as it clearly demonstrated the impact of work on the individual employee.

SCIENTIFIC MANAGEMENT: F.W. TAYLOR

Scientific Management was an attempt to uncover key aspects of work and organization which would inevitably produce efficiency. It is most commonly associated with F.W. Taylor (1911), but there were several others who contributed to the development of the Scientific Management principles, including Henri Fayol (1949) and Gilbreth (1908).

Frederick Winslow Taylor worked as an apprentice machinist and later as a superintendent at the Midvale Steel Company in the USA, starting work there in 1878. He quickly concluded, from observing the behaviour on the shop floor, that workers could work much harder than they were doing. The work was being done in a grossly inefficient way because operators were engaging in what Taylor described as 'systematic soldiering'. By this he meant that workers were deliberately restricting their output. Taylor recognized that this was a rational response on their part, because the workers believed that if they worked harder and produced more, they would not personally benefit financially as the increased profits would be creamed off by the owners. Furthermore, workers realized that if each employee produced more, they would not all be needed and some of them would probably lose their jobs. At the same time, Taylor realized that managers and supervisors could not demand any more from workers because they had no idea about how much they could expect if the job was being done efficiently. All the knowledge about the job and the best methods of completing it were tacit, in the heads of the workers who did it. Taylor's main goal was to externalize this knowledge so that it was explicit and so available to management. In order to achieve this, he believed that what was necessary was 'scientific' research which could uncover the most efficient methods and tools to carry out any particular task. He thus set out to undertake this research, which became known as 'time and motion' study.

In order to externalize this knowledge, Taylor believed that the first concern of the manager was to break any job down into the smallest possible component that could feasibly constitute a task. This made it easier to study the job 'scientifically' (and also meant that you no longer had to pay for a broad skill which took a long time to learn). Having done this, Taylor would first experiment with the tools to be used for the particular task. For example, one of his earliest experiments was in the shovelling of various materials in a factory yard. Through experimentation he worked out that a different shaped shovel head was needed depending on the density of the material which was being moved.

Taylor then experimented with the human movement in the use of the shovel, and again his aim was to uncover the most efficient use of the human muscles to perform the task. Once the 'best way' was uncovered, the manager had to calculate what output could be expected from a properly trained, suitable worker. This included the 'scientific' experimentation with rest pauses so that the worker never became overexhausted. Once the manager had this knowledge, he had to recruit a 'first class man', someone ideally suited to the demands of the job, rather than someone chosen because of friendship or family ties as was common practice at the time. Then the person would be trained in the 'scientifically' correct way to carry out the task. Lastly, to ensure that the person actually produced the maximum possible, Taylor introduced the piecework incentive system, so that the person was paid depending on the 'pieces' of output. In the example given 'pieces' would relate to the amount of material moved.

In the first 'experiment' with these ideas, a rather obtuse Dutchman nicknamed Big Hans was able nearly to quadruple output in shovelling. Later 'experiments' were not so successful, with output improving less dramatically. Nevertheless, in virtually all cases the improvement was significant. However, Taylor's methods led to violent reactions among workers, who disliked the impact on their work experience. Indeed, workers' negative reactions to these methods, implemented in an arms factory during the First World War, led the US Congress to ban Taylor's time study methods in the defence industry because they feared the industrial unrest that the methods were causing.

Taylor believed that his system was much fairer than the old, ad hoc system of work. He considered that it represented a shift towards 'a fair day's work, for a fair day's pay'. Taylor believed that it was fair because it was based on 'science' rather than rule-of-thumb. Workers would actually be paid more, in line with their increased output. What he ignored was the fact that this was at the expense of those workers who lost their jobs because the same output could be achieved with a much smaller number. The actual proportion of the profits which went to pay workers was not changed, it was simply being shared out between fewer of them. The division of the 'profit pie' between groups (employees and employers) was not changed; employees still got the same slice but it just had to feed fewer mouths. Taylor never questioned this, however, because he approached 'fairness' from a managerial perspective. This is one of the inherent weaknesses of his so-called 'Scientific Management'.

More importantly, from the focus of this book, Taylor had a very limited perspective on human needs and motivation. He saw a worker as no different from a machine. With a machine, output depends on the amount of fuel put in. Likewise, with a worker, output was seen to depend on the amount of fuel put in; however, in this case, the fuel needed was money. No account was taken of the individual's psychological needs for interesting work with some degree of challenge and autonomy. Nor was account taken of the psycho-social needs of workers for friendship and support. Indeed, Taylor explicitly tried to prevent the formation of work groups, seeing these as a potential threat to managerial control, and so to efficiency. The importance of these variables was illustrated by subsequent work.

WEBER'S BUREAUCRACY

In Taylor's analysis the individual was unimportant except in so far as he had the requisite skills and abilities to do the job in question. As long as these skills were there and the person had been trained to do the job in the 'correct way', then to ensure effective performance was a simple matter of 'fuelling' the person with money. Weber (1947) took these ideas further in looking at work organizations. He defined the characteristics of a bureaucracy and considered the ways in which these characteristics contributed to organizational efficiency. One of the most important elements of this was that individuals occupy 'offices' within organizations which have associated with them a set of clearly defined activities which the role incumbent must undertake. In this way, if the individual happens to leave a particular 'office', then a new role incumbent can simply 'step into his shoes' and take over. The individual is unimportant and so is the fact that he likes or dislikes the duties he has to undertake. As long as written procedures are followed, the job will be done in the most efficient manner.

Today, the term 'bureaucracy' is used to imply inefficient aspects of an organization, for example lots of red tape and an inability to make quick decisions. It is also recognized that people's attitudes to work are important in effecting work performance. Weber himself believed that the experience of work for an employee in a bureaucracy was not a healthy one, but he nevertheless believed that this form of organization was likely to become ubiquitous because it was based on legal-rational principles. It is now evident that this is not the most efficient form of organization because it is so inflexible. Moreover, the impact of work on the individual cannot be ignored. This had been made clear by the early Human Factor research in the UK.

HUMAN FACTOR INDUSTRIAL PSYCHOLOGY IN THE UK

The National Institute of Industrial Psychology and the Industrial Fatigue Research Board (IFRB) were both set up in the early part of the twentieth century in the UK to conduct research which would lead to an improvement in the productivity of British industry. Although separate, their research was complementary and there were individuals involved in both institutes, most notably C.S. Myers (1924). These groups conducted some of the best early research into the impact of work on the individual, although unfortunately the style of writing up the results of their studies meant that they were not very accessible to the lay reader. This can be contrasted with the writing of Elton Mayo (1949) in the USA which popularized the Hawthorne studies (see below).

The First World War spawned an important need to increase output. The common response to this was to increase the time a person worked, on the premise that they would therefore have time to produce more. Research by the IFRB was able to demonstrate conclusively that increasing the hours worked did not lead to an increase in production. A drop in daily hours from twelve to ten, for example, increased net daily output as well as reducing accidents, absenteeism, scrap work and sabotage. Taylor had, of course, demonstrated that rest pauses could increase output, but his explanation for this was purely physiological. Myers and colleagues quickly realized that this explanation was not plausible. For example, output was observed to increase immediately preceding a rest period, as well as directly after it. Taylor's machine model of man was unable to account for this. What was needed was a more complex model of man, which incorporated mental as well as physical notions of fatigue.

In Britain this led to research into the experience of monotony at work. The observed drop in work rate during the middle of a work period was accounted for by the experience of monotony. Systematic observations of people working on routine jobs demonstrated that they used many different tactics to introduce variety into their work. The interpretation of these findings was limited by the strict 'human factor' psychological model adopted by these researchers. Some members of the group did attempt to develop broader social-psychological perspectives, but in a very restricted way. For example, it was discovered that operators working on repetitive jobs in isolation were more susceptible to the negative effects of mono-tonous work than individuals working in close proximity to others.

Nevertheless, this work clearly demonstrated the falsity of the psychological assumptions underlying Taylorism. As Friedmann remarks:

> Man with the whole of his personality, is again introduced ... The abstract worker conceived by the Taylorians – a crude composite of laziness and desire for gain – yields to a complex being, both body and mind, in whom an all-important act such as work involves the whole personality.
>
> (Friedmann, 1955: 84)

The Human Factor group in the UK demonstrated very clearly the socio-psychological complexity of workers, although their analysis of this complexity was limited.

HUMAN RELATIONS: THE HAWTHORNE STUDIES

As mentioned previously, the Hawthorne research programme had wide publicity and was seen as contributing significantly to the understanding of the impact of work on the individual. However, at the outset it should be noted that two of the central findings – that workers improve their performance when someone (a researcher or a supervisor) takes an interest in them, and that the opportunity to interact with other workers boosts morale – had actually been noted during the earlier work done in the UK. Indeed, Myers and colleagues, having recognized the impact that the mere presence of an observer can have on output, had gone to great lengths to conduct research which minimized this impact. This was ignored in the early work at the Hawthorne plant.

The research was conducted at the Hawthorne works of the Western Electric Company in Chicago, USA, between 1924 and 1932. The programme of research had been instigated internally, but researchers from the Harvard Business School got involved very early, most notably Elton Mayo (1949), the professor of Industrial Relations. The research was to demonstrate the overwhelming importance of social factors on work behaviour, but the initial research was based on a broadly Taylorian perspective of workers. The research programme went through four phases which are reviewed briefly here.

1 Illumination experiments

The first phase of the research was aimed at finding the optimum lighting level for operators. Two groups of female operators were involved: the control group and the test group. In the control room the lighting level stayed constant, but in the test room lighting intensity was systematically varied. The results of this work were completely inexplicable to the internal research team that was involved. Output increased in both groups and they could find no systematic link between lighting intensity and output. Indeed, even when they had reduced the level of illumination to that of moonlight, output remained higher than the baseline level. In order to try to understand what was happening, the company bought in the help of a group of researchers from the Harvard Business School, and together they began a more systematic study of the factors affecting productivity.

2 The relay assembly test room experiments

It was decided that the problem with the first study had been that, because the group under observation had been so large, they had been unable to control systematically variables which might be affecting output. To remedy this, they decided to conduct a further series of experiments but on a small subgroup. Six female assemblers were isolated in a separate room and their work environment was varied systematically to examine the effect on the dependent variable of productivity. Changes included the introduction of rest pauses, a reduction in the working day and working week, alterations in the method of payment and the provision of a free lunch. Each change was introduced and any ensuing variation in production output was monitored. Thirteen changes in all were introduced and at each change output was seen to rise. An increase was even observed when all the perks were removed and conditions were returned back to the standard. The research team was very surprised by all these results and could not explain them. It was only later that they interpreted them in terms of improved human relations.

These 'improved human relations' were seen to constitute a variety of elements:

1   Through being separated from the rest of their work group, they came to feel special and this led them to increase their output.
2   As they had been able to choose with whom they worked (the six women had initially been able to select each other) the team spirit was stronger. This led to increased co-operation, which was beneficial to group output.
3   The observer who was present in the test room to monitor what was happening became very friendly with the women and kept them informed about what was going on. The women liked this and it helped to create a positive atmosphere.
4   More generally, the women were consulted about the changes before they were introduced and this increased participation was seen to contribute to an improved attitude to work.

The results of this study thus led the researchers to reject the idea that either money or improved working conditions could be used to increase productivity. In their place, they emphasized the need to understand the complex social situation of work, including worker attitudes, communication between workers, friendliness of the supervision and level of participation. This, in turn, led to an interest in the factors which affected employee attitudes to work and, in order to consider this, a new phase in the research programme was begun – the interviewing programme.

3 The interviewing programme

This phase of the research involved one of the most extensive pieces of field work ever undertaken in Organizational Behaviour. It involved about 20,000 interviews with employees in the Hawthorne firm. At the beginning, the interviews were conducted in a highly structured, formal way. However, it was found that a non-directive, clinical-type interview revealed much more interesting information about the feelings of the employees. It was also found that simply encouraging the individual to talk through an issue/problem was beneficial, resulting in a more positive attitude on the part of the employee. In other words, the interviews were seen to have some therapeutic benefit. However, what was also clear was that the factors influencing attitudes and behaviour in a work situation were very complex. In order to try and understand the dynamic relations between these factors, the next phase of the programme was implemented, based on observation.

4 The bank wiring room

A group of fourteen male operatives who were working on wiring, soldering and inspecting banks of telephone switch gear were segregated into an observation room. The men worked in three subgroups, each group having one supervisor. The observer studying the groups sat in the room, trying to be as inconspicuous as possible, and noted down the interactions between the men. From these observations it was apparent that there were two distinguishable cliques of men, with a few individuals who were not members of either clique. Each clique was led by an informal leader who emerged over the passage of time and who was not recognized by management. These cliques also developed informal rules or norms about how to behave, especially with regard to how much work a person ought to produce, or at least report that they had produced. Thus, daily output varied quite a lot, but the figure reported to management was constant. For men who tried to break this norm, either by producing too much or too little, sanctions were applied by the rest of the group. At first this would involve name-calling: a 'rate-buster' was someone who produced too much; a 'chiseller' was someone who did too little; and a 'squealer' was someone who 'told' anything to the supervisor. If the violation continued, more severe sanctions, including binging (a mild physical sanction in which the offending worker was hit on the top of the arm by another worker's protruding middle finger) and social isolation, were used. It was also observed that the designated supervisors were aware of what was going on, but connived with the men.

It was clear from these observations that this output norm was far below the actual capacity of the men to produce. The restriction was used by the men because they were afraid that if they increased their output significantly, the incentive rate would be reduced and the expected daily output required would increase, without any benefits to themselves. Indeed, they believed that some of the group would be laid off. As the depression worsened (and this phase of the research was begun in November 1932), the logic of doing this, from the men's perspective, increased. However, the research team were concerned less with the economic shrewdness of this group of men, and more with the social mechanisms which were revealed. The findings were thus taken to show that a worker was more responsive to the social forces of his peer group than to the financial incentives and sanctions used by management.

Conclusions of the Hawthorne studies

The conclusions from these extensive Hawthorne studies varied depending on which researcher was writing about them, but the overall conclusion was that productivity could only be improved if management could meet the social needs of workers. Counselling and leadership skills were seen as the key assets, especially for first-line supervisors. The morale and productivity of work groups could be significantly boosted if supervisors were more sensitive to the social needs of their workers, and had been trained to deal with these needs through the development of interpersonal skills (Roethlisberger and Dickson, 1939).

The research programme has come under enormous criticism for methodological slackness and the selective use of the data in drawing conclusions. For example, subjects selected to participate in the various phases of the research were not randomly selected. Therefore, it was not really feasible to generalize from their findings to the wider population of workers. Also, the research involved taking workers out of the normal working environment and isolating them in new surroundings. Again, this may not generalize back to the normal work environment. In terms of selective use of data, in the relay assembly test room it was reported by one of the research team that, following the replacement of two of the women for being uncooperative, one of the replacements actually adopted a driving leadership style (Whitehead, 1938). She urged the other five women to increase output so that she could increase her income as she had some financial problems. Yet the conclusion of the research team was that economic incentives were not an important or useful method to use to increase output. Another example is of the research team ignoring the wider context in their explanation of behaviour in the factory. The recession was clearly a factor in understanding workers' behaviour and yet this was not considered in the explanations given. The factory was treated as an isolated unit rather than as intermeshed within a national and international environment. A full discussion of these criticisms is not possible in the limited space available in this book, but the interested reader is referred to Michael Rose (1975).

While these criticisms are valid, it is nevertheless the case that the Hawthorne studies have had a lasting impact on the development of our understanding about people's behaviour in work. This research made it clear that human needs, attitudes, relationships and motives, i.e. human relations, need to be explored if one hopes to understand the impact of work on people. Moreover, the criticisms levelled against the Hawthorne studies led directly to developments in both conceptual thinking and methodological tools.

WORK AND SATISFACTION

The work of Mayo (1949) and other researchers involved in the Hawthorne studies, especially Roethlisberger and Dickson (1939), emphasized the need to consider worker satisfaction as a key ingredient in understanding behaviour in work. Mayo, in particular, emphasized that, while in the past work had been a source of personal satisfaction, much work had become meaningless to the individual employee. This proposition was endorsed by many subsequent writers who directed their attention to this issue. This was especially true among psychologists where the issues of satisfaction and motivation became a major focus. Most of the early work led to prescriptions for managers to enable them to increase the output of their workers by making them more satisfied and hence, it was assumed, motivated to work hard. Later in this book the notion of motivation is discussed in more detail. Here, it is useful to consider two of the most important of these early writers whose work was influenced heavily by the Human Relations approach – McGregor and Argyris.

McGregor: Theory X/Theory Y

The difference between the ideas of Scientific Management and Human Relations was captured in McGregor's (1960) distinction between two managerial philosophies. McGregor suggested that managers hold implicit assumptions about the nature of their subordinates which, in turn, influence the way they treat these people.

He suggested that it was possible to depict two extreme sets of assumptions, which he referred to as Theory X and Theory Y.

Theory X

On the one hand, managers who hold Theory X assumptions believe that subordinates dislike work and will avoid it if they can (as in Taylor's idea of 'soldiering'). The manager is only going to get people to exert their full effort if she uses either threats (dismissal or other disciplinary action) or inducements (bonuses, pay increases). Underlying this assumption is the belief that subordinates cannot be trusted and so must be closely supervised and controlled at all times. Scientific Management epitomizes such assumptions.

Theory Y

On the other hand, managers who hold Theory Y assumptions basically believe the opposite. They assume that subordinates are naturally active and, if given an appropriate job, can actually enjoy their work. The job of managers is to ensure that these natural inclinations are given room for expression by setting challenging goals for their subordinates, who are then left to get on and work productively.

McGregor suggested that most organizations are based on Theory X assumptions. Organizational structures are hierarchical so that there is a clear line of command, and a supervisor's job is seen to be to control those underneath her. McGregor argued that people tend to react to these conventional structures and practices negatively, with the result that the underlying assumptions become self-fulfilling – people appear to be in need of coercion. Conversely, McGregor argued, if people are given more challenge and freedom they will, in turn, respond positively. McGregor uses these ideas to argue for organizational change, including the spread of job-enlargement, participative leadership and a general decentralization of organizational power.

Argyris: human growth and development

Argyris (1957) argued that workers had become alienated because the work they were doing was not permitting them to use their capacities and skills in a mature and productive way. He argued that as we grow up we develop from a state of dependence to independence; from passivity to activity; from a narrow to a broad range of behaviour; from casual interests to in-depth interests; from a short- to a long-term perspective; and from externally imposed sanctions controlling our behaviour to internal self-regulation. Argyris did not argue that this development was due to any universal need structure, but rather that it was a product of our socialization experiences. In this way his work differs from that of Maslow (see Chapter 2). Nevertheless, the outcome is that as adults we associate maturity with responsibility and independence. The problem which Argyris depicted was that in many work situations people are unable to act as responsible adults. Rather, they are dependent on others and can do very little without asking permission. This constraint on independence, thwarting as it does the learned expectation of responsibility, produces frustration and tension. This is expressed through absenteeism, apathy, defensiveness, the creation of informal groups, the demand for higher wages and withdrawal. But Argyris saw these as responses to frustration rather than as reflecting an inherent attitude to work. The solution was not to increase control, as this would undermine the worker further, but to increase the interest in work and give the worker more responsibility and challenge.

There are problems with the theories of both McGregor and Argyris. They both have an implicit managerial bias, for example in the assumption that individual goals and organizational goals can always be mutually compatible. Furthermore, they both assume that there is one best way to manage and that organizations have simply chosen the wrong way. That is, organizations have gone for tight, authoritarian managerial control when what is needed is a participative managerial style which gives individual employees freedom and responsibility to make their own decisions. Most would now agree that there is no 'one best way' to manage. Nevertheless, the work of both McGregor and Argyris highlights the need to take into consideration employee satisfaction in the work environment and outlines the consequences of not doing so.

This concern with employee satisfaction continues to be a theme among those who seek to find the 'best' solution to managing people at work, as evidenced by the popularity of books such as *In Search of Excellence* (Peters and Waterman, 1982) which provide recipes for the successful organization. Furthermore, organizations in the West have been keen to understand the success of Japanese companies. The 'magic' ingredient is often considered to be the commitment of

Japanese employees. This commitment is, in turn, said to be fostered by management practices which encourage participation in decision-making, and generally look after the welfare of employees, for example through offering jobs for life and subsidized housing. There is now evidence that this commitment is explained better as being the product of Japanese culture, rather than as the outcome of any specific management practice (e.g. Naoi and Schoder, 1985). However, the success of Japanese companies has been used to demonstrate that 'caring' for employees and fostering organizational commitment can make economic sense.

THE IMPORTANCE OF WORKER SATISFACTION IN THE 1990s

Despite the limitations of much of the early research considered in this chapter, it did serve to highlight the importance of employee attitudes and experiences in the work context. Both the original Human Relations writings and the subsequent socio-psychological contributions all emphasized that fostering employee satisfaction would have positive benefits for the organization. This was a very different orientation to Scientific Management which had treated the worker like a money-burning machine. The difference between current conceptions of a healthy organization and the Human Relations perspective is in terms of understanding the complexity of employee needs and in the perceived contribution of satisfied employees.

The complexity of employee needs

The original idea was that satisfaction of employees was achieved by ensuring the work experience satisfied what was assumed to be a common set of needs. Today, it is recognized that employees have different needs which will alter over the course of a lifetime. Furthermore, the workforce in the 1990s is much more diverse than it has ever been before, consisting of a broad mix of workers from different racial and ethnic backgrounds, of different ages and genders, and of different domestic and national cultures. Such workforce diversity demands much more flexibility in employment practice. The emphasis is therefore on the provision of a range of opportunities and rewards which the individual can choose from to meet his/her own particular lifestyle. One example of the recognition of the complexity of employee needs is the introduction of cafeteria systems of compensation. Employees can choose from a range of potential rewards those that meet their particular requirements at the current stage of their lives.

The contribution of satisfied workers in an information technology age

There has been a suggestion that people are becoming less significant in organizational environments as information technology (IT) 'takes over'. The concept of the 'peopleless' factory and office is sometimes depicted as a scenario for the future. Any people that do work will simply be servants to the technology. This image, however, is not one which most academics would accept as the most effective. Despite the increased sophistication of new technology, the human mind is still needed to program the computers. Moreover, humans have the flexibility which enables them to respond to unpredictable circumstances. Computers do not have this capability. However, management teams who make decisions about the introduction of new technologies have a choice as to how the potentials of new technology will be exploited in their own organization.

Recognizing this, Zuboff (1986) presents us with two scenarios about how technology can be used in organizations: automating and informating. *Automating* refers to the use of technology to replace the human operator by technology. In this scenario, people become appendages to machines and are controlled by them. Ultimately, machines will replace workers. Braverman (1974) is most closely associated with this type of analysis which is the ultimate application of Taylor's Scientific Management ideas. It is based on the assumption that management needs to control labour so that management can reduce (and ultimately eliminate) dependence on worker co-operation. If technology is used to automate, it is used to control workers and eliminate their independence and autonomy.

Informating refers to the use of technology to empower the worker. The technology is used to provide the worker with information which he then uses to make the decision. The technology system would also be able to provide feedback to the individual about his own performance which he could then use to try and improve in the future. Conversely, if technology is used to automate, it could be programmed to make the decision and provide information to management about the work performance of the individual operator, which could then be used to control the worker.

Zuboff argues that these two approaches to the use of technology are possible because of the opportunities which advances in IT have made for 'textualization'. Textualization refers to the freeing of knowledge from its temporal and physical constraints so that it can be appropriated by anyone as long as they have been given the opportunities to learn how to interpret the data and act on it. In other words, one of the key features of IT systems is that they can potentially be accessed by anyone at any time. Traditional paper and oral-based systems of information transfer made this much more difficult and, in essence, it was management's exclusive access to knowledge and information which gave them their power. IT systems have the potential to redistribute knowledge and information and so redistribute power. Zuboff believes that using technology in this way to informate and empower the worker is likely to be the most successful option because people have unique human qualities of flexibility and commitment which machines, at least for the present, do not have. It is just these skills which give a firm competitive advantage if all employees are encouraged to use their skills.

Zuboff recognizes, however, that using technology in this way is proving to be difficult because of the threat which it poses to the traditional power base of managers. And, because it is managers who make the decisions about how new technology will be used, they are more likely to opt for the automating solution. Indeed, in her own case studies, Zuboff found more evidence of automating than informating.

Thus, new technology can be used to increase control over the workforce or to provide a stimulating environment where intellectual skills are developed and used by all in an innovative work environment. Successful organizations will be those that use technology to informate. For the informating solution to be successful, organizations must foster employee satisfaction and take into consideration employees' needs and desires. Many organizations fall short of this. Herriot (1992), for example, notes that many employees do not feel that what the organization expects of them is balanced by the same degree of attention on the organization's part to their own individual rights and needs.

Organizations demonstrate commitment to their employees when they provide them with high quality work environments. Quality of work life (QWL) is a term used in Organizational Behaviour to describe those organizations which have recognized that it is possible, and desirable, to achieve high productivity alongside the satisfaction of employees. Indeed, some would argue that it is only possible to achieve high productivity if employees are satisfied. QWL entails restructuring jobs so that people are given more responsibility and autonomy, creating reward systems that recognize individual and group contribution, and generally making the work setting more pleasing and responsive to individual needs through improving the physical conditions and rearranging work schedules.

This analysis suggests that the focus on employee well-being is rather different in the 1990s compared to earlier. The Human Relations perspective suggested that it is important to take into consideration employee needs so that employees are happy. The happy worker will then work more productively on the duties that have been *allocated* to her. Today, a 'healthy' organization considers that it is important to provide opportunities for employee need satisfaction in order that the organization can benefit from the full contribution of a committed and dedicated worker. It is based on the ideal that 'people are our greatest asset'. Humans make the difference between success and failure. Success increasingly depends on utilizing the unique flexibility and creativity of the human mind, to monitor and respond to an increasingly turbulent environment. Information technology may help us to monitor this environment but, by definition, if the elements of the environment are continuously changing, it is not possible to rely on particular programmed responses. Rather, the organization must rely on judgements and insight from employees who are committed to organizational success. Employees who are satisfied with their work and the work environment are more likely to show the commitment needed to operate in this proactive way.

CONCLUSION

Organizations are nothing without the people who make them up. Weber's theory of bureaucracy was an attempt to show that the people did not matter. In Weber's bureaucracy people occupied 'offices' which comprised a series of specified duties and responsibilities. The particular role incumbents were unimportant; they simply had to follow the rules and procedures as laid down in written documents. Such bureaucratic organizations are no longer efficient in today's turbulent environments, as organizations have to be much more flexible and proactive. This can best be achieved through having a committed workforce. But, in turn, generating this commitment involves understanding how the work organization impacts on individuals' attitudes and behaviour. Fostering commitment and the full use of potential can be achieved only through reducing the negative impact of the organization and promoting positive employee growth.

2 *Stress at work*

INTRODUCTION

The increasing pace of society results in pressures from a wide variety of sources, including our job. Stress has become an everyday word which we use to describe our negative response to these pressures. Among academics there is disagreement about the definition of stress. However, in general, the term is used to refer to a situation where an individual is faced with something which she perceives as threatening and where she does not feel able to cope effectively with this threat. This emphasizes the importance of cognitive factors in stress. Two individuals can be faced with exactly the same work situation, for example the annual appraisal, but one may see it as stressful while the other may feel totally at ease in the situation. In other words, it is the way a person appraises a situation that determines whether or not it is stressful. The result of stress is strain, which is the manifestation of stress, either psychologically or physiologically. Prolonged strain can result in illness which, as well as being debilitating for the individual, also has serious consequences for the work organization. For example, Kearns (1986) suggests that 60 per cent of all work absences are caused by stress-related disorders and that in the UK 100 million working days are lost every year because people cannot face going to work.

STRESS AND AROUSAL

The traditional view was that the response to stress was entirely an automatic one. It was seen as the body's innate reaction to an emergency situation, whether the source of threat was a raging bull or an irate boss. Basically, the body's metabolism was seen to be increasing in preparation for expending physical energy, with heart rate increased and muscles tensed resulting in the experience of palpitation, dry mouth and other physiological changes. It was thus assumed that there was a general arousal reaction which accompanied any kind of stressful situation (Duffy, 1962). It has sometimes been referred to as the 'flight' or 'fight' syndrome, as the arousal reaction prepared the body to flee or attack the impending threat.

More recently there has been growing concern about characterizing arousal as a unitary reaction (Hockey et al., 1986). Evidence clearly shows that it is possible to distinguish between different aspects of arousal. Lacey (1967) was the first to recognize this when he distinguished between three forms of arousal. *Cognitive* arousal refers to the increased worry and concern that accompanies a stressful situation. *Somatic* arousal refers to the increase in physiological activity (experienced, for example, in terms of sweaty palms, palpitating heart). *Behavioural* arousal refers to the increase in overt activity (e.g. getting fidgety or actually running away). Lacey demonstrated that it was possible to have an increase in the activity in one of these forms of arousal (e.g. cognitive – getting very worried) at the same time as another form (e.g. somatic – heart rate) was decreasing in activity level.

Another problem with the original arousal concept was that it assumed that the individual was passive. It ignored the fact that individuals actively attempt to cope with and ameliorate any potentially harmful effects arising from stressors in the environment. In response to this, Eysenck (1982) proposed a two-dimensional arousal system. The first system is a passive, undifferentiated arousal system. The second system is the control system which attempts to cope with the environmental stimulus which is producing the activation of the first system. If the second system is successful, the individual's behaviour will not be affected. Nevertheless, in the long term the continued activation of the compensatory second system is likely to have a price for the individual, physiologically or psychologically.

This discussion illustrates that the concepts of arousal and stress are more complex than was traditionally assumed. Nevertheless, what is true is that in situations which the individual perceives as threatening, there will be a physiological reaction as well as a cognitive and behavioural response, even though the pattern of change in these three systems may be specific to the situation (e.g. Schachter, 1957). Unfortunately, the stressors encountered in modern society are rarely ones in which a physical response is appropriate. It is unlikely that either to hit or to run from one's boss is going to be functional. However, the physiological response to perceived stressful situations still occurs and if the stress continues over a prolonged period, physical damage to the responding organs can result. This has been demonstrated in the laboratory where animals have been exposed to a stressor over a prolonged period, and have developed stomach ulcers, enlarged adrenal glands and shrunken lymph nodes. Furthermore, chronic stress can lead to a decrease in the body's ability to fight viruses and infections, making the person more vulnerable to a whole range of illnesses. In fact, it has been estimated that stress is an important element in over half of all medical problems that doctors are asked to treat.

Unfortunately, it is more difficult to study these physiological changes and their long-term impacts in field settings and in the past the emphasis in understanding work stress has been on its psychological impact, discussed below. However, recently there has been growing interest in the relationship between work stress and physiological reactions and, despite methodological problems (Fried, 1988), this early work does suggest that such a relationship can be demonstrated (Levine, 1986).

PSYCHOLOGICAL RESPONSES

Psychological responses to stress include the experience of negative emotions and an impairment in cognitive functioning. Emotional responses include anxiety, apathy and depression, anger and aggression. Cognitive functioning is impaired as we tend to dwell on the intractable aspects of the threat. After all, we have defined stress as occurring when an individual believes that he is incapable of dealing with a situation which is perceived as threatening. Thus, the individual concentrates on the difficulties and worries, and engages in self-deprecatory thoughts because he recognizes his personal limitations in being able to deal with the situation.

Such thoughts may appear to be the exact opposite of those associated with feelings of high self-efficacy (Bandura, 1977). Self-efficacy cognitions refer to the beliefs a person has about his ability successfully to execute a course of action to produce a certain behaviour. In simple terms, self-efficacy beliefs represent a form of situation-specific self-confidence. Thus, I may believe that I can effectively present a seminar on stress to a group of managers (high self-efficacy belief) but believe that I will not be able to give an entertaining speech at my best friend's wedding (low self-efficacy belief). These judgements of personal capabilities have been shown to be important determinants of motivation and, as such, high self-efficacy is associated with good mental health (see Chapter 5). However, it is also clear that the psychological stress response is not simply the extreme, negative end of a stress-efficacy continuum. It is possible to have low self-efficacy beliefs and yet not to experience stress. A person may not feel that they are able to do well in a particular situation (e.g. I may not believe that I will get a promotion that I have applied for), and so have a low self-efficacy belief, and yet not feel threatened by the situation, and so not experience a stress response. This is why it is important to distinguish between stress and mental health. The absence of stress does not necessarily imply good mental health.

WORK STRESS

The focus of this book is on the organization, and what we are concerned with here is the issue of whether work is a direct cause of stress and, if so, how the organization can help to reduce this stress. As we will see, this might either involve changing the organization so that stress is removed from jobs or introducing programmes which help individual employees cope with the stress which they are experiencing. From an organizational perspective, it makes sound economic sense to try and reduce the adverse effects of stress. For example, Cooper (1986) uses financial statistical data to estimate that American employers spend about $700 million a year replacing men below retirement age due to CHD (coronary heart disease) incapacity. Clearly not all stress is work-related but there is enough evidence now available to show that work can be stressful and so result in the physiological and psychological consequences discussed above.

In trying to understand the causes of work stress it must be remembered that there are few jobs or job situations which are inherently stressful. Rather, it is the way in which the job demands are appraised by the role incumbent which will determine whether the job is perceived as stressful. Unfortunately, this has not always been recognized in research in the area, which has often simply involved correlating reported levels of job demands with levels of psychological strain. Furthermore, it is not very helpful to look at the demands of a job in isolation from the context in which it is being done. Two university lecturers may be asked to cover the same number of modules in a year, but one lecturer has access to postgraduate helpers, technology to make the job more efficient (e.g. computerized scanners to read multiple-choice examinations automatically), a well-stocked library, computers so that student essays can all be typed and so more easily read, and a pleasant campus environment. The other lecturer has none of these resources. It is likely that the second lecturer will experience more stress. Payne and Fletcher (1983) refer to such factors as constraints, although a more general description might be resources available, which can make the achievement of job demands more or less difficult and stressful.

Finally, the ability to cope with a job will depend on the quality of social support from colleagues, superiors, clients, etc. A demanding job is less likely to be stressful if a person knows that her boss is aware of the difficulties and will be sympathetic, for example, if she fails to meet a deadline. By contrast, the person who knows that her boss will simply chastise her if she is unable to meet a deadline, is more likely to experience the situation as stressful.

When we look, therefore, at the job factors that have been associated with stress, we must take all these factors into account and recognize that any job situation is moderated by the person's perception of the job demands and his perceived ability to meet these demands. This, in turn, will be moderated by:

1   The resources available which can constrain or make task fulfilment easy.
2   The social support given to the person (see Figure 1).

Having recognized this, it is also true to say that some jobs are potentially more stressful because of their nature, and it is possible to identify certain job and organizational features which contribute to the experience of stress. These factors are reviewed briefly below.

The main reason for considering job and organizational features which contribute to stress is because it suggests that organizations can also help to prevent or reduce the occurrence of stress, with

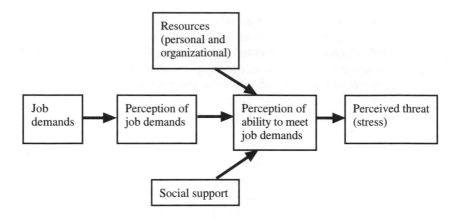

Figure 1   Job factors associated with stress

positive payoffs for both the individual and the organization. Organizations are increasingly recognizing this fact and many are active in trying to reduce stress among their employees. However, these initiatives vary tremendously, basically in terms of whether they concentrate at the level of the individual, where the emphasis is on helping the person cope with the stress, or at the level of the organization, where the emphasis is on actually reducing the degree to which the job causes stress in the first place. Such initiatives are considered in Chapters 3 and 4. Here, we are looking at the factors which actually cause stress in the first place.

WORK-RELATED CAUSES OF STRESS

There are many factors within the work environment which have been associated with stress and there are many ways of categorizing these. Cooper and Marshall (1976) developed one of the earliest systems of categorization and this system is still used extensively today. They identified forty interacting factors which they grouped into seven major categories of managerial stressors. Although this work was focused on managerial employees, the categories have also been found to be useful when looking at stress among other groups. Five of the seven categories are tied directly to the person's job: factors intrinsic to the job; role in the organization; relationships at work; career development; and organizational structure and climate. The sixth factor relates to factors outside the work environment: extra-organizational sources of stress, including family, financial difficulties and conflict between work demands and outside commitments. The final factor relates to individual variability: characteristics of the individual, focused mainly on personality differences and Type A behaviour. These categories will be used to consider, in turn, the various factors which have been found to relate to stress in work.

1 Factors intrinsic to the job: occupational demands

Research has shown quite clearly that certain jobs are more stressful than others. For example, the jobs of fire-fighter, airline pilot and miner expose incumbents to fairly high levels of stress, while the jobs of librarian, office cleaner and bank clerk generally do not. The interesting issue is to discover what exactly makes one job more likely to result in the experience of stress than another. Certain features have been identified as generating high levels of stress. Using data from the Position Analysis Questionnaire, Shaw and Riskind (1983) found five factors which were most useful in predicting job stress:

1   Making decisions.
2   Constant monitoring of devices or materials.
3   Repeated exchange of information with others.
4   Unpleasant and dangerous physical conditions.
5   Performing unstructured rather than structured tasks.

The more these features are present as general conditions of the job, regardless of the specific tasks involved, the more stress a person is likely to experience.

2 Role in the organization: role conflict

A person plays a number of roles in her life, often simultaneously: employee, wife, mother, daughter, friend, club member. Associated with each of these roles are a number of expectations which define how a person should behave in that role. There are strong pressures on people to conform to these expectations and various sanctions which can be applied if the individual steps outside these expectations. For example, as a mother I am expected to go and pick up my child from school if she is sick, and if I do not go, I will be considered an irresponsible parent. Similarly, as a lecturer I am expected, at certain times, to take seminars and lectures with groups of students. If I do not turn up to a seminar, I may be disciplined by the head of department. The problem is that at times these role expectations may conflict. Thus, if I am telephoned to go and pick up my child three minutes before I am due to take a seminar, I will be in a situation of role conflict.

This experience of conflicting demands is very common in work settings and there are different types of role conflict that may be identified:

a Intrasender conflict

This occurs when the same person sends conflicting messages. For example, a boss who tells a subordinate, 'I don't mind how you get this done, just do it as quickly as possible' and yet who has already said, on another occasion, 'don't break any rules'. This will cause a conflict if the only way to get the job done on time is to ignore a safety test which is supposed to be performed on every job.

b Intrarole conflict

This occurs when different people have different expectations about what a role incumbent should do. Merton (1957) developed the idea of a role set, which refers to the network of others who interact with a particular role incumbent. For example, the role set of a production manager might include subordinates, other managers, superiors, staff specialists, shareholders, trade union representatives, customers, suppliers and sales people. The expectations of two or more of these members of a role set may be incompatible. Such intrarole conflict is very common in organizations, and has been found to be especially prevalent among supervisors who are caught in-between the expectations of management and workers. Also, such conflict has been found to be a problem for employees working in matrix organizations. In a matrix organization, an employee will be working for two bosses, her functional manager and a project manager. This can cause problems when the two bosses make conflicting demands on the individual. This was why in classical management theory there was an emphasis placed on creating organizational structures with a unitary chain of command. Matrix structures violate this principle in a bid to improve horizontal communication and so reduce lead times and improve quality. The potential for intrarole conflict, however, is increased.

c Interrole conflict

This occurs when two roles held by one person are in conflict. For example, the roles of mother and career woman have often been found to conflict and lead to stress (Davidson, 1989), as suggested in the example in the introduction to this section.

d Person-role conflict

This occurs when the personal attitudes or values of the individual conflict with what is required from him in a particular role. For example, if a student sees a friend cheat in an examination, there may be conflict between the expectations of trust between friends and the values of the individual which include an abhorrence towards cheating.

e Role ambiguity

This is not so much to do with a conflict of expectations as a lack of clarity as to what the expectations actually are. This may occur for any of the following reasons:

1 Because the individual does not understand what is expected of her.
2 Because the individual understands what is expected, but is unclear how she is going to meet those expectations.
3 Because the individual's perception of what the job ought to be differs from what she is being expected to do by members of the role set.

Such role ambiguity is very common in organizations, especially when a person first starts in a job. This is because many of the expectations are not explicitly articulated and can only be learnt by observation of others. For example, there may be an expectation that little work is done on a Friday afternoon after 3.00pm, but it is unlikely that a boss will actually tell a new employee this.

f Role overload

This occurs when the expectations and demands of the job exceed the ability, or at least the perceived ability, of the role incumbent. Role overload can be either quantitative or qualitative. *Quantitative role overload* occurs in a situation where a person is required to do more work than is possible within the time allotted for the job. For example, where a teacher is required to carry out assessment tasks with a large class of thirty-five pupils within a week, with each child requiring two hours of individual attention. *Qualitative role overload* occurs when a person does not have, or does not believe that she has, the abilities or skills to perform the job that is required of her. For example, where a person is promoted to the job of supervisor and is subsequently asked to develop budgetary plans for her department without being given any training in how to do this.

g Role underload

This occurs when the expectations and demands of the job under-utilize the abilities of the role incumbent. While role overload is often acknowledged as a problem, role underload is less likely to be recognized although it has been found to be a serious cause of job stress. Role underload, like role overload, can be either qualitative or quantitative. *Quantitative role underload* occurs when a person has little to do in the job, and results from the ensuing boredom in 'sitting around doing nothing'. For example, where a secretary is only given documents to type that last him half the working day. *Qualitative role underload* occurs when the jobs that have to be done are not mentally stimulating or challenging, as is common in many routine jobs. For example, where a graduate is employed as a clerical officer, undertaking routine filing all day.

An important point to note with both role overload and role underload is that it is the individual's perception of the job which is important. The same job can be overloading to one person and underloading to another and vice versa. For example, consider the case of the secretary who is only given a limited amount of typing to do, such that he has no 'work' to do for half the day. One individual in that job might experience intense boredom and stress in the job, while another individual might enjoy the job because he decides to use his 'spare' time at work to develop his skills or interests, for example learning a new language or simply reading. Nevertheless, some jobs by their very nature are more likely to lead to the experience of role overload (or role underload) for the job incumbent.

3 Relationships at work

Most stress frameworks include relationships with co-workers (bosses, colleagues and subordinates) as a source of occupational stress. Indeed, theory and research focusing on psychological burnout (the experience of being worn down – or out – by repeated exposure to stress) contends that social interactions are the critical stressors (Leiter and Meechan, 1986). For example, Leiter and Maslach (1988) found that nurses, when asked to identify sources of stress in their jobs, cited interactions with co-workers ten times more often than interactions with patients.

The importance of relationships at work is also highlighted by research which has shown how responsibility for people is much more clearly related to stress than is responsibility for other types of resources. A person in work may be responsible for financial resources (budgets, accounts, taxes, etc.), for physical resources (equipment, procuring supplies, distributing finished products, etc.) or for human resources (i.e. people). A manager may well have responsibility for all three types of resources, but other managers will have responsibility for only one or two types. Research has found that it is those with responsibility for people who are likely to experience the most stress from their jobs.

As an example of this relationship stress, we can think of a firm having to lay off or make redundant certain employees because of the recession. It will fall on certain managers to relate the 'bad news' to the chosen employees. Having to observe the distress which this news is likely to generate on individuals who have worked for them, perhaps very well for several years, is a cause of stress for many managers.

Research suggests that not only is it the case that poor relationships at work can cause stress, but that good relationships at work can serve as a buffer, helping the individual cope with other sources of stress in the work environment. For example, Oullette-Kobasa and Pucetti (1983) studied managers in a public utility who were experiencing high levels of work stress. They found that those managers who felt that they had a high level of support from their immediate superior reported fewer physical symptoms associated with stress than did managers who did not feel they were well supported by their boss.

There are a number of ways in which such social support can help to reduce the amount of stress experienced. First, friends might be able to suggest useful strategies for dealing with the stressful event that the individual had not thought of. Second, friends might encourage the individual to reappraise the threat and to see it as more under her own control. Finally, friends may help the individual to deal with and reduce the negative feelings generated by the stressful event. Thus, the old adage 'a problem shared is a problem halved' does have some truth.

4 Career prospects

There are two distinct groups of factors that are related to career prospects as a source of stress. First, *lack of job security*. This source of stress is particularly acute during times of recession, as people fear that they will be made redundant. Indeed, in research looking at the impact of unemployment, it has been found that it can be the period of uncertainty, before the actual names of those who are going to lose their jobs are revealed, which is the most stressful. There can actually be a sense of relief experienced once the person knows that she is going to lose her job as then she can start to make plans to cope with this. Having said this, the negative impact of unemployment is now very well documented, as will be demonstrated in Chapter 5.

The second way in which career prospects can be a cause of stress is related to *status incongruity*. This refers to a perceived mismatch between the aspirations of an individual for career progression and the reality of promotion. The most common cause of stress here is when a person realizes that he has reached his 'career ceiling' and at a point below that to which he aspired. This often occurs at middle management and in middle age and has sometimes been related to the so-called 'male menopause', on the outdated assumption that it is only males who aspire to 'get to the top'. This status incongruity is common because, in the early years of work, people tend to be ambitious and rise quickly through the bottom layers of the organizational hierarchy. However, by definition, the 'room at the top' is limited and so the majority will not rise above this middle level. The individual must then come to terms with the fact that he will not rise further in the hierarchy and will probably suffer an erosion in status before he finally retires. The stress is thus caused by the frustration of career ambitions and the individual must cope with the disappointment.

This problem is becoming more acute as organizations reduce the number of levels in the management hierarchy in a bid to become flatter and so more responsive to market demands. This gives very little scope for upward mobility, frustrating more people at an earlier stage in their career. It is suggested that the lack of upward mobility will be compensated for by the horizontal development of the individual. Increased status will be accrued, not by being more senior in hierarchical terms, but by having a broader range of skills and experience. Unfortunately, this does not coincide with people's career aspirations which remain entrenched in the idea that upward mobility is the only sign of increased status. Thus, this problem of status incongruity is likely to become an increasing problem in the immediate future.

While this is the most common form of status incongruity, stress can also result from a situation where an individual has been promoted to a level at which she does not feel able to cope. This is also a threatening situation for the individual. The individual does not perceive that she has the ability to deal with the demands of the job, thus leading to role overload.

5 Organizational structure and climate

The final source of work stress relates to the fact of having to work in an organization and all the restrictions on personal freedom that this entails. In Chapter 5 we consider the research on the impact of unemployment which points to the stress that accrues from not having a job. Jahoda (1982) identifies a number of latent functions of work, the removal of which, when unemployed, she suggests, leads to a reduction in mental health. One of these functions of work is that it provides a time structure to the working day. Most employees have to arrive at work by a certain time (even if they are on flexi-time), have their breaks at particular times and then leave at the end of the stipulated working day. From the point of view of those unemployed, not having this structure can lead to a disintegration or disorientation of time which, for many people, is a negative experience. However, for those in work, the restrictions on their freedom to choose when to do things and what to do can also be experienced as negative.

This lack of freedom relates to a more general problem of not being in control of what happens in work. Democracy is a well-established principle in the Western world, but within the context of work many decisions are taken which affect individuals fundamentally, though without those individuals being involved at any stage in the decision-making process. For example, there have been situations where employees first learnt that their company had been subject to a hostile takeover through news transmitted on the mass media. In Germany, there is a system of works councils to which employee representatives are elected. The management board have to consult with these works councils about any decisions which will affect employees. In the UK there is no such system and, indeed, the government has resisted the adoption of the European Social Chapter, a fundamental component of which concerns the rights of employees to consultation and information.

Much research has illustrated that giving employees access to greater participation in decisions leads to lower staff turnover and higher productivity, and that when employees are not given opportunities to participate, it leads to lower job satisfaction and higher levels of physical and mental health. Most employees feel that they know a great deal about their work so that they could contribute usefully to decisions concerning it. When they are unable to get involved, they experience frustration and helplessness at not being able to control their own fate. This, in turn, can lead to the experience of stress.

The discussion so far has concerned causes of stress that stem from the job itself and the work environment. However, to understand the causes of stress at work, two other sets of factors must be considered: factors related to the home–work interface and factors related to individual differences.

6 Home–work interface

Stress experienced at work is often taken home and affects life outside work. Thus, the manager harassed at work may take out her frustration on the family. At the same time, stress experienced outside work will be carried into the job. For example, if an individual is experiencing problems with a marriage, this is likely to affect work performance. There can also be a reciprocal relationship, such as when a person is under a great deal of stress from work overload which affects her home life. In turn, this might contribute to marriage problems. Tensions may arise because one partner is always having to work late and bring work home which the other partner does not feel is reasonable. This type of stress is particularly acute among female workers (see Chapter 6) who have to maintain a dual role as worker and mother. This has been found to be a major cause of stress among female managers (Davidson and Cooper, 1983).

Another example of a possible source of home–work interface stress is caused by the requirement to be mobile, for those who want to progress in their career. Traditionally it has been the husband who has needed to be mobile, with the wife not working, or at least not pursuing a career. Constant moving has, in itself, been found to be stressful for the family. However, with dual career families the problems become more acute as moving for one partner's career will typically mean the other partner making sacrifices to her career prospects.

7 Individual differences

It has already been made clear that stress is not inherent in the situation, but is determined by whether the person perceives or interprets what is happening as threatening. Research has also made it clear that, in the face of a perceived stressful situation, individuals differ in how well they are able to cope. Some suffer ill effects after exposure to brief periods of relatively mild stress while others are unaffected by prolonged exposure to much higher levels of stress. Research in this area has demonstrated several personal dispositions that are important.

a The Type A behaviour pattern

People classified as Type A show high levels of competitiveness, irritability and time urgency. They are always in a hurry. Individuals who exhibit the opposite characteristics are classified as Type B. As might be expected, the constant push to excel exhibited by Type A individuals has been found to be adversely related to health. Research has found that those classified as Type A are more than twice as likely as Type Bs to experience serious heart disease. There are three important findings relating Type A behaviour with stress:

1   Type As tend to *perceive* themselves as being more under stress than Type Bs. As we have seen, this cognitive appraisal is fundamental in determining the impact of a situation.
2   Type As tend to *respond* to stress with a more pronounced physiological reaction than Type Bs.
3   Type As actually tend to *behave* in ways that increase their work load and generate conditions most persons would describe as stressful.

It is clear, therefore, that those exhibiting Type A behaviour patterns are more at risk from the adverse effects of stress because they actually create more stressful work experiences for themselves.

For example, Kirmeyer and Biggers (1988) observed civilian radio dispatchers working in police departments. Before the observation, they measured these individuals for their level of Type A behaviour. They found that those who scored higher on Type A behaviour were more likely to initiate work, to engage in and complete more work, and to divide their attention between two or more simultaneous tasks. Changing their behaviour patterns, so that they 'slow down', is likely to have an extremely beneficial effect on the health of Type As. Some stress management programmes are directed towards achieving this.

b Hardiness

An individual's level of hardiness has also been found to relate to how vulnerable she is in the face of stressful events. In fact, hardiness refers to a cluster of characteristics (Kobasa, 1979) with hardy people scoring higher on: *commitment* – deeper involvement in activities engaged in, including their jobs; *control* – belief in personal ability to influence important life events and the outcomes they experience; and *challenge* – the perception of change as an opportunity to grow rather than as a threat to personal security.

It appears to be the combination of these characteristics which gives an individual a higher resistance to stress, although research suggests that commitment and sense of control are more important components than challenge (Hull et al., 1987). For example, Oullette-Kobasa and Pucetti (1983) studied executives in a large public utility and found that those who scored higher on a measure of hardiness reported better mental health than those who scored low, even when they had recently experienced major stressful life changes.

c Optimism

Individuals also differ in terms of their general level of optimism/ pessimism. Optimists tend to approach things in a positive light, expecting favourable outcomes. Pessimists, in contrast, tend to approach things in a negative light, always expecting the worst. Research has found that optimists are much more stress resistant than pessimists. For example, Scheier and Carver (1985) found that those classified as optimists were much less likely to report physical illness during a high stress period such as final examinations.

Part of the reason for this difference appears to be because of different approaches to stressful events by optimists and pessimists. Optimists are much more likely to focus on solving the problem through planning and acting to reduce the stress. They are also more likely to seek social support from friends and others who may be able to help them. Pessimists, on the other hand, give up very quickly and often deny that the stressful event has even occurred (Scheier et al., 1986).

CONCLUSION

In this chapter we have looked at what stress is and noted that the term is often used in rather diverse ways. This has impeded the development of theory in the area and generated considerable controversy over the usefulness of the term. Nevertheless, it is clear that the term has meaning in everyday language and psychologists have begun to tackle the definitional problems. Thus, recent research has adopted a cognitive-based interactional model in which stress occurs as a result of cognitive appraisals that one's coping resources will be taxed, or even inadequate, to meet the demands imposed by a particular situation. According to this model, it is not the situation which is stressful, but the individual's appraisal of the situation in relation to their perceived abilities to cope.

Nevertheless, it is clear that there are certain situations which are more likely to lead to such an appraisal and the research in the area of work-based stress has concentrated on identifying those situations. We have looked at these aspects of work under five headings: factors intrinsic to the job; work role factors; relationship factors; career-related factors; and factors related to the organizational climate. In addition, it was noted that if we want to understand the causes and impact of stress in work, we need to consider personal characteristics and the interface between the home and work environments.

Despite acknowledging individual differences in terms of both appraisal of events and personality characteristics, it is clear that certain organizational structures and procedures are more likely to lead to stress. Organizations that promote worker passivity and rely on external controls will find that this leads not only to a high potential for stress but that this also leads to high levels of ineffectiveness, waste of talent and compliance rather than commitment. Yet, as we have seen, success in the 1990s depends on utilizing human capabilities to the full. However, creating an organizational environment which encourages the use of the potential of *all* employees is not simply a matter of reducing those features of work which are likely to lead to stress. The individual who is not suffering from work-related stress (or indeed any other kind of stress) is not necessarily in good mental (or physical) health. For example, I may not feel stressed but I may also not feel confident, happy, interested, fulfilled and so on.

The healthy organization not only tries to tackle the problem of employee stress (see Chapters 3 and 4), it also actively seeks to enhance employee health (see Chapter 5). This will have benefits not only for the well-being of individual employees, but will also provide the necessary conditions for the development and utilization of employee potential. For example, the inflexibility of organizational structures and procedures restricts opportunities for many employees whose life and career patterns do not fit the traditional mode. Increasing organizational flexibility offers the potential to tap a much more diverse range of people. Likewise, reducing role overload for those at the top of the hierarchy can be achieved by giving employees lower down the hierarchy more decision-making power. This can reduce the role underload experienced by the lower-level employees, and create the conditions necessary for the development of skills and competencies among the whole workforce. These opportunities will be considered in Chapter 5 after the more defensive stress reduction techniques have been reviewed.

3   *Helping individuals to cope with stress*

INTRODUCTION

There are three distinct ways in which an organization can take action to reduce the negative effects of stress on its employees. However, only one of these (primary initiatives) will also promote physical and mental well-being, and lead to the positive employee contribution discussed in the Introduction.

1 Primary initiatives

Any initiative introduced by an organization which actually tries to reduce the causes of stress is considered to be primary. For example, it was seen in Chapter 2 that a lack of participation in decisions in work could be an important source of stress. An attempt by the organization to increase the level of participation in decision-making through an organizational change programme would be classed as a primary stress reduction initiative. More positively, increasing the level of involvement will give employees the opportunity to use their abilities and skills more fully (see Chapter 5).

Unfortunately, despite the fact that organizational structures and practices are often primary factors in the onset of stress for an individual, most stress reduction initiatives are not of this kind and so do not aim to remove the sources of stress. Rather, they are aimed at helping the individual cope with stress that either may arise (secondary) or has already developed (tertiary).

2 Secondary initiatives

Secondary initiatives include any programme introduced to help individuals develop greater resilience to sources of stress. By developing greater resilience, individuals are better able to cope with potentially threatening situations. Such initiatives include stress management training and also programmes aimed at improving the lifestyle of the individual in terms of both diet and exercise. These approaches are considered in Chapter 4.

3 Tertiary initiatives

Tertiary initiatives include any programme that focuses on helping the individual cope with stress that has already developed. Tertiary initiatives are the focus of this chapter.

INDIVIDUAL FOCUSED STRESS REDUCTION INITIATIVES: TERTIARY LEVEL ACTION

Four different examples of tertiary level initiatives are included in this chapter. First, we will look at relaxation training which attempts to reduce the physiological changes that accompany stress. Second, we will examine strategies which aim to change the way an individual cognitively appraises the situation so that it is perceived as less threatening. Third, we will consider programmes which have been set up to deal with specific behavioural manifestations of stress, e.g. alcoholism. Finally, we will consider the strategy of providing employees with access to generalized counselling facilities where they can go and talk through their problems.

Reducing physiological stress responses: relaxation training

The use of relaxation as a means of anxiety and stress reduction is not new. Many Eastern religions have been using techniques such as yoga and meditation for many centuries. The theoretical rationale for teaching individuals to relax when they experience a stressful situation is that relaxation induces the physiological effects opposite in nature to those induced by stress. Specifically, relaxation produces a decrease in sympathetic nervous system activity and causes an increase in parasympathetic nervous system activity. Relaxation, therefore, results in a reduction in heart rate, blood pressure, sweat gland activity, EEG activity and somatomotor activity (Wallace and

Benson, 1972). In conjunction with these physiological changes, relaxation also promotes psychological changes. For example, Shapiro and Giber (1978) cited studies that found relaxation reduced fears and phobias, and was associated with positive subjective experiences.

There are different types of relaxation training, for example meditation and autogenic training, but the most commonly used method is based on the technique of *progressive relaxation.* This technique was developed by Edmund Jacobson (1938), originally to help hospital patients who appeared tense. The training teaches people to contract and then relax specific muscles. Muscle tension is taught to enable people to recognize when they are tense. Relaxation is taught so that people can reduce this physical tenseness and relax voluntarily. The training starts with a focus on one muscle group, adds another when the first is relaxed and progresses through the body until total relaxation occurs. Relaxation thus relaxes the mind by first relaxing the body (Greenberg, 1983).

The original technique described by Jacobson took several years of practice to learn, but subsequent research has shown that benefits can result in several weeks of three daily practice sessions of just five minutes each (Curtis and Detert, 1981). While progressive relaxation training can be fairly complex, it is possible to gain benefits from following a simple relaxation procedure:

1 Sit comfortably with your eyes closed in a quiet location.
2 Slowly repeat a peaceful word or phrase over and over to yourself in your mind.
3 Take deep, but comfortable, breaths, inhaling through the nose and exhaling through the mouth.
4 Avoid distracting thoughts by keeping a passive mental attitude.

Individuals within organizations may be taught relaxation techniques to help them reduce high levels of experienced stress. More usually, such techniques are taught as part of a stress management programme (see Chapter 4) which is directed at teaching individuals skills which will help them to cope better with stressful situations that they may encounter in the future. Studies evaluating the effectiveness of relaxation techniques illustrate that they can have tremendous benefits in reducing stress and anxiety (e.g. Rice, 1987). For example, Kohn (1981) found that individuals trained in progressive muscle relaxation showed lower heart rate and fewer performance errors under conditions of high noise stress. However, it is now clear that individuals differ in terms of how effective they find such techniques. Murphy (1983) reported that between 20 and 40 per cent of participants in either biofeedback or muscle relaxation training were unsuccessful at lowering EMG 25 per cent from baseline levels. This is why many stress management programmes include multiple methods. However, this has made it difficult to evaluate the effectiveness of specific aspects of the training.

Murphy (1984) reviewed thirteen studies which had attempted to measure the effectiveness of work site stress management programmes. All of these studies included a relaxation exercise for lowering arousal level and creating a deep state of relaxation. Taken together, the studies showed that relaxation was associated with significant decreases in systolic and diastolic blood pressure, subjective anxiety and reported ability to cope with stress. However, in several of the studies, similar results were also reported for the control group (i.e. a comparison group who had not been taught relaxation skills). In general, more research is needed to evaluate the effectiveness of relaxation skills in reducing the stress experienced in stressful situations outside the training setting.

Furthermore, while it appears that relaxation can help many people cope with experienced stress by reducing physiological arousal, it does not help to remove the causes of this stress. It is a 'sticking plaster' remedy, stopping the blood flowing from a cut. It does not help to prevent the person from injuring himself in the first place.

Changing cognitive reactions: rational–emotive therapy

In the first edition of one of the earliest books on occupational stress, *Stress at Work* (Cooper and Payne, 1978), there was only one chapter on stress reduction. This was a chapter by Ellis in which he discussed how his rational–emotive therapy could be used to encourage a person to 'help himself' cope with the stress he was experiencing. In reality, few organizations today would use rational–emotive therapy per se. However, cognitive therapy would often be an important element of a more general counselling programme.

Rational–emotive therapy is based on the idea that people choose to be under stress because of the way they appraise a situation. That is, they irrationally choose to appraise the situation as involving demands which are beyond their abilities. The solution involves teaching individuals to become more aware of their belief system so that they can modify 'irrational' beliefs as a means of reducing stress. The therapy thus involves encouraging individuals to modify their negative perception of a situation.

This idea is clearly based on an interactive, cognitive model of stress. When individuals perceive situations as threatening, dangerous or out of control, the stress they experience rises. Some people take this further and when exposed to such a perceived situation, they start to engage in negative 'self-talk'. They tell themselves over and over again how horrible and unbearable it will be if they fail, if they are not perfect or if they cannot get others to agree with their point of view. The aim of cognitive therapy is to make people aware of this irrational and self-defeating quest for perfection. The assumption is that, once the person is aware of how irrational he is being, he will be able to modify his appraisal of potentially threatening situations and think about things in a more 'rational' way.

For example, if I have just failed an important set of accountancy examinations, so that I cannot get the promotion that I had expected, I may feel that this has ruined my life and be thoroughly depressed. Rational–emotive therapy would aim to encourage me to change my perceptions of this life event so that I reappraised it. It is clearly not 'the end of the world' and maybe I could see it as opening up new opportunities, rather than simply as cutting off expected options. For example, if I had got the promotion, I would have had to work longer hours and this would have impeded my ability to play in the squash team for my local club.

This type of training may be useful in some situations and for some individuals who have a tendency to make particularly negative cognitive appraisals – to see fairly innocuous events as life-threatening. However, the problem with this approach is that it focuses the blame on the individual. The stress is the result of her irrationality. This alleviates any need for the organization to consider ways in which the job and organization could be changed to reduce the likelihood that employees will find certain situations threatening and therefore stressful. For example, it may be that, in this company, failing accountancy examinations is a regular occurrence because the company does not give employees the necessary time off to study. But, by focusing on encouraging individual employees to alter cognitions and so reappraise what has happened to them, the company is spared the need to consider how organizational practices are actually contributing to the stress experienced by those employees.

Changing behaviours: Employee Assistance Programmes

In the 1960s and 1970s many companies, especially in the USA, introduced programmes concentrating on alcohol- and drug-related problems. These programmes were generically called Employee Assistance Programmes (EAPs). Alcoholism has been a particular target of EAPs. It has been referred to as 'industry's billion dollar hangover', because evidence has illustrated that an alcoholic employee is far more costly than a non-alcoholic employee, as measured by indices such as sickness absence and work accidents. Moreover, the mortality rates of alcoholic employees are two to three times higher than for a comparison group of employees controlled for age, sex, socio-economic status and geographical location. The costs of this to individual firms are greater in countries which do not have a national health service, because employers have to contribute to health care costs. Nevertheless, in the UK, the national cost of alcoholism is still enormous.

The reason for considering alcohol and drug programmes is that stress is seen to be a dominant cause in substance abuse. Clearly there are social and cultural factors which need to be taken into consideration in understanding why people drink excessive alcohol or turn to drug-taking. Nevertheless, psychological factors are also relevant. For example, a number of psychological models have been put forward to explain alcoholism. One model suggests simply that alcohol can directly reduce tension. Another model suggests that alcohol can reduce cognitive self-awareness leading to a decrease in negative self-evaluation after some kind of failure. Finally, it is suggested that alcohol causes selective impairment of emotional memory so that the individual can escape from unpleasant feelings. While these models vary in detail, they all see alcohol consumption as a learned behaviour used to cope with stress. As alcohol is an addictive drug, this drinking is reinforced and eventually leads to alcoholism.

The actual evidence linking the use of alcohol to job stress is limited. One of the major problems is that research has to rely on self-reports of alcohol consumption. Employees will try to deny or cover up an alcohol problem for fear of disciplinary action. However, what evidence there is supports the suggestion that drinking can be associated with high levels of job stress.

As mentioned, EAPs were introduced initially to deal with alcohol and drug problems. However, EAPs have since developed well beyond the substance abuse area and now cover a wide variety of personal problems, including marital, financial, parent–child difficulties and other psychological difficulties (Wrich, 1980). The programmes themselves vary in detail but are generally consistent in the method used, which has been termed 'constructive confrontation'. The confrontation is between the supervisor and the employee, with the focus on a deterioration in work performance, *not* on problem drinking. Thus, it does not matter that the employee has been to the pub during the lunch hour. What matters is that she returned to work late and is not able to perform her required duties efficiently. The employee is offered the opportunity of assistance to help her deal with the problem under the EAP. If the work does not improve, the confrontation may need to be repeated with more serious consequences attached to failing to improve (with the ultimate sanction being the loss of the job).

EAPs which focus on reducing alcohol and drug consumption and other psychological problems, and on putting in place policies and procedures for dealing sensitively with employees who have problems, have generally been heralded as successful. Unfortunately, the studies which have been done have been methodologically weak, as few have employed comparison groups (i.e. groups matched with the 'problem' group but without the alcohol addiction) and none has involved random assignment of employees to different treatment or control groups. This makes it impossible to conclude that it is the particular treatments employed that have led to the beneficial effects, as opposed to a whole range of other factors which might have a bearing on the employees' problems. Nevertheless, the research which has been done would suggest that EAPs can be successful if introduced and managed sensitively (MacLeod, 1985). For example, Wrich (1984) of United Airlines estimated that for every dollar spent on the company's EAP programme, the company gets back $16.35 in the form of reduced absenteeism alone.

Nevertheless, EAPs deal only with reducing the negative behavioural impact of stress. EAPs do not attempt to treat the environmental factors which were causing the stress in the first place and which may have prompted the individual into excessive alcohol consumption or some other stress-related, negative behaviour.

Counselling

Industrial counselling programmes are usually traced back to the classic Hawthorne studies conducted at Western Electric in the mid-1920s and early 1930s (see Chapter 1). One aspect of the research involved interviews with approximately 20,000 employees and the main conclusions from this were that:

1   The complaint, as stated, was often not the real source of the individual's difficulty. Consequently, taking action to deal with this stated source did not ensure that the difficulty was resolved.
2   Giving employees the opportunity to talk freely in many cases led the problems to disappear.
3   More generally, the opportunity to talk about problems gave many employees a 'new enthusiasm' for their work.

On the basis of these conclusions, Western Electric developed a counselling service which could be used by any of its employees. This is seen as the precursor to the development of other counselling services provided in the context of employment. However, most services offered to employees focus on treating troubled employees rather than counselling 'normal' employees, as the latter tends to be seen as outdated paternalism.

Counselling is more broadly based than rational–emotive therapy which is a specific form of therapeutic counselling, based on changing cognitions. Counselling as a generic method can be introduced to help employees cope with stress of all kinds. A counselling session may lead an individual to reappraise a situation (change cognitions), but it may also encourage the person to think through other strategies which she can use actually to cope with the problems which she perceives (change behaviours). For example, a probationary teacher is given a strong indication that she is going to fail her probationary year. This is experienced as threatening and stressful. According to rational–emotive therapy what the person should do is reappraise the situation so that it is no longer threatening, for example by deciding that it does not matter if she fails as she did not want to be a teacher anyway. For some, perhaps those not suited to teaching as a profession, this may indeed be the best approach to take. However, for others a more problem-focused approach which tries to encourage the person to cope with the problem might be much more useful. For example, if the problem is an inability to keep control in the classroom, it might be better to encourage the individual to go and talk to an experienced and supportive teacher to learn some of the 'tricks of the trade' for maintaining discipline among a group of thirty five-year-olds.

The work of Carl Rogers

In counselling, a variety of techniques are used to encourage the person to think through, for himself, in a non-threatening environment, his perceived problems. Most counselling begins from the premise that we have within us the resources to find solutions to our problems. What we need is the opportunity to explore solutions within the context of a supportive but non-directive relationship. This approach to counselling stems from the work of Carl Rogers (1961) who wrote from a phenomenological perspective. The phenomenological approach assumes that the best way to understand behaviour is to consider it from the internal frame of reference of the individual. Moreover, Rogers asserted that the organism has one basic tendency and striving – to actualize, maintain and enhance the experiencing organism. That is, Rogers believed that the basic motivating force of human behaviour is the actualizing tendency – a tendency towards fulfilment or actualization of all the capacities of the person. A person will always choose to grow rather than regress; to fulfil potential within the limits of heredity. This growth or actualization motive is also the central idea of the work of Abraham Maslow, discussed in Chapter 5.

From this basic belief, Rogers developed his non-directive or person-centred form of counselling. This assumes that, given the right opportunity, every individual has the motivation and ability to change, and that the individual is the best person to decide on the direction of any change. The right opportunity depends on establishing a supportive relationship with someone. In counselling, this relationship is between the counsellor and the client. The role of the counsellor is to act as a sounding board while the individual explores and analyses personal problems. The counsellor is there to facilitate exploration by the individual of his own thoughts and feelings, and to assist him in arriving at his own solutions.

THE SELF-CONCEPT

The central construct in Rogers' work is that of the self-concept, which constitutes all the perceptions and ideas that characterize the

'I' or 'me': what I am and what I can do. A person will always try to behave in ways that are consistent with his self-concept. Problems arise when there is a mismatch between the self-concept and reality, and/or between the self-concept and the ideal self, which is the individual's idea of the kind of person he would like to be. For example, ideally I may want to be an outgoing, extroverted person, but I see myself as a shy, introverted person. I will therefore be unhappy with myself.

The individual's self-concept may not necessarily reflect reality, as for example when a person is highly respected and successful, but still feels herself to be a failure. Rogers believes that such incongruities develop because the person has had to deny part of her natural feelings in order to be accepted by parents and others. The more the person has to deny her real feelings and to accept the values of others, the more negative she will feel about herself. The aim of counselling is to encourage the person to start to think positively about herself again.

THE SUPPORTIVE RELATIONSHIP

The revaluation of self is possible if the person is given the opportunity to think through solutions for himself within a supportive relationship. Rogers considered that there were three essential ingredients needed for the development of a supportive relationship between the client and the counsellor: warmth, empathy and genuineness.

Warmth refers to the counsellor's acceptance of the client for what he is. The counsellor must be able to communicate this acceptance to the client and also the belief that the client has the ability within himself to find solutions. Empathy refers to the ability to understand the world from the client's frame of reference and to communicate that understanding to the client. Finally, the counsellor must be genuine, not operating behind a professional façade. Rogers believed that a counsellor who possessed these attributes would be able to facilitate self-exploration by the client which, in turn, would lead the client to uncover his own solutions.

Several organizations, recognizing the costs of stress, both to the individual and the organization, have introduced counselling services. The aim is to help the individual cope more effectively with the stress that is being experienced so that the costs to the organization are reduced. The aim is not to reduce the source of stress. The Post

Office was one of the first organizations in the UK to introduce a counselling service for employees. Any employee could make use of the service and there were guarantees given that the problems discussed in the counselling sessions would be kept confidential. While the service had some success, there was also an unexpected side-effect. In the course of talking through their problems employees became aware of how it was their job which was largely to 'blame' for the stress they were experiencing. The result was that, rather than returning to their employment happier and more content, some employees who had used the counselling service actually became more discontent and even left the organization. This emphasizes the point that although we need to take into consideration an individual's appraisal of the situation if we are going to understand the experience of stress, it is nevertheless the case that some jobs and environments do place pressures on people such that almost anyone would feel threatened. In such situations, stress is almost inevitable and no amount of counselling will eradicate it. The Post Office has now abandoned its counselling service.

Other companies are also experimenting with introducing counselling services, but not necessarily by employing their own counsellors. Some companies have arrangements with independent counselling providers. Employees can use the counselling services free of charge, and can access them through picking up the phone and dialling a particular number. An advantage of this form of counselling is that there is more likelihood that confidentiality will not be breached. In the Post Office, the issue of confidentiality was a perceived problem even though employees were told that it was guaranteed. Nevertheless, the same fundamental problem exists with this external provision of counselling in that it does not actually change the fact of a job that continually places the incumbent under pressure.

CONCLUSION

The stress reduction initiatives focused on in this chapter vary in terms of how they attack the problem. Relaxation training concentrates on reducing the increased physiological activity which accompanies stressful experiences. Rational–emotive therapy focuses on changing irrational cognitions which lead to the belief that the individual cannot cope with the situation. EAPs focus on the maladjusted behaviour, attempting to change the overt manifestation of stress first. Finally, counselling, to some extent, brings all of these approaches together in trying to help the individual cope more effectively with the stress that is being experienced.

There has been a growth in the number of companies introducing these types of initiative. This indicates a willingness by many corporations to take responsibility for helping employees (and occasionally dependants as well) cope with job stress, as well as a wide variety of personal and family problems. Yet all the programmes examined in this chapter can be labelled as tertiary, as they focus on helping to reduce the negative effects of stress on individual employees. They concentrate on rehabilitation rather than prevention. They do not focus on the removal of the factors causing the stress. The premise is that if the employee is helped to cope with the stress, not only will he as an individual feel happier but the organization will benefit from an improvement in work performance. None of these programmes actually attempts to alter the job and work environments which may be contributing to the stress reaction in the first place. Thus, for their full potential to be realized, such programmes will need to be incorporated within a primary prevention strategy. In this respect, the information provided by employees using these tertiary services can help to identify the stress-invoking aspects of the job and work environments. This information needs to be fed back into the organization and action taken to reduce the stressful aspects. The major problem with doing this is that individuals who use the programmes must be guaranteed full confidentiality. Information must therefore be in terms of broad trends and used to pinpoint groups or departments where stress is high. This information can be used as a starting point for further investigation and ultimately organizational change.

Stress reduction programmes may always be necessary, as not all stress is induced directly from the work environment. The person who is experiencing stress because of marital or financial difficulties may still suffer from impaired work. The provision of some kind of stress reduction service may well be beneficial to the organization if it helps the person to cope more effectively with the stress being experienced. The individual's work may improve in consequence. Also, some would argue that it is never going to be possible to remove all the potential sources of stress from the work environment, so that the provision of stress reduction programmes will always be needed. However, on their own tertiary level, initiatives will only plaster over the problems. They will not promote the positive mental health which is necessary if workers are to make their full contribution to the organization.

4 *Increasing individual resilience to stress*

INTRODUCTION

In this chapter we will look at programmes which some organizations have introduced which target people who are not suffering stress or ill-health. These programmes can be generically referred to as work site health promotion programmes. They can include an array of organizational activities designed to 'promote the adoption of personal behaviour and organizational practices conducive to maintaining and/or improving employee physiological, mental, or social well-being' (Wolfe et al., 1993). The range of programmes which this might include is very broad, including smoking cessation, stress management, weight control, exercise and fitness, health risk appraisal, high blood pressure detection, nutrition education, prevention of back problems and accident prevention programmes (Pelletier, 1991).

The objective of health promotion programmes is to promote good health among employees and detect the very early signs of ill-health. In this way, programmes can build up a resilience in the individual so that he is less likely to suffer breakdown in a potentially stressful situation. Thus, they are secondary stress management programmes as defined in Chapter 3. Three types of programmes will be considered in this chapter which cover a broad spectrum of approaches to health promotion:

1   Programmes which aim to improve the lifestyle of the individual so that she is more resistant to pressures from work or elsewhere.

Such initiatives are based on the premise that a physically healthy individual is more productive, and is more resistant to ill-health and stress. As an example of this we will concentrate on corporate fitness programmes.

2   Programmes which aim to train managers to be more aware of the early signs of stress and take action before the stress begins to impair performance.

3   Career planning or development initiatives which encourage the individual employee to think through and plan her career so that she is less likely to suffer stressful threats and disappointments.

The growth of health promotion programmes is based on the recognition that much illness is preventable if people change their lifestyles and attitudes. Whether or not the job per se directly causes the stress is not important. If people can be educated to change their behaviour and attitudes so that they are more resilient to all types of pressure, this should benefit both the individual, who will experience improved mental and physical health, and the organization, which will benefit from a less stressed, and by implication more productive, workforce.

HEALTHY LIFESTYLES

Research has demonstrated that it is possible to build up a 'stress tolerance' by improving physical fitness. People who are physically fit appear to be less vulnerable to the adverse effects of stress than those who are not fit (Brown, 1991). Improving physical fitness involves attention to two aspects of lifestyle: nutrition and exercise.

Nutrition

In the UK and most of the Western world the problem with diet is related more to an excess than to a deficit of particular nutrients or calories. The primary effects of poor diet are an increase in the likelihood of developing both coronary heart disease and cancer. Moreover, a shift in eating habits can enhance the body's ability to cope with the physiological effects of stress. The problem is that the typical diet is too high in fat (especially saturated fat) and cholesterol, too low in complex carbohydrates, too high in sodium and too high in alcohol. Reduced intake of saturated fats and salt, and an increased consumption of vitamin-rich fruits and vegetables, can promote improved physical health and can help the body resist the harmful, health-related effects of stress (e.g. Keys, 1984; Shekelle et al., 1981; Willet and MacMahon, 1984).

Despite the evidence which clearly demonstrates the harmful effects of a bad diet, national surveys still show that many people in the UK continue to have diets which contain too much salt and saturated fats. Some companies have attempted to change eating habits through changes in the cafeteria provision. For example, Cadbury have had a canteen system for some time which gives employees an indication of the nutritional content of the various foods and drinks on sale. This can be coupled with a promotion of foods which are more healthy. Some school canteens are similarly promoting school dinners which are nutritionally balanced, in a bid to introduce healthy eating at an early age. These are steps in the right direction, but little is known about how effective such campaigns are.

An important aspect of these campaigns is that they do not attempt to force people to eat healthy foods, for example by only providing healthy food in the canteen. A variety of foods are offered: chips as well as jacket potatoes, chocolate pudding as well as fruit. But people are given the opportunity to make informed choices about their diet as they are provided with information which can help to educate them about the nutritional content of food and its impact on the human body. The argument is that if an individual is forced to eat healthy food, he will not necessarily change his attitude to his diet so that outside the work canteen he will continue to make unhealthy choices. Only when the individual understands for himself the benefits of a healthy diet is he likely to change his total food consumption and become more health conscious. But the choice is up to him. The role of the organization is to educate and make the healthy options accessible and appealing. It is not to dictate the behaviour of employees.

Exercise

Exercise, like nutrition, has been shown to have numerous health benefits. The most important benefits are:

- Reduced risk of coronary heart disease (e.g. Haskell, 1984).
- Better control of blood pressure in cases of mild hypertension (e.g. Paffenbarger et al., 1983).

- Prevention of brittle bone disease (e.g. Krolner and Taft, 1983).
- Management of non-insulin-dependent diabetes (e.g. Siscovick et al., 1985).
- Maintenance of muscle strength and point flexibility (e.g. Deyo, 1983).
- Management of body weight and hence reduced risk of obesity-related diseases (e.g. Blair et al., 1985).
- Reduced stress, enhanced mood and self-esteem (e.g. Hughes, 1984).

An appreciation of such benefits, coupled with evidence about the lack of exercise taken by people in the UK, led the authors of the UK national fitness survey (a survey of the levels of fitness among different groups in the UK) to conclude that 'an increasingly active society will have a major impact in reducing the economic and social costs caused by chronic ill-health or premature death and improve the quality of life for **millions of people**' (Allied Dunbar, 1992: 3).

In terms specifically of stress, research has shown that physical exercise can help an individual to resist the harmful effects of stress in two ways. First, there is a growing body of evidence to show that people who exercise regularly show considerably lower rates of various stress-related illnesses compared to people who do not exercise. Second, exercise can help a person cope with stress that is experienced by reducing the unpleasant feelings and the physiological strains that accompany it (Biddle and Mutrie, 1991). At the same time, it is clear that a majority of the population do not take much, if any, physical exercise. For example, the Allied Dunbar National Fitness Survey (1992) revealed that over seven out of ten men and eight out of ten women fell below the age-appropriate activity level necessary to achieve the kinds of health benefits discussed above. The recognition of the beneficial effects of exercise, coupled with an increasingly inactive population, has encouraged some companies to introduce corporate fitness programmes. These are programmes funded, or part-funded, by the employer which aim to encourage employees to improve their fitness. The next section will consider such programmes in more detail and review evidence about their effectiveness.

Corporate fitness programmes

Compared to the 1890s, jobs in the 1990s are much more likely to involve sedentary activities. A recent survey in the UK demonstrated that about 80 per cent of men and 90 per cent of women were not in occupations which demanded physical activity as an integral part of the job (Allied Dunbar, 1992). Many people work in 'desk-jobs' which involve little or no physical activity. The walk to the canteen at lunch-time may be the most active part of the working day. At the same time, as seen, it is clear that increased exercise is related to numerous health benefits, physical and psychological, and generally helps to build up a resistance to stress-related illness.

Clearly, even though a job does not involve much physical activity, people can take part in some form of exercise outside the working day. However, many do not. Recognizing this, companies have sought to encourage physical activity through the provision of exercise facilities for employees and the promotion of exercise programmes (Gebhardt and Crump, 1990). A growing number of studies have demonstrated the benefits of such programmes (Baun and Bernacki, 1988). These benefits are said to include:

1   Increased resistance to stress and enhanced ability to cope with the negative effects of stress (see above).
2   Increased commitment to the company and other positive attitudes among employees (Holzbach et al., 1990).
3   Reduced absenteeism (Jones et al., 1990).
4   Enhanced productivity (Blair et al., 1986).
5   Reduced health care costs (Breslow et al., 1990).

The growth of corporate fitness programmes has been most prevalent in the USA where the major concern has been to reduce escalating health care costs. There is ample evidence that, in the short term, participants in an exercise programme are absent less often and expend less on health care as compared to non-exercising employees (e.g. Baun et al., 1986). However, where studies have been continued over longer periods, the beneficial effects of exercise on absenteeism and health care costs have reduced. The most significant reason for the reduction is the high level of dropout from exercise programmes. This is partly due to employees leaving the company, but also because of the problem of low exercise adherence. These problems will be discussed below. For companies in the UK, the existence of the National Health Service means that the motive to reduce health care costs is of less immediate relevance to individual companies. Nevertheless, there remain the suggested benefits of improved performance and enhanced commitment.

Participation in corporate fitness programmes

Most of the research in this area has been done in the USA and Canada, where such programmes are more extensive. In general, the expected recruitment rate to a corporate fitness programme is around 20 to 40 per cent of employees, but only one-third to one-half of the users will exercise on a regular basis at vigorous intensities (e.g. Shephard, 1986). Also, it is common to find that employees who are already physically fit are more likely to be recruited to the corporate fitness programme and to adhere to its programmes, compared to employees who are not fit. This suggests that corporate fitness programmes are simply making it easier and cheaper for those employees who already engage in physical exercise outside work to pursue their hobby. They are not attracting the 'unfit' employees who would really benefit from an involvement in physical activity. However, there are examples where recruitment and adherence rates have been much better. Furthermore, there are also less tangible benefits which may accrue to the company which offers corporate fitness programmes, influencing for example recruitment and retention.

Cases of more successful corporate fitness programmes are characterized by enthusiastic support from management, a predominance of white-collar employees, a high-profile experimental programme at the outset and a corporate orientation to health. For example, Canada Life Assurance initiated a corporate fitness programme in its head office in Toronto in 1978 (Song et al., 1982). Employees could register for two or three thirty-minute exercise sessions per week, which were held in the converted basement of the HQ office block. The sessions were either before work, in the lunch hour or after work and the registration fee was $10.00 for every two months. This money was used by the fitness co-ordinator to purchase 'prizes' for those who met certain standards of programme adherence and exercise participation.

In the first six months that the programme was operated, about 47 per cent of the 1,280 employees made at least some contact with the fitness co-ordinator. A number of these only came to have the initial fitness test and never participated further. Another group dropped out completely and others continued to attend but on a very irregular basis. The last group was the largest and comprised those who continued to attend two or more sessions a week on average. After seven years the programme was still attracting substantial support, with 400 active members. The programme was also found to encourage increased participation in community physical activities, both among those who did not participate in the corporate programme, and as a supplement for some of those who did.

The Canada Life project was also fairly successful in recruiting those not fit initially. This was seen to be due, first, to the initial publicity of the programme which was directed at those who were unfit, encouraging them specifically to join. Second, members were assessed at the outset in terms of their physical ability and directed to classes graded according to ability. This meant that recruits were less likely to become discouraged because they could not live up to the expectations of the instructors or the performance of other group members. Finally, the instructors progressed the classes at a deliberately slow pace so that individuals did not feel threatened and did not suffer injuries. Also, the aim of the initial programme was to encourage eventual lay leadership of the programme (employees themselves taking the classes). This was eventually achieved.

The fitness programme introduced by General Foods Corporation in New Jersey, USA, is an example with a lower level of recruitment and adherence. The programme also tended to attract those already physically fit (Morgan et al., 1984). General Foods constructed a Health Fitness Centre, including medical and exercise testing facilities, a large, covered, indoor/outdoor jogging track, a gym, a weight training room, outdoor jogging and skiing trails, and shower and locker areas. Employees could join as members for a small monthly fee which was deducted from the payroll and they could use the facilities in their own time. This is the general pattern, although companies differ significantly in the fees for membership. There are also a handful of firms which allow employees to exercise during company time.

General Foods hired trained professionals to organize a variety of exercise programmes, including jogging, aerobic sports, aerobic dance, strength-building, flexibility and relaxation. As space at the facility was limited, members had access for two and one-half days per week. Initially, 13 per cent of eligible employees took up membership, with those who worked close to the facility being more likely to join (22 per cent). What was more encouraging was the finding that at a follow-up evaluation after twenty months, 53 per cent of the men and 62 per cent of the women who had been inactive at the start of the programme were still participating regularly in exercise sessions. Thus, the programme had encouraged some employees to take up regular exercise, albeit a minority of the total population of employees.

Corporate fitness programmes and enhanced performance
Unfortunately, many of the studies evaluating corporate fitness programmes have methodological weaknesses. However, the growing body of evidence would suggest that there can be positive effects from such programmes. For example, Bernacki and Baun (1984) studied the effects of exercise on work performance. Individuals were classified as high or low performers before an exercise programme was introduced into the company. This classification did not change after participation in the programme had begun. However, a significantly greater proportion of those designated 'high performers' participated in the exercise programme than did low performers. Thus, while high performance was associated with exercise, this was not a causal relationship. This suggests that increasing the exercise levels of sedentary employees is not likely to benefit performance. Nevertheless, the provision of corporate fitness facilities can still contribute to enhanced performance through the selection process. Individuals must choose to work for a corporation. If a company provides an exercise facility, this might attract those interested in developing or maintaining their fitness. These people are more likely to be highly motivated and to achieve high levels of performance. Putting effort into inducing non-exercisers to exercise may well be of secondary importance with only moderate levels of success given the generally low adherence rates among this group. However, as the Canada Life Assurance example illustrates, success can be achieved if resources are appropriately directed.

Shephard (1986) concludes that for a corporate exercise programme to recruit significant numbers of employees, effort must be put into an appropriate shaping of behavioural intentions. This will require a long process of education to promote attitudes and values which endorse the merit of exercise. The goal must be to create a social norm in which regular physical exercise becomes an accepted part of corporate life. Furthermore, once the individual employee has been induced to participate in the programme, an effective system of external rewards will need to be used to maintain the individual's participation until such time as adherence is sustained by the internal rewards of exercising. Finally, consideration needs to be given to enabling factors such as flexible hours of work, child care and family programmes, so that intentions to exercise can be translated into behaviour. Baun and Bernacki (1988) suggest that the effort expended in developing a corporate culture in which exercise and good health become an inherent employee desire and responsibility will reap tremendous rewards: 'stronger, healthier employees who are absent less, consume fewer health care dollars, and are more productive and happier at work' (Baun and Bernacki, 1988: 346).

The growth of corporate fitness programmes looks set to continue, propelled by the sometimes exaggerated claims from companies which have introduced them. While there are clearly some beneficial effects for individuals and organizations where a corporate fitness programme has been introduced, more research is needed to establish the conditions which maximize the benefits. Otherwise, the benefits will be seriously limited by the problems of both recruitment and retention (Brennan, 1982). Research is needed which can establish how to improve participation and adherence to such programmes. Research needs to identify:

- Factors which predispose an individual to participate, for example knowledge, attitudes, beliefs, values and perceptions which create an intention to get involved in physical activity.
- Factors which enable those intentions to be translated into action, such as personal and corporate resources, as well as the individual's personal activity skills.
- Factors which reinforce the behaviour, ensuring the individual adheres to the fitness programme.

Research to date illustrates the potential of corporate fitness programmes, with benefits for both the organization and the individual. It is likely that more companies will introduce such programmes in the future. Once research has established how to maximize participation and adherence, the benefits are likely to be substantial.

STRESS MANAGEMENT TRAINING

Like the promotion of healthy lifestyles, stress management focuses on health promotion rather than stress reduction. In fact, stress management training is not a technique per se. Rather it refers to a collection of techniques that seek:

1   To foster among employees an awareness and recognition of environments and experiences that may lead to stress.
2   To educate managers to be aware of the early signs of stress both in themselves and in other people.
3   To teach managers how to reduce their level of arousal or stress through techniques such as relaxation, meditation, biofeedback and various cognitive-focused methods.

Such programmes do not focus on those who are already suffering from high levels of stress. They aim to prevent stress escalating rather than to cure those who are already suffering the negative effects.

In general, studies evaluating stress management programmes have confirmed their effectiveness for reducing anxiety, depression, somatic complaints, sleep disturbances, muscle tension levels, blood pressure and urinary catecholamines (e.g. Charlesworth et al., 1984; McNulty et al., 1984). However, as with the research on corporate fitness programmes, much of the research has been methodologically weak (Murphy, 1988). Often there has been no follow-up to assess the stability of the changes over time. Where such follow-up has been done, the changes are typically not sustained and there is a regression to the baseline. Furthermore, very few studies have examined the relative effectiveness of different training methods. Thus, a management stress programme might include relaxation training, biofeedback and cognitive-refocus training. But there is seldom a systematic attempt to identify which of these components is responsible for any observed change. Indeed, this has led some to conclude that, while doing something appears to be better than doing nothing, the specific technique used does not matter much. Studies are further restricted by the fact that, for practical and ethical reasons, they have to rely on employees who volunteer for stress management training. This restricts the ability to generalize results to a wider population.

One example of a better controlled study (Bruning and Frew, 1985) systematically compared a variety of stress management techniques for their effect on various physiological measures: pulse rate, blood pressure and galvanic skin response. The methods compared were management skills training, which included goal setting, time management and conflict resolution; clinically standardized meditation; physical exercise; and a combination of these methods. The study found that each technique was effective in reducing pulse rate and blood pressure, although the largest decreases occurred in the group that undertook the skills management training. They also found that the techniques had a differential impact on the physiological measures, suggesting complex patterns of interaction at the individual level.

Stress management and organizational functioning

While an improvement in individual health might be a motive in itself, most organizations introduce stress management programmes in the belief that there will be a positive payoff for the organization, for example an increase in job satisfaction and productivity, and a decrease in absenteeism, turnover and accidents or injuries. Results from different studies vary, partly because of the many methodological weaknesses already referred to. A study reported by Murphy (1988) which used supervisory ratings of employee performance concluded that training in biofeedback, muscle relaxation or cognitive skills did not result in significant improvements in work performance. In one example of research, the effectiveness of a cognitive-behavioural stress programme was assessed. This involved six training sessions which focused on changing cognitions (negative self-statements and irrational beliefs), increasing assertiveness and fostering social support. A group of twenty-eight workers received the training and a waiting list of twenty workers was used as the control group. Outcome measures included productivity and absenteeism. The results showed significant increases in productivity and decreases in absenteeism over the study period. Unfortunately, these changes were evident for the control group as well as for those who actually received the training. This study emphasizes the importance of including a control group in the research design and points to the limitations of the many studies which do not include such a group.

In summary, despite the increasing popularity of stress management programmes in work settings, the findings related to their effectiveness are equivocal. Some are highly critical of such programmes, referring to them as a 'band-aid' solution. That is, they try to cover up the stress rather than remove its causes. Thus, in reviews of stress management programmes it is found that the majority focus on the individual as the target of change and do not include interventions aimed at modifying the stressful aspects of the work environment itself. If it is jobs and work environments that are the predominant causal factors in the onset of stress, then clearly such individual-focused initiatives are likely to have limited success. Nevertheless, as was pointed out in the last chapter, such programmes may always have a place in work settings, as there will always be stress which employees experience from outside the workplace. It would therefore seem appropriate to continue to include such programmes, but only as a supplement to interventions directed at organizational change. Such programmes could then play an important role in health promotion rather than in stress reduction.

CAREER PLANNING AND DEVELOPMENT

The literature on career development is concerned with how promotion systems, placement decisions, career tracks and human resource management can either inhibit or facilitate the career of the individual employee (e.g. London and Stumpf, 1982; Rosenbaum, 1984). There are two divergent perspectives on such career development activities (Nicholson and Arnold, 1989):

1   *Organizational responsibility*: the dominant approach adopted by organizations is a paternalistic one. It is based on the premise that management has the responsibility for designing and operating career systems for employees. Career planning involves designing internal career paths that will satisfy the strategic needs of the organization as well as the psychological needs of the employees.
2   *Individual responsibility*: the alternative view, and the one increasingly emphasized in the academic literature (e.g. Herriot, 1992), is that people benefit most if given the opportunity to build and plan their own careers.

Career development is typically seen as an organizational responsibility because the overriding concern is to improve the current performance of employees and to provide a pool of talent for the

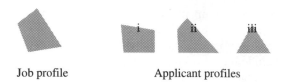

Job profile   Applicant profiles

Figure 2   The psychometric approach: matching a square peg to a square
hole

future. Thus, organizational effectiveness is the primary consideration, with the needs of the individual of secondary importance. In
many companies, while there might be lip service paid to the idea that
individuals need to take responsibility for their own actions, in
practice it seems the individual is treated as a passive recipient of
organizational decisions (Fletcher and Williams, 1985). This is true
both of the initial selection of an individual employee and of
decisions made about the subsequent career development of that
individual. This is because the traditional view of both selection and
development is a *psychometric* one (Herriot, 1984). Selection and
development decisions are viewed as decisions which are the sole
prerogative of senior managers within the organization. The role of
these managers is to put up hurdles over which both potential recruits
and current employees must jump in order to get a job, or be
promoted vertically or horizontally.

The psychometric approach is based on the notion that jobs are
made up of a range of specified tasks and that to be able to carry out
these tasks, a person with a particular set of abilities and attributes is
required. Individuals vary in their abilities and attributes and these
can be assessed. Thus, both selection and career development involve
the assessment of individuals by management to find the person with
the best match to the desired abilities and attributes. It can be
described as a process of trying to match the 'shape' of the job with
the 'shape' of the person, as depicted in Figure 2.

The alternative view, and the one promoted in the recent academic
literature, emphasizes that both selection and career development
should be viewed as reciprocal. The individual has to make a
decision, as well as the organization. The individual has to make a
decision as to whether she feels that the job or promotion being
offered fits in with her own expectations. Herriot describes this as a

Job   Individual

Figure 3   The exchange approach: negotiating job and individual fit

process of 'exchange' (Herriot, 1984). The individual and the organization exchange information until a mutually agreed decision is made. This decision is made on the basis of the open negotiation of expectations by both parties. Either party can break off the exchange at any point if it is felt that there can never be an agreement which matches the expectations of both parties. From this exchange perspective, both the job, in terms of the tasks involved, and the characteristics of the individual are seen to be more flexible than from the traditional, psychometric perspective (see Figure 3). Jobs can be successfully carried out in more than one way so that there is not a fixed requirement for a particular set of attributes and abilities. Moreover, the abilities and characteristics of the individual are seen to be less rigid, as behaviour is seen to be as much the result of environmental circumstances as individual attributes.

Self development

In terms of career development, this exchange perspective places the emphasis on the individual employee who will be an active agent in planning her career, rather than a passive recipient of organizational decisions about her career. While the dominant pattern within organizations remains one where it is senior management which takes control of the career process, there is evidence that promoting individual involvement in career development is increasing. Such involvement usually places emphasis on encouraging the individual to put effort into planning her career. Career planning can be defined as a deliberate process for: becoming aware of self, opportunities, constraints, choices and consequences; identifying career-related goals; programming of work, education and related developmental experiences to provide the direction, timing and sequence of steps to attain a specific career goal (Storey, 1979).

One of the reasons why organizations continue to adopt the

traditional approach to career development and why individually oriented career planning approaches are avoided is the fear that the latter will lead to certain negative consequences. For example, the fear is that an employee will raise his expectations as a consequence of being encouraged to think about his career, and that he will, in consequence, place increased demands on the training and development facilities. Also, it is feared that there will be increased turnover as individuals leave the organization, having been made aware that it cannot offer them what they really want in terms of a career. Evidence from the USA suggested that these fears were not justified in practice. For example, rather than increase expectations following career planning sessions, individuals were found to become more realistic about their present circumstances and future prospects (Williams, 1982).

More recently, however, research in the UK has indicated that these fears might be justified. For example, Fletcher (1991) found that candidates who had been unsuccessful on a development centre (see below) showed a drop in self-esteem. Robertson et al. (1991) found that, after going through a development centre, some individuals had become less committed to the organization. This may be because going through the process had driven them to think clearly about their own expectations and abilities, as against the expectations and requirements of the organization. Where these did not match, the effect of the development centre was reduced commitment. However, it could still be argued that this would be beneficial to the organization in the long run. It would mean that those for whom the organization could not satisfy career expectations would self-select out before a crisis was reached either for the individual or for the organization. It could also be argued that if such a self-awareness process and negotiation had been experienced prior to the individual actually starting work in the organization, i.e. during the selection process, then the negative outcome from the development centre would have been less likely.

Methods to encourage career planning by individuals

A range of methods can be used to involve individuals in their own development and career planning. The most popular are career workshops, career counselling and development centres.

Career workshops

Career workshops vary greatly but, in general, they aim to foster a climate in which participants can take stock of their achievements to date, and give careful thought to the future direction of their lives and careers. The emphasis is typically on including life goals, as well as specific work-related goals, as the two are so clearly interlinked. Initially, the focus is on promoting self-analysis: who am I and what have I done with my life to date? This involves the individual in exploring both achievements and disappointments in life. Such self-analysis provides the basis for assessing one's personal strengths and weaknesses, which can be used in planning for the future. Thus, individuals are encouraged to go on from here and think about their future by establishing career and life goals, and assessing what needs to be done to achieve these.

The unique aspect of a career workshop is that the learning will typically be achieved in groups. Individuals will often complete an exercise alone, for example listing life achievements to date, but then go on to share this analysis with the group. The use of such group exercises and discussions allows participants to exchange ideas and information within a supportive atmosphere.

Career counselling

The main type of career counselling that is offered can be described as crisis counselling. It is offered to try and help an individual cope with a career crisis. The most obvious example of this would be counselling offered when a person is made redundant. The objective of such counselling is to encourage the individual to look at how she can best 'salvage' her career. Such counselling would not help the individual to actually find another job, but would encourage her to think through the options, which might include, for example, the pursuit of a totally new career trajectory or indeed the acceptance of early retirement.

Such crisis counselling can be distinguished from developmental counselling. Here there is no immediate crisis, and the objective of counselling is to get the individual to take the responsibility for identifying her development needs and for thinking through the training and experience opportunities which might help her to address those needs.

In both cases the counselling approach is more likely to be non-directive (see Chapter 3), as the objective is to encourage the individual herself to take responsibility for planning her career, and for making decisions about training and experience. However, a directive approach is also possible, especially during crisis counselling. In a directive approach, the counsellor would be more proactive. For example, the counsellor might make suggestions about options the individual has which she would have been unlikely to think of herself.

Development centres

Assessment centres are becoming increasingly popular as a method to select people for jobs (Shackleton and Newell, 1994). Assessment centres involve using multiple methods of assessment on groups of job applicants to assess various attributes of each candidate which are deemed to be relevant to job success. The assessment methods may include psychometric tests, interviews, work simulation exercises, and a variety of group methods used to assess a candidate's personal and interpersonal skills. For example, a group exercise may include a group of candidates being given a problem to solve, within time limits. The behaviour of each individual candidate is observed and recorded to assess, for example, his ability to get on with others, his ability to influence others, his ability to express himself clearly, and his ability to think logically and clearly.

While assessment centres are still used mainly for this purpose, the same exercises and techniques are increasingly being used for training and development purposes (Newell and Shackleton, 1993). A development centre could be used in the traditional psychometric way, with career decisions being made *for* the individual *by* the assessors on the basis of his performance of the different tasks. However, at least in the literature if not always in practice, the emphasis of a development centre is on providing the individual with an opportunity to think about his career. Even the fact of participating in a development centre may encourage such a process, especially if the individual is exposed to activities which would become a part of the job if he was promoted. However, from a developmental perspective, the most important factor is the provision of feedback to the individual about his performance on the different tasks. This gives the individual useful information which can be used to make career plans. The interviews that are typically part of a development centre can then be used like a developmental counselling session, providing the opportunity for the person to talk about the career implications of this new-found self-knowledge.

For all three types of career development programme discussed, the major problem is establishing an environment in which the individual feels that he is not being judged and can therefore experiment with ideas about his future career. One factor that will affect this is the role of the person conducting the workshop, counselling or development centre. If that person is an employee of the organization, for example someone from the personnel function, then it is less likely that the client will feel confident that what he says will not be 'used as evidence against him'. In such circumstances it is less likely that the participants will open up (Fletcher and Williams, 1985).

Stress and career development

Models of stress generally include career development factors as a significant causal factor in the onset of stress (see Chapter 2). However, the research assessing how far career planning can reduce this stress has been limited. What research there has been has demonstrated that the causes of career development stress vary over the course of the life cycle. In the formative years of work, stress is seen to derive from disillusionment and frustration as career expectations are thwarted. This occurs because organizations, in attempting to attract the best young recruits, tend to 'overglamorize' the job which the person will be doing and exaggerate the speed at which the corporate ladder can be climbed. Young people thus enter their first job with unrealistically high expectations. They quickly become disillusioned with the reality of work.

At a later stage, problems of balancing commitments to work and private life dominate. In many organizations, there is a code of practice, often unwritten, which states that if an individual wants to progress up the organizational hierarchy they have to work excessively long hours. If such progress up the hierarchy is going to occur, it is likely to be between the ages of twenty and forty. Yet this is also the time when most couples that have children would be starting their family. Conflicts are therefore inevitable between the demands of a young family and the demands to work excessive hours. This conflict is especially apparent for women who tend to bear more of the responsibility for the family (Newell, 1993). A recent survey of managers demonstrated that women who are successful are much more likely to have foregone getting married and having a family than their male counterparts (Coe, 1992).

In the middle years, there is the problem of personal failure as one recognizes that career ambitions are not going to be met. Organizational hierarchies are arranged as a pyramid, with a broad base and a pinnacled top. The opportunities to progress are therefore severely limited, especially in the upper echelons. Given that many of those who start at the bottom (or even the middle) are ambitious to work their way up the hierarchy, there are inevitably going to be a lot of employees who do not match up to their early ambitions.

Finally, at the end of a career, there is the problem of winding down to retirement. Retirement can be a particularly unpleasant experience as the person moves from being a full-time employee, with a fully structured active day, to being a full-time retired person, with no set pattern to the day. In fact, the experience can be very similar to unemployment and occurs for the same reasons (see Chapter 5). In terms of Warr's vitamin model, the individual has moved from a situation where perhaps the job provided all the necessary psychological 'vitamins', to a situation where she must find activities herself to provide the needed vitamins (see Chapter 5).

Given these various problems with career development that have been identified, the introduction of initiatives which encourage the employee to plan his career more effectively would appear to have a significant potential for promoting more positive outcomes for the employee and the organization. Clearly, however, the career planning issues are different at the various stages of a career, as outlined above.

Formative years

Job changing is especially prevalent when an individual first enters the labour market with between 30 and 50 per cent of young people leaving their first job within the first three years of work. Research has shown that the same level of turnover is also evident among graduates (Parsons and Hutt, 1981). In the above study, the authors concluded that the reasons for the high level of turnover were that many of the graduates 'felt their abilities were not being used, were dissatisfied with the general nature and pace of work and saw limited opportunities for career development ahead of them'. Such problems are much less likely to materialize if organizations adopt an exchange perspective during the recruitment and selection process. If such an approach is adopted, new recruits would have the opportunity to discuss their own expectations, and compare these with the demands of the job and organization. Unfortunately, few organizations adopt such a perspective. Rather, in a bid to attract the 'best' candidates, the more typical approach is to present a very glossy image of the job and company. The aim of most recruitment publicity is thus to impress, rather than to give the potential applicant a realistic picture of what she will be doing if she is offered the job. The consequence is raised expectations which are thwarted when the individual actually experiences the reality. Unless the economic circumstances are particularly bad, the likely consequence is that the individual leaves the company.

The solution is to provide a more realistic picture of the job and the company. For example, Wanous (1977) advocates the use of a realistic job preview. This would involve giving the potential recruit as much information as possible about the job and company, perhaps including the opportunity actually to spend time working in the job that is being offered prior to actual acceptance. This might involve some costs, but compared to the costs of, for example, a graduate leaving after two years on an expensive training course, they would be insignificant. The challenge is thus to get candidates to self-select out not only so that those finally selected suit the job, but also so that the job suits them.

Premark and Wanous (1985) undertook a meta-analysis of twenty studies which had assessed the impact of realistic job previews. The results showed that such information had lowered applicants' optimistic expectations of what the job would be like, so that more actually left the selection procedure voluntarily before a decision had been reached by the organization. However, those that actually started work were more committed, more satisfied, performed better and were less likely to leave than were those who had not had such a realistic job preview.

Early career
At this stage, the problems are related to managing the interface between home and work. This is because this is the life stage where the person is most likely to be establishing his career and progressing up the organizational hierarchy. At the same time, it is also the period when he is likely to be establishing a family. The problem is that both these activities are potentially very time-consuming. Especially in the UK, climbing the career ladder involves demonstrating commitment through working long hours (Colgan and Tomlinson, 1991). This is not conducive with spending time with a growing family. In

the past this dilemma has been resolved because the mother of the child would not have a career and so could take sole parenting responsibility. The father was therefore released from most parenting duties. This remains the dominant pattern, even though more women both work and raise a family (see Chapter 6). However, there is increasing evidence that men, as well as women, would like to see change (Pleck, 1985). The solution would be for the organization to adopt a more flexible approach to career development, which allows an individual opportunities to progress at a later age, if the choice is made to devote less time to work and more time to the family in the early career stages.

Some organizations, for example the main banks, do have policies which allow either men or women to take career breaks to look after children. However, not only have very few fathers actually availed themselves of such opportunities, anecdotal evidence also suggests that if they had done so, their careers would have been 'blighted' for life. Indeed, the knowledge of this may well be a cause of the low take-up of such schemes by men. Organizations not only need to establish the structures which allow careers to be more flexible, they also need to change attitudes which typically remain thoroughly traditional (Newell, 1993).

Middle years
The major problem in the middle years is the realization that career aspirations are not going to be achieved. This is likely to become an increasing problem as organizational hierarchies flatten, so that opportunities are even more constrained at the top. The solution to this is to concentrate on horizontal as well as vertical development. The growth of interest in management competencies is a reflection of this concentration on horizontal development. Here, the emphasis is on developing skills across a broad range. Nevertheless, frustration can still be experienced, as individuals continue to use the metaphor of career ladder, with its emphasis on hierarchical success. The fact that they are not climbing a career ladder can be perceived as a personal failure. However, such frustration is less likely if the individual has been given the opportunity to realistically plan her career from an early stage, through one of the methods discussed above. If the individual has been encouraged to take responsibility for her career then she is less likely to be frustrated by decisions made by superiors about the direction her career should take.

Retirement

The final stage is when the individual moves into retirement. Again, the challenge is for organizations to adopt a more flexible approach. Some individuals might like the sudden and dramatic break from full-time employment to full-time leisure and find no problems in making the adjustment. Others find this experience very traumatic (as evidenced by Victor Meldrew in the BBC comedy series *One Foot in the Grave!*). Such people may prefer to be given the opportunity to adjust more slowly, perhaps through gradually reducing the hours of work. Also, the opportunity to engage in career planning should encourage the individual to prepare for the end of a career. It has been shown that such preparation can have very positive effects on the transition to retirement. Organizations can encourage such planning, either as a special activity for those coming up to retirement, or as part of the overall career development strategy which focuses on employees taking responsibility.

CONCLUSIONS

The initiatives covered in this chapter have value in their own right, as they can promote the well-being of employees. However, they do this not by changing the work itself but by changing the individual – making her fitter, physically and psychologically, and so more resilient to the stresses of work. For example, to encourage employees to be more physically active is important for the overall health, physical and psychological, of the individual. It may not directly lead to improved work performance but it has been argued that the provision of such opportunities will make it more likely that the organization can attract and retain potentially competent employees.

The problem with the initiatives covered in this chapter, however, like those covered in the previous chapter, is that, while they have value in responding to individuals who are experiencing stress, they address only part of the underlying cause. What is needed is a shift from traditional views of stress as a personal problem located within individuals, towards seeing it as an indicator of the ineffectiveness of working environments, systems and practices. Stress needs to be seen within the context of the organizational, political and social climate. Without this perspective, stress becomes inappropriately personalized. The final chapter in Part I analyses how work itself can be modified to contribute to the development of positive mental health.

5 *Work, positive health and improved performance*

INTRODUCTION

The Introduction emphasized that work can have a significant impact on an individual's mental and physical health. This impact can either be detrimental or enhancing. In Chapter 2 we considered the detrimental impact as we looked at how work can lead to stress, and all the attendant mental and physical problems associated with stress. In Chapters 3 and 4 we considered ways of reducing the negative effects of stress. However, this does not necessarily lead to positive mental health. In this chapter we consider positive mental health and analyse how the work environment can promote this. More importantly, we consider how and why this is important for an organization.

Most effort in psychology has been directed at understanding ill-health and identifying a recognizable pattern or syndrome of symptoms (e.g. a stress syndrome). This approach is based very firmly in a medical model of illness. However, there have also been attempts to understand the more general components of mental health, that is, the gradations of mental health among people who are themselves basically healthy. Much of this work has been done under the heading of the more specific topic of motivation. This is because good mental health is generally associated with being keen, eager, interested, etc., that is, with high levels of motivation. Poor mental health is associated with low levels of motivation – with lethargy, boredom, apathy, etc. We will first look at a specific model of mental health which incorporates several theories of motivation, but which has a broader focus than motivation alone. This model will then be used to analyse the features of work which contribute to mental health. It is argued that if an organization wishes to make full use of employee potential and encourage full commitment, it must concentrate on the work itself. As Kanter argues, 'the job makes the person' (Kanter, 1993: 3). It is the qualities embedded in the design of the job and its context which evoke behaviours from the job holder. This behaviour can either be a positive contribution to the organization or a negative (or at least neutral) one.

COMPONENTS OF MENTAL HEALTH

Warr (1987) discusses five components of mental health: affective well-being, competence, autonomy, aspiration and integrated functioning. We will discuss each of these briefly, bringing in, where relevant, the motivation theories which have been developed to analyse human effort in the work context. We will then consider the environmental model which Warr has developed to explain how certain features of work affect these aspects of mental health.

1 Affective well-being

This is the most general aspect of mental health and relates to our overall feeling – feeling good or feeling bad. However, Warr considers that it is more useful to think of two independent dimensions of affect, rather than just one. On the basis of previous research, he separates arousal and pleasure, each viewed as a continuum from positive to negative, as seen in Figure 4. Any affective state is thus represented by its level of arousal and pleasure. For example, feelings of depression are characterized by low levels of arousal and pleasure. The feeling of anxiousness would be described as low on pleasure but high on arousal. The feeling of being relaxed relates to high levels of pleasure and low feelings of arousal. Feeling cheerful and happy indicates high levels of both arousal and pleasure. While good mental health is generally associated with quadrants 1 and 2, mentally healthy people will also experience affects in quadrants 3 and 4 (see Figure 4). The distinguishing feature between the mentally healthy and unhealthy is the length of time which they spend in the various quadrants. The mentally healthy person may experience tension and gloom, but these feelings typically will not last a long time. The person with poor mental health is likely to experience the majority of her time in the negative states.

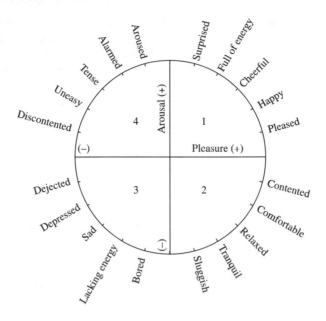

Figure 4   A two-dimensional view of affective well-being
Source: Warr, 1987: 27

2 Competence

This refers to the degree to which individuals believe that they will be successful in the things they do. Mentally healthy individuals have a high (although not unrealistic) opinion of their own abilities. Competency beliefs depend in part on a person's skills, but there will always be a cognitive dimension. Two children may have an identical level of skill (e.g. to swim fifty metres), but while one child believes that he can achieve this, the other child does not. Research has shown quite conclusively that the person who believes they can be successful will do better than the person who does not, all other things being equal. Bandura (1977, 1983) has developed a whole theory of motivation based on this idea, which he refers to as self-efficacy. Many studies have illustrated the power of self-efficacy beliefs. For example, children were given an IQ test and, in addition, were asked how competent they believed they were in mathematics. They were then given a maths test. Results showed that at each level of competence, as measured by the IQ test (high, medium and low), students who believed that they were more competent (high self-efficacy beliefs) did better than students who had a low opinion of their competence (low self-efficacy beliefs). Bandura explains this in terms of the effect of self-efficacy beliefs on a person's motivation. That is, the higher your belief in your own competence, the more effort you will put into ensuring success. This can be explained in terms of two dimensions which underpin process theories of motivation. Process theories seek to identify the relationships among the variables that contribute to the level of effort (i.e. motivation) an individual expends in a given situation.

a Expectations
If you have a high level of self-efficacy you are likely to have a high expectation of success in a particular endeavour. This notion of expectation is an important element in several process theories of motivation. For example, in Vroom's (1964) expectancy theory of motivation, *expectancy* is one of three components which determine the level of effort (i.e. motivation) that a person will expend on a given task. The other two elements are *valence*, which refers to the value that is placed on the likely outcome of an act; and *instrumentality*, which refers to the degree to which the person believes that there is a relationship between good performance and the attainment of a valued reward. In a situation where the expectancy, instrumentality or valence is low, the level of motivation is correspondingly low. For example, if you have an examination to sit, the theory suggests that your level of motivation, or the effort you expend on working for this examination, will depend on:

1 *Valence*: the value you place on the outcome, which would be passing or failing this exam. It might be an exam which you very much want to pass (high valence) or it might be one which you are not really bothered about (low valence).

2 *Expectancy*: you might want to pass the exam and believe that if you work hard, your performance will improve (high expectancy) or believe that, however hard you work, you simply do not have the ability to improve your performance in the particular subject being examined (low expectancy).

3 *Instrumentality*: you might believe that your performance will improve if you put in extra effort and that this will lead to the

valued reward of passing (high instrumentality), or that, however good your performance, this will not lead to the valued reward (low instrumentality), for example, because you believe that your particular examiner never passes anyone on their first attempt at this exam and this is your first attempt.

b Goals

A high level of self-efficacy belief will also ensure that a person sets herself reasonably difficult goals and works hard to achieve those goals, persevering in the face of difficulty. This is an important component in Locke's (1968) goal theory of motivation. This theory suggests that setting specific and difficult, but attainable, goals can increase motivation. People with a low self-efficacy belief will assume that they can achieve little. In consequence, they are likely to set relatively easy goals to start with. Furthermore, they are likely to give up more quickly if they do not see any movement towards these goals, as this would simply be used as confirmation of their low belief in their abilities.

Not all incidents of low competence belief should be taken as evidence of low mental health, as clearly every individual will have certain areas where they are incompetent or less than fully competent. Rather, it is a person's general approach to tasks, i.e. whether there is typically a positive belief that these can be achieved successfully, which reflects good mental health, or whether there is typically a negative belief that failure will occur, which reflects low mental health.

3 Autonomy

The concept of autonomy is captured very well by Argyris (see Chapter 1). Argyris (1964) describes the development of a child as she moves gradually from a state of total dependence as an infant to being an independent person as an adult. As an independent person, she then relies upon personal judgements in deciding a course of action and, in consequence, feels responsible for the outcomes of that action. This can be contrasted with the individual who does not achieve this stage of autonomy and always feels that it is other people that determine what happens to her: 'she becomes a straw in the wind, a piece of driftwood carried by currents'. The healthy person is thus independent and responsible. There are two psychological theories which are clearly related to this concept of autonomy.

a Locus of control

The concept of locus of control (Rotter, 1966) subsumes this idea of autonomy. Rotter suggests that individuals differ in seeing the causation of events and their reinforcing consequences as either internal (under their own control) or external (beyond their own control). While there will always be examples of situations where an individual has little, if any, ability to influence events, this is considered to be the exception. In most situations the individual is seen to have at least some control over his actions and so is held responsible for the outcomes. Individuals who do not believe that they are in control of their lives (externals) are considered to have poorer mental health. The person with good mental health believes that he is able to resist environmental influences and determine his own opinions and actions (internals).

b Attribution theory

The element of autonomy is also an important component of attribution theory. Attribution theory suggests that we always look for the *causes* of both our own behaviour and the behaviour of other people. We want to attribute behaviour to something. There are basically two types of attribution that we can make. We can attribute behaviour to:

1   *Internal factors*: a person (or ourselves) has behaved as she has because of factors within herself. If we attribute behaviour to internal causes, we can decide that this is either due to *effort*, the person has done well because she has worked very hard (or failed because she has not worked hard enough); or that it is due to *ability*, the person has done well because he has a natural talent for this type of activity (or has done badly because he lacks talent).
2   *External factors*: the person (or ourselves) has behaved as she has because of outside pressures. External attributions may be that the behaviour was either caused by *luck* (good or bad), or that the person was helped (or hindered) by *other people*.

Research has shown that the attributions we make tend to have certain biases, thus resulting in common errors in how we perceive behaviour. For example, we tend to recognize the external influences on our own behaviour but in considering the behaviour of others we tend to underestimate such factors and so perceive their actions as stemming largely from internal factors. This is important because it is only when we make an internal attribution that we hold a person responsible for their actions. Thus, when a person makes a mistake in a work situation we tend to hold them personally responsible for this, seeing it as due to either a lack of effort or a lack of ability. We tend to ignore the many factors in the situation which may have contributed significantly to the mistake.

In terms of attributions for our own behaviour, while we are more able to recognize external factors which have contributed to the outcome, there is a tendency to be biased depending on the outcome. If we have been successful, we tend to attribute this to internal factors – of course I managed to win the contract, I put a lot of effort in and have a flair for selling. On the other hand, if things turn out rather badly then we find all sorts of external 'excuses' for this – of course I did not manage to win the contract, the product I was trying to sell was weak and the competition was particularly strong. Up to a point this is a healthy way to respond as it helps to protect and boost our self-esteem. Poor mental health is characterized by a tendency to make personal attributions in exactly the opposite way – to attribute successes to external factors while taking the blame when things go wrong.

4 Aspiration

Good mental health is seen to require more than passive contentment with the status quo. The healthy person aspires to better himself and makes active efforts to achieve this. The need theories of motivation developed by Maslow (1954) and Herzberg (1966) have emphasized this aspect of health in particular. Need theories consider what motivates our behaviour.

a Maslow's need hierarchy

Maslow's (1954) hierarchy of needs identifies five levels of need. The two lowest levels in the hierarchy are *physiological* and *safety* needs – the need for food and water, and the need for shelter and a sense of security. The satisfaction of these needs is necessary for basic survival. Maslow suggests that if these needs are not satisfied, people will put all their effort into finding ways of satisfying them. However, once satisfied (and Maslow assumed that these needs would be basically satisfied in the developed world), these needs are no longer motivating and the person will move up the hierarchy to the next level of need – *social* needs. This refers to the need for friendship, companionship and affiliation. Once these social needs are satisfied, they no longer motivate and the individual moves up to the next level and is motivated by *esteem* needs, or the need to feel that one is respected and appreciated by others around one. The final level in the hierarchy is termed *self-actualization*, which is seen as the striving to fulfil one's personal potential. According to Maslow, healthy people are those who are motivated at this level. They have satisfied all the lower-level needs and are moving towards the actualization of what they might be. Maslow feels that this need can never be satisfied completely as there are always more aspects of the self that can be developed. However, the healthy person is continuously aspiring to fulfil her own ideal nature, striving to overcome environmental and personal constraints.

b Herzberg's two factor theory

In a similar way, looking specifically at the work environment, Herzberg (1966) suggests that the features of work which determine motivation are aspects which enable the individual to grow psychologically. He calls these factors *motivators*. Motivators are intrinsic features of the job which give the person a feeling of achievement, responsibility and recognition, and thus allow scope for personal growth. Herzberg distinguishes this set of motivator factors from what he calls hygiene factors, which include aspects of the work environment such as pay, company policy, quality of supervision, physical work conditions, relations with others and job security. These hygiene factors can be a focus of dissatisfaction for workers, but cannot motivate the expenditure of extra effort.

While there has been much criticism of the need theories of Maslow and Herzberg as explanations of motivation, they nevertheless do help us to understand this component of aspiration which is linked to mental health. This is because these theories are concerned with satisfaction rather than motivation. They consider the factors which people in general find satisfying. However, the process theories of motivation have demonstrated clearly that the link between motivation and satisfaction is not always direct – happy workers do not necessarily work harder. Such satisfaction theories are relevant, however, because mentally healthy people are generally considered to be satisfied. Nevertheless, the mentally healthy person is not considered to be the person who accepts the present state and has no desire to improve herself or the environment in which she lives. Mentally healthy people aspire to improve both themselves (to self-actualize) and their environment.

In contrast, it is also possible to have unrealistically high aspirations which can never be achieved. This is likely to lead to distress, as the person continually fails to achieve her goals. An example of this is the research which has shown that unfulfilled career aspirations can lead to stress. Career aspirations often remain unfulfilled because they were initially set unrealistically high.

5 Integrated functioning

This final feature of mental health discussed by Warr refers to the person as a whole and considers the interrelationships between the first four components. It is a difficult feature to define, but suggests a person who is 'balanced' and 'in harmony'. For example, Jahoda (1958) emphasized that a mentally healthy person was someone who was consistent in character, had a unified outlook on life and was able to successfully accept or resolve mental conflicts. Integrated functioning is also sometimes considered in relation to the balance a person finds between the different aspects of life – love, work and play. A mentally healthy person is considered to have found a balance between the importance of family relations, paid employment and leisure. So, the 'workaholic', who can only find time for work, is not considered to exhibit good mental health.

This last point illustrates how the concept of mental health is socially constructed. The components of mental health considered above are deemed to define the healthy person in Western society in the twentieth century. At other periods in history, and in other cultures, a very different concept of mental health may exist. For example, independence and autonomy are considered to be positive features in our society, whereas in other cultures and periods of history these same features would be used to suggest that the person was unhealthy or even ill, the healthy person being the one who exhibited strong dependence on others. As an example, even until recently, women in Western societies were not expected to be too independent. It was considered 'correct' for the woman to remain dependent first on her biological family and then on her husband. As another example, Muslim tradition dictates that women are not expected to want to have any autonomy in the choice of marriage partner.

Thus, the concept of mental health must always be situated within a particular context and seen as a manifestation of cultural or societal norms. The components of mental health discussed here are features which have been defined by Western society in this century. Furthermore, different writers emphasize different aspects of mental health, so that there is no agreed definition, rather the components considered above are those which summarize different approaches. The 'fuzziness' of the concept needs to be borne in mind as we turn to consider factors in the work environment which are thought to influence the development of positive mental health in our society. We will argue that it is important for organizations to provide work environments which promote positive mental health because mentally healthy employees have precisely those attributes which are necessary to the survival of organizations in the 1990s and beyond.

ENVIRONMENTAL FEATURES WHICH AFFECT MENTAL HEALTH

We are not born mentally healthy or mentally ill, except perhaps in extreme cases of ill-health where there is a strong genetic component, such as schizophrenia. But even here it is clear that environmental factors play some role in the course which the illness takes. Psychologists have thus sought to describe features of the environment which influence the development of a mentally healthy person. In this context, much research has been done to identify childhood experiences which inhibit or advance the development of a healthy adult. In this book we are concerned with features of the work environment which might affect the well-being or mental health of the adult employee. Less research has been carried out in this area, but there is a growing literature which does identify features of the work environment which can have an impact. Somewhat perversely, one of the richest sources for understanding the impact of work on mental health has come from studies of those without work – the unemployed. The next section will consider briefly some of this research.

The impact of unemployment on mental health

Research on the impact of unemployment dates back to the Depression of the 1930s. From this early work there emerged a stereotyped picture of this impact. This stereotype had two central themes.

1 A stage reaction

It was suggested that, on becoming unemployed, an individual would typically pass through a range of experiences and emotions which were common to most people who lost their job. While there were various versions of these stages, the most commonly cited model depicted four (Eisenberg and Lazarsfeld, 1938):

1   *Shock*: on first becoming unemployed, the individual would typically react with shock, not able to believe that it had actually happened to him as an individual. This reaction was said to occur even though unemployment was widespread and so the probability of a person losing his job was high. This shock was often manifested in physiological symptoms, such as a loss of appetite and insomnia.

2   *Optimism*: once the initial shock had been overcome, the individual was said to go through a 'holiday' period. The person expected to find work fairly soon and so decided to use the unexpected free time to engage in activities which he had previously not had time for. This might have involved DIY around the house or the pursuit of a leisure interest. This stage was also said to be the most active period in terms of searching for work, with the individual using a variety of avenues to look for work and making many job applications.

3   *Pessimism*: one of the negative effects of the optimism stage was found to be that because the individual was applying for many jobs, he was also receiving a lot of rejections. Despite the fact that a person might know that the competition for a job is very fierce, being told that 'you are not good enough' for a particular job (however politely worded) is a very demoralizing experience. Repeated rejections, even in someone with an initially high sense of self-esteem, is likely to have a negative impact. The result of this was said to be that the individual entered the next stage in the cycle, that of pessimism. The person is much less certain about his chances of finding work and becomes distressed and anxious.

4   *Fatalism*: the final stage in this model was reached when the individual gave up hope of ever working again. The individual had come to believe that he was not capable of holding down a job and accepted and adapted to the status of 'unemployed' or even 'unemployable'. The individual was then said to have a 'broken attitude'.

2 Negative mental health

The second feature of the stereotype was the notion that unemployment had a characteristically negative impact on mental health. It was found to lead to feelings of personal inadequacy, a loss of personal identity, a loss of drive, boredom, loneliness, social isolation and an experience of disintegration of time. Thus, while it was suggested that there was a stage of optimism, experienced near the beginning of a period of unemployment, this was found to be short-lived for most. So the characteristic impact of unemployment on mental health was negative.

When unemployment again surfaced as a major social problem in the 1970s and 1980s, renewed research effort was put into considering the psychological impact. Initially, researchers used the stereotype from the 1930s and argued that, despite the reduced poverty associated with unemployment in the 1970s and 1980s, the same characteristic pattern of response could be identified. However, as the research became more sophisticated, it became apparent that individuals varied quite considerably in their responses, and so research concentrated on identifying factors which moderated the impact of unemployment. For example, it has been found in several studies that a strong social support network can help to buffer an individual against some of the negative impact of unemployment (Gore, 1978). Thus, today, it is recognized that the 1930s stereotype is not universally applicable. Nevertheless, it must still be acknowledged that, for the majority of people who lose their jobs (or indeed, for young people who are not able ever to find a job), the experience is a negative one and mental health declines.

Unemployment and the meaning of work

From the perspective of this book, what is important is that writers have sought explanations for this negative experience by examining the meaning of work. One of the most important early contributions in this respect came from Marie Jahoda (1982), who was involved in important research in the 1930s and who continued to work in this area in the ensuing period. Jahoda suggests that in understanding the meaning of work we need to consider the functions which it fulfils for the individual. She identifies two broad classes of functions. *Manifest functions* are concerned with the objective reasons why people work. That is, we work in order to gain the monetary reward which we use to pay for the things we need in order to live, and to pay for luxuries. While the unemployed lose this monetary reward, this in itself does not fully explain the negative impact of unemployment; otherwise unemployment would be no different from poverty and research has shown that there are important differences. The second set of functions to which work contributes Jahoda calls *latent functions* and these, she suggests, are more helpful in explaining the impact of unemployment. It is the removal or deprivation of these latent functions which accounts for the reduction in mental health – the reduction in affective well-being, feelings of competence, autonomy and aspiration, and integrated functioning. Jahoda identifies five latent functions of work:

1   *Work imposes a time structure on the working day*: work provides a structure to our lives and helps us to organize our daily existence. We may at times resent this imposed time structure, for example when we have to get up early to get to work on time, but its absence can lead to an uncomfortable experience of the disintegration of time, as is sometimes felt by the unemployed.

2   *Work implies regularly shared experiences and contacts with people outside the family*: work helps to tie us into the fabric of the community and gives us access to a pool of experience and contact. Without this arena for regular contact, the unemployed may become socially isolated and withdrawn from the community and society.

3   *Work links a person to goals and purposes which transcend her own*: whatever the specific nature of employment, a job does provide a person with a feeling of doing something of purpose, whether this is collecting the refuse or healing the sick. Without this daily experience that efforts can be combined to achieve something of use to society, the unemployed may experience feelings of uselessness, of being on the scrap heap.

4   *Work defines an individual's status within society*: at least in Western, contemporary society, to ask someone 'who are you?' normally results in the person providing an answer in terms of her job, following, perhaps, the provision of a name. When someone has lost a job, she may suffer from an undermining of personal identity.

5   *Work enforces activity*: work makes us get out of bed, go to work and engage in some kind of activity to satisfy the job require-

ments. Lacking this compulsion, those who are unemployed may become lethargic and bored, unable to find the self-motivation to 'get up and do something'.

Jahoda suggests that the negative impact of unemployment can be accounted for in terms of the individual being deprived of these latent functions of work. Of course, activity outside the formal job environment could provide access to each of these needed elements of life, but it is suggested that when a person (or even a society) has always relied on employment to satisfy these needs then it is difficult to find substitutes. Thus, for many women thirty years ago, employment was not the arena in which these functions were fulfilled, and it was suggested that the experience of unemployment was different for women as compared to men. However, the important factor would be the degree to which these functions of work are satisfied if a person loses a job. Where a person can find activities which substitute by fulfilling these latent functions, for example taking up voluntary work, a hobby or caring for the family, the negative impact is likely to be reduced. Indeed, a large number of moderating variables has been identified by recent research. These variables have been found to influence the impact of unemployment, and writers have attempted to explain their moderating impact in terms of how they substitute for these latent (or manifest) functions of work. For example, as seen, having more social support has been found to reduce the negative impact of unemployment (Gore, 1978). This might be because social contacts are maintained even though friendships during working hours have been curtailed.

There are those who argue that this deprivation account of unemployment is misleading as it portrays people as reacting passively to an environmental experience. They suggest that it would be more realistic to see people as responding *actively* to things that happen in their lives, making plans and seeking ways of coping with difficulties encountered. The interested reader is referred to Fryer and Payne (1984) for a full account of these ideas. This action-centred approach is clearly important, but it does not help to identify those features of a work environment which might influence a person's mental health. The deprivation account is useful as it focuses on features of work which can influence mental health. For example, one of the latent features of work is that it provides a person with 'something to do'. While the removal of this enforced activity may lead to boredom and lethargy among the unemployed, it is clear that jobs differ significantly in what this 'something' actually is. In some jobs the tasks are very mundane and there is little variety, while in other jobs the tasks may be intrinsically interesting and of wide variety. This is likely to have a differential impact on the mental health of the job holder. Thus, we can take the deprivation model further and consider how jobs vary in terms of the latent functions which they satisfy and how this impacts on mental health.

Warr's vitamin model

The most comprehensive attempt to consider the environmental features of work which affect mental health has been the work of Peter Warr (1987). He developed what he called a vitamin model. He outlines nine environmental features which will be present to a greater or lesser extent in a job. Each of these features of work is considered to be a necessary contributor to mental health, just as each vitamin is a necessary contributor to physical health. When the feature is not present, the person will be deprived and mental health will be adversely affected, just as when the body is deprived of one of the essential vitamins, physical health will suffer. The increasing presence of these environmental features of work will increase mental health, but only up to a certain plateau level, just as an increase in vitamins will improve health, but after a certain level of vitamin intake is reached, no further improvements will occur. Indeed, with certain vitamins there is the possibility that a person can have too much and then health will actually suffer. In a similar way, Warr suggests that for certain of the environmental features the level can become too high and mental health will suffer. We will first consider the nine environmental features and then consider their impact on mental health.

1 Opportunity for control

Jobs vary in the degree to which they enable the individual to control activities and events. Some jobs give the worker the freedom to schedule tasks, set objectives and decide how to achieve those objectives. Other jobs allow the worker very little input in any of these decisions. In Chapter 2 a lack of control was considered to be an important cause of stress, so that one can expect that jobs which do not allow the worker much, or any, control over what to do and/or which do not allow the outcome of actions to be predicted will be detrimental to mental health. Conversely, where the job offers a lot of opportunity for control mental health will be enhanced.

2 Opportunity for skill use

The opportunity both to use the skills one already has and to develop new ones is assumed to have a positive impact on well-being. Such opportunity enables one to achieve one's goals and aspirations which are seen to be important in mental health (see Maslow above). Where a job provides little opportunity to use and develop skills it is likely to be detrimental to health.

3 Externally generated goals

People in work occupy roles and associated with a role is a set of normative expectations about how the role occupant should behave in different situations. For example, as a lecturer I am expected to take certain classes, be available to students at various times, undertake designated administrative duties and engage in certain research-related activities. Thus, the requirements of a role provide a structure to the activities and allow the person to focus on the attainment of goals. This is likely to have a positive impact on mental health. By contrast, the job in which expectations are ambiguous or where demands are few (see Chapter 2) is likely to have an adverse effect on the role occupant.

4 Variety

In some jobs the task requirements are repetitive and the person stays in one place doing the same thing over and over again. This is unlikely to promote mental health. Where the job involves a wider variety of tasks in various locations this is likely to stimulate more interest and hence promote mental health.

5 Environmental clarity

This refers to the degree to which the job environment provides feedback to the individual about his performance. Feedback enables a person to know the consequences of actions taken, to predict outcomes in advance and to take steps to avert negative consequences. Also, environmental clarity relates to the degree to which role expectations are explicit and generally accepted by those in the person's role set (see Chapter 2). It is expected that where there is clarity, mental health will be improved and where this clarity is lacking, mental health will suffer.

6 Availability of money

Clearly, jobs differ in the financial rewards. This in itself may not affect mental health, but the absence of money is likely to restrict a person in many ways which will affect mental and physical health. For example, having to worry how the next bill will be paid is likely to be stressful, and not having money to pursue hobbies is likely to be inhibiting and frustrating.

7 Physical security

Job environments that involve adverse physical conditions such as cold, danger and lack of space, and/or psychological insecurity because they are not permanent, are likely to pose a threat to the individual, which in turn can affect mental health. Jobs where the environment is comfortable and permanent are consequently assumed to promote feelings of well-being.

8 Opportunity for interpersonal contact

Interpersonal contact is important for a number of psychologically important reasons. For example:

1   It provides the opportunity for friendship which is seen as a strong human need. Maslow's hierarchy of needs places social needs at the third level, just above basic survival needs.
2   It provides a person with a form of social support or help in the face of problems and difficulties.
3   It is often necessary to work with others to achieve one's goals. As an individual it may not be possible to have influence in work, but in coalition with others this becomes more possible.
4   It provides guidance on how to behave. For example, in a new job the person does not know how to behave, for instance with respect to the new boss. The person then looks to colleagues to see how they relate to the boss, for example in calling him/her by the first name or by the surname.

Thus, it is assumed that where job environments restrict access to interpersonal contact, mental health is likely to be adversely affected. As an example, it has been found that many home-based workers miss social contact. Successful home-working schemes have there-fore incorporated mechanisms to establish interpersonal networks among those who are working from home, either by ensuring regular meetings between members or setting up links electronically.

9 Valued social position

Positions or jobs exist within social structures. Jobs will have differing amounts of status attached to them depending on the value attributed to the activities associated with the role. This is the result of a social construction. There is nothing inherent to say that a doctor should be accorded more social status than a receptionist. While people may differ in the esteem in which they hold different jobs, there is also widespread agreement within society about the status which derives from particular positions. Those who hold a valued social position may be able to maintain higher levels of self-esteem and confidence, which is an important aspect of mental health, as we have seen.

Contribution of environmental features to mental health

These nine environmental features are the structural factors which will affect mental health at work. However, Warr also considers the process by which they operate, as outlined above, through his analogy with vitamins affecting physical health. The important aspects of this process are that:

1   While a deficiency in an environmental feature will impair mental health, an increase in that feature, beyond a required level, will lead to no further improvement in health.

2   For some of the features an addition beyond the required level will lead to a reduction in health, while for other features any addition will have no effect. The analogy is that too much of certain vitamins (A and D) will result in toxic poisoning and so reduce health; while for other vitamins (C and E), though you can have a deficiency, once the required level is reached, any additional intake will have no adverse or positive effect (see Figure 5). Warr considers that six of the environmental features operate like the A/D vitamins and three operate like the C/E vitamins.

   A/D vitamins: externally generated goals, variety, environmental clarity, and opportunities for control, skill use and interpersonal contact are all considered to be features which, if they have a low presence, will be damaging to mental health. However, if they are in an overabundance, this will also be damaging. For example, if a person is constantly required to develop new skills, this might pose a threat, as she does not feel able to cope.

C/E vitamins: availability of money, physical security and valued social position are considered as environmental features where mental health is unlikely to be affected by having too much of them. Only a deprivation of these essential features will impair mental health.

One point to note is that with all of these environmental features, the optimal level is not fixed as people will differ in what they need. In the same way, with vitamins, the optimal level will vary depending, for example, on body weight. With the environmental features what is optimal will depend not only on people's level of skill and experience, but also on their *perception* of their ability. This will determine whether they believe that they have the resources to meet the requirements of the situation. This issue of perception and belief was dealt with in more detail in Chapter 2.

Clearly, these nine features overlap to a considerable degree, but Warr argues that including them all provides a more comprehensive treatment of the environment. There is also clear overlap with Jahoda's (1958) latent and manifest functions of work, with the vitamin model expanding some of these functions. The importance of such models is that they provide a starting point for considering the impact of a job on a person's mental health. The vitamin model suggests that a job which contains limited vitamins (amounts of the nine environmental features) will have an adverse impact on mental health. By definition, to improve mental health in work, it will be necessary to improve the extent to which a job incorporates these features. The influence of these features on mental health should be considered in terms of what has been said in this chapter about what constitutes positive mental health, and what was considered in Chapter 2 about poor mental health or stress. For example, the need for job variety can be seen as deriving from the importance of competence and aspiration to good mental health. Conversely, too much variety is likely to be perceived as a threat, as the person does not believe that she can cope. In Chapter 2 we saw that perceived threat is a major precursor to stress.

When considering different organizational approaches to improving health and reducing stress at work, it is necessary to consider how far, if at all, they actually change the job environment to incorporate more of the 'vitamins'. The main criticism against the stress reduction and resilience techniques discussed in Chapters 3 and 4 is

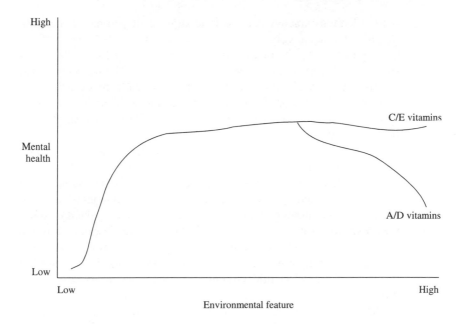

Figure 5 Contribution of environmental factors to mental health
Source: Warr, 1987: 10

that they focus on helping the individual cope with stress, rather than actually attempting to change the environment per se. The vitamin model would suggest that this can only be a short-term solution as it does not attempt to make the environment itself any 'healthier'.

CONCLUSION

We have considered in this chapter what is meant by 'good mental health' and looked at features of the work environment which can contribute to this. Of course, experiences outside the work environment, for example domestic circumstances and relationships, can also contribute to mental health. Furthermore, there will be an interaction between experiences outside work and experiences within work. For example, if a person, in his spare time, is organizing a local party political campaign which is very demanding and time-consuming, he may not be able to cope with responsibilities in work which normally he would find easy. But the important point is that the work environment can contribute significantly to mental health – positively or negatively.

From a moral point of view this can be considered important in its own right. To enhance the environment of work in the ways described in this chapter will contribute to the mental health or well-being of employees. More importantly, while it is more difficult actually to 'prove', healthy employees are likely to provide the crucial element for organizational success in the 1990s. Koopman describes how in 1978 he became aware of a dilemma within the company at which he was working – everything in the organization seemed to be in place, systems, procedures, technology, a booming market, but something was wrong. The 'something wrong' he diagnosed as a lack of commitment among employees – 'we had a lot of trained men but no committed soldiers' (Koopman, 1991: 5). He describes how he started to 'unlock' the human resources by democratizing the workplace, giving power and autonomy to the workers – increasing the level of mental health 'vitamins' available in the work environment.

Peters and Waterman (1982) similarly stressed the importance of employee commitment for successful businesses. However, as Herriot (1992) stresses, individuals will only continue (or start) to give this commitment if there is a reciprocal commitment to the individual on the part of the organization. Creating healthy work environments, i.e. environments which contain the necessary 'vitamins' for good mental health, is the only way to demonstrate that reciprocity. If the individual employee feels that he is simply being 'used' by the organization and is expendable if the economic fortunes of the company change, then it is unlikely that he will make the kinds of personal sacrifices that Peters and Waterman describe individuals as making in 'excellent' companies in order to achieve what the organization expects of them.

The example of Rover

Organizations need to consider changing jobs and work environments so that employees will want to contribute positively to the work organization. This is epitomized by Rover who acknowledge: 'Without a doubt, the successful businesses of the 1990s will be those who can attract, retain and motivate employees to use their full talents in the interest of the firm' (Bower, 1994). Employee attitude surveys conducted in the late 1980s had revealed that most Rover employees did not feel the best use was made of their talents or that they were given sufficient challenge in their job. They also felt that they were not particularly involved in problem solving, did not enjoy a relationship of mutual trust with their boss, did not have clear opportunities to develop themselves and did not receive recognition for their contributions and achievements. In other words, virtually all the environmental 'vitamins' at work were low and, in consequence, motivation and commitment to Rover were seen to be poor. Influenced by its partnership with the Japanese company Honda, Rover responded to these challenges by radically changing the work environment to harness the potential of all employees and to win their maximum contribution. The changes which were introduced can be clearly linked to the 'vitamin' model.

1 Opportunities for control

The organizational hierarchy was reduced from eleven layers in the manufacturing organization to six, and organizational units were created of between 3,000 and 10,000 people. The outcome of the move to a 'lean organization' was that responsibility was devolved to shop floor direct workers because there were far fewer middle managers and indirect workers to control and supervise them.

2 Opportunities for skill use

The increased responsibility of workers meant that they needed to use a broader range of skills. These skills needed to be developed. Rover created the Rover Learning Business (RLB) in 1990 to encourage such skill development. RLB was set up as a separate business within the Rover company and its aim is to provide assistance to everyone in Rover who wants to develop themselves. The emphasis is very clearly on learning – doing something for oneself – rather than training, which most people see as having something done to them. One of the first schemes launched by RLB was the Rover Employee Assisted Learning Programme (REAL). Under this programme, any employee is entitled to receive up to £100 a year for pursuing virtually any kind of learning programme. For example, employees have been financed to learn to swim, to learn a language, to develop IT skills. The initiative is intended to create a learning culture where people accept and are keen to update their skills and knowledge continuously.

3 Externally generated goals

One of Rover's main goals was to improve quality. To ensure that this goal was recognized by all employees, not just those at the top of the organization, Rover implemented a Total Quality Improvement (TQI) programme. To guarantee that all employees were aware of these corporate goals, over 500,000 training hours were devoted to TQI programmes covering all Rover employees. All employees are therefore aware of the Rover vision – 'to be internationally renowned for extraordinary customer satisfaction' – and TQI Steering Groups establish local quality improvement goals and measures which are cascaded to all employees through Quality Action Teams (management directed) and Discussion Groups (voluntary, shop floor teams).

4 Variety

One of the most important changes has been the introduction of teamwork. The teams have responsibility not only for production, but also for housekeeping, continuous improvement of processes/ products, quality control and inventories. This has inevitably increased the variety of work for shop floor workers who are no longer simply involved in a single routine job.

5 Environmental clarity

Rover had found that there was a lot of dissatisfaction about traditional approaches to feedback through appraisals and performance reviews. A new voluntary system of Personal Development Files was therefore introduced. This builds on the concept of Records of Achievement, and involves the individual employee, working with his line manager, thinking through career objectives and making plans to develop personal skills through gaining broader experience. Although it is based on a two-way commitment between the employee and manager, the emphasis is on personal responsibility. The individual owns the personal development file (a robust, pizza-box style plastic case) which is his personal record and plan. The system enables the employee to think through, with the support of his manager, what he wants from his work and how he can satisfy those goals.

6 Money

Interestingly, there were no financial incentives offered to Rover employees for accepting most of the changes that have been introduced.

7 Physical security

One of the most publicized aspects of the changes at Rover has been the introduction of a new employment contract for all permanent staff (the New Deal). The key feature of this contract is that it offers security of employment. While this does not actually guarantee that no one will ever receive a compulsory redundancy notice, it does emphasize Rover's commitment to its employees and provides a promise that the company will make every effort to find a job for all its workers. However, the contract also emphasizes the need for employees to be flexible – it does not guarantee that the employee will stay in the same job throughout his career. Indeed, it was this need for flexibility which led to the introduction of the New Deal. Rover has recognized that what it requires is a skilled and competent workforce who will be able to contribute to the success of the business. Resources are therefore put into training and developing employees so that they will acquire the skills which the company will need in the future, not simply the short-term skills which the company needs now. The result is that Rover can virtually guarantee job security because it will be ensuring that employees actually have the skills which will be needed.

8 Opportunities for interpersonal contact

The car industry was renowned for its lack of interpersonal contact as individuals worked on assembly lines in noisy environments which prohibited conversation (Goldthorpe et al., 1968). The move by Rover, and other car manufacturers, to teamwork has therefore radically changed the opportunities for contact with colleagues. Furthermore, Rover has introduced Discussion Groups, Quality Action Teams and Workshops whose aim is to encourage involvement of all employees in working together and ensuring the best possible working environment.

9 Valued social position

Another feature of the New Deal was that it eliminated the separate hourly paid and salaried staff grading structures, and created a single scheme based on a reduced number of occupational classifications. No employee now has to clock in, and there are single status terms and conditions.

Rover has thus recognized the importance of creating a healthy work environment where employees will be motivated to contribute to the company success. The success of this strategy is evident, with Rover now acknowledged as a very healthy company – so much so that it has been acquired by BMW who recognize its new-found strength. This takeover would never have occurred in the 1980s when Rover was simply seen as a massive tax burden by the British government who almost gave the company away to British Aerospace.

The changes introduced at Rover can be contrasted with the current strategy in other organizations which are attempting to increase flexibility through reliance on contract workers (Handy, 1989). For example, IBM has dramatically increased its use of contract workers. Contract workers are used precisely because they are expendable – they can be kept on or let go at the end of a contract at the will of the company. While this does provide the flexibility for the organization in the short term, it is likely to be at the expense of a healthy and committed staff. Contract work ignores the need for security. Moreover, it is also likely to create deficiencies in other environmental vitamins. For example, organizations are less likely to put resources into the training and developing of contract staff, and so there will be less opportunity for such staff to develop and utilize new skills.

Thus, while there is clearly a need for much greater flexibility of employees within an organization, the short-term solution of using contract workers is unlikely to be in the long-term interests of the company, at least if these contract workers are treated as mere resources to be brought in and displaced as the company needs them. Such a human resource policy can be compared to the original Scientific Management ideas of F.W. Taylor (see Chapter 1). It might look more economical from a pure short-term, monetary calculation, but it ignores the fact that employees contribute more than a 'pair of hands'. This was true of the early part of this century and is even more true today when the intellectual skills and dedication of employees are much more important than the physical skills which have largely been taken over by machines. The short-term reliance on contract workers will not lead to the development of the skills and commitment which will be needed to be competitive in a global market.

Nevertheless, organizations need to be increasingly flexible. While this means that organizations cannot guarantee jobs for life in the old bureaucratic sense – a job in one function where you gradually worked up the career hierarchy – they can guarantee *employability* (Kanter, 1993). Although specific jobs may disappear, companies can ensure that they continually invest in retraining and career counselling to upgrade people's skills so that they will always be employable, whether inside the company or outside. To do this will involve concentrating on providing the organizational environment that ensures the growth and development of all employees.

The current organizational demand for adaptability, innovation (Clark and Staunton, 1989) and proactive responsiveness (Zuboff, 1986) depends on employees who are willing and able to take responsibility, think creatively, contribute to teams, develop and utilize multiple skills, and so on. In other words, employees who are competent, independent and have high aspirations, i.e. have high mental health. Creating healthy work environments which contribute to the well-being of employees at the same time, therefore, develops the very skills and attributes which are essential for organizational success. Work environments which do not provide challenge, responsibility, variety, learning opportunities, and so on, will therefore not foster the human skills which are needed for organizations to respond to the dynamic and competitive environments in which they find themselves.

Part II
The organization and minority groups

6 *Discrimination at work*
The intolerance of diversity

INTRODUCTION

In Part I we considered the general effects of work on mental health, both positive (well-being) and negative (stress). This analysis has concentrated at the individual level, considering how the subjective and objective work environments affect the individual's well-being, and, in turn, how this affects performance in work. Now we will turn to consider how specific groups are adversely affected in work because they are discriminated against by a variety of more or less subtle processes.

All organizations have to make discriminations between individuals. This is the basis of selection and promotion, as the organization seeks to find the person who is most likely to satisfy the requirements of the job. From the individual's perspective, it is also important that she finds a job which matches her expectations and abilities. The problem occurs when these discriminations occur on the basis of unfair and irrelevant criteria, for example the colour of a person's skin or their sex. It is this unfair discrimination which we consider in this chapter.

Unfair discrimination occurs on the basis of criteria which are not relevant to the capacity to carry out the job. For example, a selection decision made on the basis of family ties is unfair to all those applicants who might actually have been better suited for the job but who did not have the 'right connections'. Apart from discrimination based on nepotism, other forms of unfair discrimination are based on stereotypical views about the relationship between particular types or groups of people and their ability to carry out different jobs. For example, the assumption that 'young women will leave the organization to raise a family' will disadvantage an individual female candidate in competition with a similarly qualified male candidate for a job opportunity, irrespective of whether this particular female candidate will either want to have a family in the future or want to give up work even if she does.

There are a number of sources of unfair discrimination, including discrimination based on sex, race and ethnic background, age, religion, disability and sexual preference. Each of these sources has its own independent roots. In this chapter we will concentrate on the two forms of discrimination which affect the largest proportion of people – sex and racial discrimination – and consider their causes and consequences. This background is necessary if we are to examine ways of reducing discrimination in employment. This issue is considered in Chapter 7 which examines equal opportunity strategies which organizations are adopting, and their effectiveness.

Unfair discrimination has an adverse impact on individuals subjected to it. Such individuals are less likely to be able to find satisfying jobs which make full use of their potential and are more likely to end up in jobs at the bottom of organizational hierarchies. Such jobs are much more likely to be deficient in the environmental vitamins which produce good mental health, as outlined in Chapter 5. Furthermore, such jobs are more likely to include features which are associated with stress, as outlined in Chapter 2.

The problem is that groups which suffer discrimination do not fit easily into the dominant structures and processes characteristic of most organizations, because these have been developed around the white, able-bodied, heterosexual, young to middle-aged, male, family breadwinner. Organizations find it more difficult to accommodate individuals who are different – they are intolerant of diversity. Organizations need to develop a much greater flexibility to accommodate non-traditional groups, if individual members of such groups are to be able to utilize their potential within work fully. Governments have responded to the problems of discrimination by introducing various pieces of legislation which make it illegal to discriminate.

EQUAL OPPORTUNITIES LEGISLATION

It is only possible to give a brief overview of the Equal Opportunities (EO) legislation in this chapter, but this provides a useful background for considering the evidence of continued discrimination.

The Equal Pay Act, 1970 and the Equal Pay (Amendment) Regulations, 1983

The Equal Pay Act, 1970 sets out to eliminate discrimination between men and women in pay and other terms and conditions of employment contracts such as bonus payments, piecework, sick leave and holidays. Under this act a woman has the right to equal pay and terms of contract when she is employed:

1   *On like work*: where a man and woman are doing work of the same or a broadly similar nature.
2   *On equivalent work*: in jobs which have been rated as being equal (or equivalent) under a job evaluation scheme, pay must be equal.
3   *On work of equal value*: the act was amended in 1983 by the Equal Pay (Amendment) Regulations which came into effect from January 1994. The amendments were introduced as a result of proceedings against the UK government by the European Commission. Under Article 119 of the Treaty of Rome, which Britain had signed on joining the EC, governments are obliged to enact measures which enable an employee to claim equal pay for work of equal value, free of sex discrimination. The amendment gives a woman the right to equal pay and conditions of employment when she is employed on work of equal value. Under this condition, there is no need for the job to be similar, or for there to be a job evaluation study. It simply needs to be shown that, in terms of skill, effort and decision-making, the job of the woman is of equal value to the organization as the job of a man. For example, a cook at Camel Laird claimed that her work was of equal value to painters and joiners. The cook was awarded equal pay although the case went to an appeal.

This equal value amendment was needed because many existing pay structures and differentials were, and are, based on traditional views and attitudes, reflecting a system of values which is rooted in past traditions. These traditions are based on the premise that it is the male who is the breadwinner and who therefore needs to be paid a 'family wage'. Women are simply working for pin money or to support themselves and so can be paid less. The amended Equal Pay Act raises the possibility of questioning and challenging the traditional system of values which sees female labour as 'less worthy'. It provides a vehicle through which women can actually challenge the status quo legally. Unfortunately, although there have been a few test cases which have actually done this, the numbers are so small that they have had little impact on the general regard for 'women's work'.

Details of average earnings suggest that the act and the amendments have had relatively little impact. Prior to 1975, women's average hourly earning were 63 per cent of men's. Since 1989, the Equal Opportunities Commission (EOC) published separate figures for white-collar and manual workers which show that women's pay still lags considerably behind men's in 1993. In manual work, women on average earned 28 per cent less than men and in white-collar work, they earned on average 33 per cent less. Furthermore, women make up 68 per cent of the five million employees earning less than the Low Pay Unit poverty threshold. The act has reduced blatant discrimination in terms of women's pay. However, equal pay will never be a reality until the problem of equality of opportunity is tackled. This is what the Sex Discrimination Act set out to address.

The Sex Discrimination Act, 1975

The 1975 Sex Discrimination Act (SDA) is typically thought of as an act to prevent discrimination against women but, in fact, it applies equally to both sexes. The SDA states that it is 'unlawful to treat anyone, on the grounds of sex, less favourably than a person of the opposite sex is or would be treated in the same circumstances'. Thus, in Jeremiah v. Ministry of Defence there was found to be unlawful discrimination because only the men had to do unpleasant jobs.

The act covers discrimination in different areas of life. In employment, it is against the law to discriminate on the grounds of sex and marital status. This includes discrimination in recruitment and selection, advertisement of jobs, and access to promotion and training facilities. The act applies to both *potential* and *present* employees.

The act identifies both direct and indirect discrimination:

1   *Direct discrimination*: this involves treating a woman less favourably than a man because she is a woman, for example by not considering women for a management training course.

2   *Indirect discrimination*: this occurs when a condition is applied equally to men and women but where women have greater difficulty in fulfilling that condition and the condition cannot be justified. For example, it was adjudged that the age condition applied in the Civil Service for promotion to the Executive Officer grade resulted in indirect discrimination. Individuals over the age of 28 could not obtain promotion to this grade. This was adjudged to discriminate against women as they were often raising a family in their twenties and so would be less likely to be ready for promotion by this age limit.

There were specified circumstances where the SDA, 1975 did not apply. However, many of these areas were repealed under the Employment Act, 1989. Nevertheless, there remain specific circumstances where it is lawful to discriminate because of a Genuine Occupational Qualification (GOQ). For example, there are some restrictions on the employment of women in jobs which would lead to particular risks for women because of their childbearing capacity. This includes a restriction on the employment of women in manufacturing processes which involve the use of lead and the use of ionizing radiation. It is lawful to discriminate against women for such jobs.

Unlike in some other countries, for example the USA, positive or reverse discrimination is not legal in the UK. Positive discrimination refers to the practice of discriminating in favour of women (or other previously disadvantaged groups) so that their presence in a particular job is increased: for example, selecting a woman for a job, even though a male candidate was better qualified and experienced. This would be illegal in the UK. However, positive or affirmative action is legal. This enables an employer to take action to encourage women to a job where they were previously under-represented: for example, by including in an advertisement that applications from women are especially welcomed. It is also legal for an employer to put on special training and development programmes for women in order to enable them to get to a standard where they can compete on equal terms with male candidates.

The Race Relations Act

The first Race Relations Act was implemented in 1968 and was consolidated and extended in the Race Relations Act, 1976. The legislation itself is very similar to the SDA, making it a basic legal obligation on employers to deal equally with applicants from different racial backgrounds. Racial grounds are defined as including colour, race, nationality (including citizenship) or ethnic or national origins. As with the SDA, the Race Relations Act distinguishes between direct and indirect discrimination, making both unlawful. Again, as with the SDA, there is some scope for positive action, but not for positive, or reverse, discrimination.

The impact of legislation

Despite this legislation women and ethnic minority members continue to dominate in specific jobs, and to be represented at lower levels in organizational hierarchies. One of the reasons for this has been the law itself. The laws have been presented above in simple form. In reality they are highly complex (e.g. during a House of Lords debate, Lord Denning described them as 'beyond compare ... no ordinary lawyer would be able to understand them') and their enforcement is fraught with difficulties.

If a woman or racial minority member feels that s/he has been discriminated against s/he can take the case first to the Advisory, Conciliation and Arbitration Service (ACAS). If an agreement cannot be made between the person bringing the case and the offending employer, the case can go on to an industrial tribunal. Many cases do not go to a tribunal because they are settled before they reach this stage, although the number of cases reaching the tribunal stage has shown a steady increase over time.

For those cases that reach an industrial tribunal there has been a ceiling to tribunal awards of £10,000. However, the European Court of Justice has recently ruled that this limit on compensation is in breach of European law. Future compensation awards made through industrial tribunals can therefore be expected to increase. Furthermore, in 1993, industrial tribunals were also given the power to restrict press reporting of sexual harassment cases.

These changes to the implementation of EO legislation should make it slightly easier for individuals to pursue their cases and get compensation. However, going through the process can still be a traumatic experience. Thus, a study by the EOC of ninety-six sex discrimination complainants (only six of them men) found that over half admitted that they had found the experience stressful. On the positive side, ninety-four said they were pleased that they had fought the case, with the responses indicating that this had helped the victim to 'regain respectability' and 'gain peace of mind' once the injustice had been acknowledged (*Financial Times*, 22 July 1993). To some extent the psychological trauma of going through with the case has been recognized by the Court of Appeal rulings in 1987 that payments for 'injury to feelings' should be realistic, and that aggravated and exemplary damages could be awarded. Nevertheless, the EOC and the Commission for Racial Equality (CRE) still believe the level of compensation is too low, given the stress that is associated with a discrimination case.

The problem is that even if there is a clear case of discrimination in employment, it is extremely difficult to find the necessary proof. If a woman (or man) feels that s/he has experienced unfair discrimination in employment s/he has to provide prima facie evidence to prove that s/he has been discriminated against. This is extremely difficult to do, even with the EOC or CRE supporting the individual. It can also be a very time-consuming and demoralizing experience, even if the outcome is favourable.

The most clear example of this came from the recent case of Alison Halford who finally settled out of court her long-standing sex discrimination claim against Northamptonshire Police Authority, Her Majesty's Inspector of Police Sir Philip Myers, the Home Office and the Chief Constable of Merseyside. Miss Halford had risen in the police force to assistant chief constable, but had failed in nine attempts to win promotion to deputy chief constable. She claimed that her career and promotion prospects had been blighted by sexual discrimination, including sexual innuendo and harassment; the police 'canteen culture'; and the pressure to 'be one of the boys'. The case took two years to get to a tribunal, with the defendants doing all in their power to delay the hearing. During that time all the tacky tricks that could be pulled out to blemish Miss Halford's character were used: how she had gone into a swimming pool in her bra and pants with male colleagues after a party; how she drank pints; and how she called her boss a 'prat' and told an acquaintance, while off duty, to 'sod off'! Little wonder that she agreed to settle out of court.

Moreover, aside from the problems of actually enforcing the legislation, there are also more fundamental reasons for continued discrimination in employment which mean that the law itself cannot hope to change the status quo. Real change demands a complete overhaul of basic attitudes towards males and females of all races and backgrounds, as well as major innovations in organizational structures and processes. We will look first at the position of racial minority members and women in employment, and then briefly examine some of the causes which have been suggested.

RACIAL MINORITIES IN EMPLOYMENT

Just over three million people from ethnic minorities live in Britain, which represents 5.5 per cent of the population. Almost half of this ethnic minority population was born in Britain, and nearly three-quarters are British citizens. In Britain, there are no laws (e.g. apartheid) which discriminate against people on the basis of their race, colour or ethnic origin. Theoretically, therefore, members of all races should enjoy equal access to housing, employment, education, etc. However, the reality has been and remains very different, with members of racial minority groups being disadvantaged in most aspects of life. And what consistently comes out as the most important factor in understanding ethnic discrimination in the UK is the colour of a person's skin. Thus, a 'white' Italian man is likely to suffer much less prejudice in trying to find a job in the UK than is a 'black' West Indian man. And this, despite the fact that the West Indian 'black' is actually a third generation British citizen who has always lived in this country, while the Italian 'white' has only lived in the UK for six months. Thus, when we are talking about problems of ethnic minorities in work, we are actually talking about the problems of people with black or brown skins, whether West Indian, African or Asian.

The first systematic study of such discrimination was undertaken by Political and Economic Planning (PEP) (Daniel, 1967). They sent pairs of applications to a wide range of jobs which had been advertised in six towns and cities in England. The application pairs were matched for qualifications and experience, and the only substantial difference between them was in the racial origin of the applicant. In each case one of the pair was a white person and the other was someone of a different racial origin – West Indian, Indian, Pakistani, Italian or Greek. One-third of the employers rejected the black applicant (West Indian, Indian or Pakistani) while offering to take the white applicant for further screening. The Greek and Italian applications were used to assess whether the crucial variable was being an immigrant or being black. The Greek and Italian applications resulted in significantly less discrimination, demonstrating that it was skin colour which was the factor being used by employers to discriminate.

A similar study was carried out in Nottingham between 1977 and 1979 by the local Community Relations Council (Hubbuck and Carter, 1980). In this study three written applications were made for each vacancy – by a white person, a West Indian and an Asian, with qualifications and experience held constant. This study found an even higher level of discrimination. Over 40 per cent of employers rejected the black applicants while offering the white applicant an interview. Yet this study was done ten years after the Race Relations Act had been implemented.

More recently, the Policy Studies Institute (PSI), the successor to PEP, repeated the experiment to examine how far there had been changes in racial discrimination (Brown and Gay, 1985; Brown, 1984). The study was undertaken in 1982 and involved a three-applicant procedure, replicating the earlier, small-scale Nottingham study. The research was conducted in three cities – London, Birmingham and Manchester. In nearly a quarter of the cases two applicants received positive responses while the third was rejected. This figure was made up of only 4 per cent of white applicants but 10 per cent of each of the Asian and West Indian applicants. Moreover, a third of the employers rejected two applicants and made a positive response to the third. In nearly all these cases it was the two black candidates who were rejected.

Taking all the valid tests together, 90 per cent of the white applicants were successful, compared with 63 per cent of the Asian and West Indian applicants. The white applicant was over a third more likely to receive a positive response than either of the two black applicants. This discrimination occurred across all job categories and in all three cities. The authors of this report conclude:

We can say confidently that a minimum of one in five of the employers in these job categories discriminate against both Asian and West Indian job applicants and at least a further one in eight discriminate against either Asian or West Indian applicants; in total at least a third of all the employers discriminate against one or both groups of black applicants.

(Brown and Gay, 1985: 19)

A comparison of the level of discrimination over the three studies showed that there had been no reduction in racial discrimination, and perhaps even an increase. Thus, despite Race Relations legislation, 'direct discrimination persists as an additional and powerful impediment to any economic progress by blacks' (Brown and Gay, 1985: 29).

The type of discrimination which these studies demonstrate is unlawful in this country under the Race Relations legislation. However, it is extremely difficult to prove. In most of the cases of discrimination in these studies the 'victim' was sent a polite letter 'explaining' the reasons for his/her rejection, for example because the other applicants were better qualified. The applicant would have no reason to suspect that s/he was a victim of racial discrimination. Moreover, even if s/he did suspect this, there would be no easily available evidence to support this.

WOMEN IN EMPLOYMENT

There has clearly been a dramatic change in the numbers of women in paid employment since the end of the Second World War. In 1951 only 22 per cent of married women were economically active (Hakim, 1981), while by 1990 the figure was over 70 per cent. This is because women have dramatically reduced the length of time spent out of employment looking after their family. In the 1990s most women who start a family will return to paid employment after a relatively short period at home. The return to employment will very often be on a part-time basis, at least at the outset. This return to part-time work is often associated with a demotion to a lower category of work than that held previously (Beck and Steel, 1989). This is because part-time jobs are typically only available in the most junior positions in the organization. The assumption is that a person needs to be highly committed and motivated to work in more senior positions which carry responsibility. It is further reasoned that if a person is only 'prepared' to work part-time then they are clearly not demonstrating this commitment. This is a very clear example of how organizations have been structured around the dominant male career path, characterized by an unbroken, full-time career.

It is these two related factors which are perhaps most important in understanding the employment position of women. That is, for the majority of women their careers are not continuous, but interspersed with at least one period of 'home' employment. And, furthermore, a majority will work part-time for at least a period in their employment. This pattern is not illustrative of the typical male career which will be full-time and unbroken, except perhaps where he has been made redundant during the recession. Despite some well-publicized examples of the 'house-husband', the man who stays at home to look after the family while the woman goes out to work, the actual number of households where this role reversal occurs is very small.

Thus, despite the increasing numerical equality in the participation of males and females in employment, this has not led to dramatic changes in the status of women in employment. The majority of women in work remain in jobs associated with the female caring role and at the bottom of organizational hierarchies, earning substantially less, on average, than men in work (Dex, 1987; Shipley, 1990). This is especially true of women who work part-time. In other words, 'women's work' remains both horizontally and vertically segregated.

In terms of *vertical segregation*, while it is true that the proportion of women in management is increasing (as illustrated by successive Labour Force surveys: see *Employment Gazette*, April 1990), women still account for less than 30 per cent of all managers. More significantly, at senior executive levels the numbers of women remain negligible at about 1 to 2 per cent (e.g. Hirsh and Jackson, 1990). The further up the organizational hierarchy one goes, the fewer women one finds proportionate to men. This is true even in female-dominated professions like nursing and teaching.

In terms of *horizontal segregation*, women remain restricted to a narrow range of jobs associated with the traditional 'caring role' of the female. Even in professions like law and medicine, professions where women have increased their representation quite dramatically over the last twenty years, they are dominant in certain specialisms within the profession and virtually unrepresented in others. Thus, in medicine women are found in paedology, gynaecology and gerontology, and in law women are 'steered' into family, rather than commercial, law (e.g. Podmore and Spencer, 1982).

The police forces of England and Wales exemplify both vertical and horizontal discrimination (Home Office figures reported in the *Independent*, 1 July 1992). In terms of horizontal discrimination, it is clear that women are under-represented in the police forces overall. They average only 15 per cent of all constables. In terms of vertical discrimination, if promotion opportunities were fair, we would expect to see this 15 per cent of women reflected in the grades up the hierarchy. However, in the forty-three police forces in England and Wales, there were no women chief constables or deputies; only three assistant chief constables; eleven chief superintendents; and twenty-nine superintendents. In fourteen of the forces there was no woman above the rank of inspector.

EXPLANATIONS OF DISCRIMINATION

A Explanations of racial discrimination

Psychological explanations of racial discrimination are useful, although we also need to consider broader sociological and economic issues. There are three main interpretations:

1   Macrosocio-psychological and structural explanations which consider *intergroup hostility* (including racial hostility) as an expression of the struggle of power, income and prestige.
2   Psychological explanations which consider prejudice and hostility from the perspective of the *personality* of those perpetrating the racial 'crime'.
3   Cultural explanations which look at the ways in which society teaches each new generation what are considered to be appropriate *beliefs* regarding other groups, including various racial minority groups.

1 Intergroup hostility

Ethnocentrism is the belief in the unique value and rightness of one's own group. The concept of ethnocentrism is fundamental to understanding discrimination and prejudice. It is not possible to avoid elements of ethnocentrism as one is socialized to the behaviour and beliefs of one's own society. These behaviours and beliefs come to be accepted as 'natural' so that other behaviours and beliefs are viewed as 'unnatural'.

However, ethnocentrism alone cannot account for the kind of widespread racial discrimination which exists in our society. To understand this it is also necessary to consider how ethnocentrism serves the dominant group(s) in society in the struggle for power and wealth. For example, in examining the growth of the system of slavery in the southern states of the USA it is vital to consider economic forces. The belief in slavery as a just system had been declining in this area throughout the seventeenth and eighteenth centuries, basically because the use of slaves gave no major economic benefit. However, the invention of the cotton gin and other mechanical devices for the processing of cotton cloth began to make cotton agriculture more profitable from about 1800. Exports to Europe increased dramatically and the effect of this increase was to make the price of cotton and land values increase sharply. In turn, this greatly increased the value of slaves who were needed to run the vast cotton plantations which began to emerge. It is not a coincidence that at the same time an extensive literature began to appear, justifying the exploitation of slaves on the grounds that the 'Negro was inferior and subhuman'. Racial prejudice and the exploitation of blacks was perpetuated because it was able to bolster the power and wealth of the dominant white groups. This analysis also helps to explain why slavery thrived in the southern states of the USA long after it had been abolished in the north.

From this perspective, the designation of inferior groups comes from those in the powerful positions at the top of society. It underpins, and is an expression of, their right to rule. It acts as a mechanism to improve the economic position of the powerful within society even further. However, prejudice and discrimination also occur among those near the bottom of the social ladder and, in fact, has typically been found to be greater here. It is suggested that prejudice here is as an expression of the need for security among whites at the lower end of the social scale. Again, intergroup hostility, displayed in acts of prejudice and discrimination, arises from basic economic sources.

The explanation most usually given for this greater prejudice is that it arises because lower-class whites see a direct and immediate competitive threat from minority groups, for example in employment and housing. In consequence, they exhibit greater hostility. It should be noted that the evidence that lower-class whites are more prejudiced is based on verbal questionnaires. It may well be that middle- and upper-class whites are better able to disguise their prejudice, and/or that they have more skilful rationalizations and verbal disguises for their prejudices. Campbell depicts this well in his description of the racial hostility surrounding the issue of bussing in the USA (segregation of black and white children in schools):

Who were the people with the brickbats forming the crowd in front of Central High School in Little Rock, screaming and crying, 'They're in. The niggers are in,' on September 23, 1957? They were the rural and lower class urban (white) riffraff. But who were the people who built a new high school on the western edge of the city and planned to keep its attendance area lily-white, by this act securing a private public school for their kind and releasing Central High School to the residents of the city's inner zones? This was the urban middle class, the Southern moderate. Understanding community processes, and controlling the mechanisms of decision, they had no need to resort to violence; they had alternative methods of securing their ends.

(Campbell, 1961: 137)

A more recent example in the UK occurred where a mother from an inner city area in Birmingham asked the Local Education Authority if they could find another school for her daughter because in the local one over 95 per cent of the pupils were black. There was an outcry against this, with the family being accused of racial prejudice. However, this was largely driven by the white middle class who sent their own children to the suburban schools where it was ethnic minority groups who were the 5 per cent minority.

From this perspective, discrimination is not simply an individual eccentricity. It is tied into social structures and privilege systems. Change will therefore require attention to occupational structures, access to training and education, and to presently protected opportunity channels. Moreover, from this perspective it would be predicted that, even if the present discrimination against blacks were resolved, some other minority group would become the focus of prejudice.

2 Individual personality

The above considers the structural, economic sources of inequality and prejudice. However, from the perspective of an individual minority group member there is a big difference between a landlord, employer or teacher who is a relatively tolerant person, and the landlord, employer or teacher who is hostile. It also makes a difference whether or not the behaviour of those with whom s/he interacts is governed by stereotypes, guilt or self-hatred. It is therefore also important to consider factors which differentiate between more and less hostile individuals, even though they appear to face the same or similar economic situations. It is on this level that psychologists have tended to focus, seeking to understand the processes involved in the generation of hostile tendencies. We will consider two different theories – the theory of the authoritarian personality and frustration-aggression theory.

A THE PREJUDICED PERSONALITY TYPE: THE AUTHORITARIAN
PERSONALITY

The seminal work in this area was produced by Adorno et al. who wrote a book entitled *The Authoritarian Personality* (1950). They suggested that they had identified that prejudice is part of a complicated personality syndrome, which is itself a manifestation of a basically insecure person. Such a person sees life as threatening, looks upon all human relationships in competitive, power terms and has a desperate need to cling to whatever appears to be strong, and to disdain and reject whatever is relegated to the bottom. It was suggested that this insecurity stemmed from having had a harsh, capricious and unloving childhood. The group of researchers, working at Berkeley, developed a personality test (the F Test) to measure this personality syndrome which they termed an authoritarian tendency.

The theory that there was an identifiable personality trait which could be implicated in the interpretation of racial hostility generated an enormous interest in the academic world. A number of methodological shortcomings of the original research were highlighted (e.g. Krug, 1961) and others were critical of the original interpretation of data (e.g. Bass, 1955; Ray, 1980). These and other criticisms do not necessarily mean that the study of personality is irrelevant to our understanding of prejudice. Rather, they make it clear that we need to move beyond simple models in which personality is alone seen to relate to prejudice and discrimination. There are three major ways in which the theory of the authoritarian personality can be extended to improve our understanding.

1   *Functional alternatives*: while it may well be the case that some people who suffer from feelings of anomie and powerlessness are hostile to minority groups and support totalitarian political movements, this is unlikely to be true of all those suffering in this way. Some will find alternative ways to express their insecurities. The functional alternatives chosen by any given individual will

depend upon that person's total situation.

2   *Group differences*: much research in the past has ignored group or cultural differences in the expression of anti-minority feelings. Some communities express, in general, more hostility towards minority groups. If such group differences are not taken into account in research that is undertaken then these cultural elements are being confounded with individual personality elements to make the interpretation of the results very confused.

3   *Interactions of situation and tendency*: it is important to distinguish carefully between attitudes and behaviour. A person with a tendency towards prejudice will not necessarily engage in discriminatory behaviour. All the work on attitudes is relevant here. Attitude research made it clear sixty years ago that there was a complex relationship between attitudes and behaviour. The classic study illustrating this was carried out by Richard La Piere (1934). La Piere travelled extensively throughout the United States in the company of a Chinese student and his wife, staying at hotels and visiting restaurants. On only one occasion was the Chinese couple not treated hospitably. Six months after this La Piere sent a letter to each hotel and restaurant visited asking if Chinese clientele would be accepted. Over 90 per cent of the replies to this letter were negative, stating that they would not accommodate Chinese guests.

Thus, I may say and even believe one thing but act in a way which is very different, and even contradictory. A person's behaviour cannot be understood solely with reference to his/her internal prejudices. This reflects a more general truism that needs to be taken into consideration in all studies of the individual – that behaviour is a function of P (the Person) and S (the Situation). I may be hostile towards black people but if my boss is very strongly against racial prejudice, I am unlikely to exhibit discriminatory behaviour at work. Conversely, if my boss is racially prejudiced I may find it very difficult to offer an opportunity to a black candidate whom I have interviewed for a job, even if I believe that this would be the best candidate, as I believe my boss will find this unacceptable.

B FRUSTRATION AND PREJUDICE

Psychologists have also analysed prejudice as the product of frustration. The frustration-aggression hypothesis (Dollard et al., 1939) states that all individuals have goals which they strive to fulfil. We desire to attain these goals in order to satisfy our needs. In striving to fulfil our goals and so satisfy our needs we all experience frustration at some point. For whatever reason we are unable to meet a goal which we have set ourselves. This may be due to personal limitations, environmental obstacles or other people inhibiting us. For example, a young girl may have a burning desire to be a vet, but if she does not have the ability, cannot afford to go to university or finds that her parents are against this then her goal is unlikely to be fulfilled. Our reaction when our goals are blocked is often aggressive. This, then, is the frustration-aggression hypothesis: when we are frustrated in achieving our goals we react with aggression and hostility. For example, if I leave my house in such a hurry in the morning that I leave my keys inside, my immediate reaction might well be to stamp my foot, hit the door or shout some verbally aggressive remark!

In relating this to prejudice and discrimination, it is suggested that because it is often impossible to react aggressively against the source of our frustration, we instead displace this aggression onto minority group members who are often an 'easy target'. In this way certain individuals become 'scapegoats'. However, it is difficult for us to be entirely comfortable with this situation as we would have to admit that we are actually retaliating against an innocent party. In order to overcome this dissonance (the occurrence of two mutually inconsistent or contradictory beliefs), we look for justifications as to why the scapegoats 'deserve' our hostility. This involves defining the scapegoats in negative terms. Furthermore, these negative terms are extended to cover all members of the minority group so that a stereotype emerges which helps to rationalize prejudice towards the whole group.

The actual source of the displacement will depend on the situation. For example, Dollard et al. (1939) suggested that the ease with which many Germans adopted the anti-Semitic sentiments of Hitler could be explained as an outcome of the many frustrations German people experienced between 1914 and 1933. But the choice of Jews as the target group was not random. It can only be explained by considering the total situation in Germany at that time.

It is important to realize that frustration does not always lead to aggression and hostility, so that this scapegoating theory of prejudice is partial. At best we can say that frustration may make a person more susceptible to prejudice. However, not all those who are frustrated will develop hostile feelings towards racial minority groups. It is one element to consider in attempting to understand discrimination, but it needs to be understood within the wider context of an individual's experiences. To examine this context in more detail we can consider the part which culture plays in the maintenance of prejudice and discrimination.

3 Cultural factors in discrimination and prejudice

We do not react or think uniquely in all situations we come across. This is particularly true of our relationships with other people. If we had to make a decision about how to greet and react to every new person whom we met, life would be unbearably complex. Instead, we rely on standard conventions. We shake hands if the person is an adult to whom we are formally introduced, but we would be thought of as very strange if we greeted a small child in the same way. These are standard ways of responding and thinking which we learn through our socialization. Such *cultural conventions* help to reduce the complexity of life. They can also at times increase the complexity, especially in cross-cultural interactions. Greeting someone from another country can be quite embarrassing as the two people attempt to use very different methods of greeting, perhaps kissing versus shaking hands. Our response to people from minority groups can also be seen as part of the standard cultural equipment which each member of a particular social group learns through a process of socialization.

Cultural explanations are a necessary additional factor to consider in our understanding of racial discrimination. Intergroup conflicts and individual personality deficits can help us understand why prejudice and discrimination exist. They are not, however, useful in explaining why it is one particular group, rather than any other, which is the source of the hostility. Why black people rather than people with red hair? In order to understand this we must consider the historical factors that have become embedded within a particular society's culture. From the cultural perspective, an attitude towards a minority group can be seen as a learned way of responding.

Such learning processes manifest themselves in *stereotypes*.

Stereotypes refer to the existence of a set of beliefs about the personal attributes of a group of people. The earliest work on stereotypes was undertaken in 1933 by Katz and Braly. They asked one hundred students to use a list of eighty-four traits and to choose the five traits they thought were most typical of each of ten groups – Germans, Italians, Irish, English, Negroes, Jews, Americans, Chinese, Japanese and Turks. The students had no problems in completing this task, even though most had had little or no contact with these groups. Moreover, there was substantial agreement among the students about the attributes assigned to the different groups. For example, Negroes were seen as superstitious, lazy, happy-go-lucky, ignorant and musical; Germans were seen as scientifically minded, industrious, stolid, intelligent and methodical. Such stereotypes are invalid but their existence cannot be ignored.

Despite some research that suggests that stereotypes are changing, it is still clear that cultural stereotypes of different racial and religious groups exist. And they are sustained because they help to 'explain' things which would otherwise be inexplicable, for example why so many black children excel in sport at school but not in their academic subjects. And these stereotypes are important because research has illustrated how they can become self-fulfilling prophecies. The belief that West Indian children are not going to be good at academic subjects but will excel in sport leads to differential reinforcement of their sporting and academic work to create the result which was anticipated. But it is the expectations, informed by the stereotype, which lead to this, rather than the innate qualities of the child. For example, Word et al. (1974) trained black and white 'job applicants' so that they would respond in similar ways in job interviews. They then recorded job interviews and found that with the black applicant there was less eye contact, the interviewer expressed less interest, made more speech errors and gave the interviewee less time. The result was a far less satisfactory interview for the black applicant. In turn, this led to poorer performance by the black candidate, so contributing to a vicious circle.

While evidence suggests that stereotyping has declined over the last twenty years, prejudice and discrimination have not been reduced in line with this. Indeed, racial riots and racially motivated attacks appear to be on the increase in several countries, including Britain. To explain this writers have begun to employ the concept of *symbolic racism*. This explains prejudice and discrimination as being the result of the majority white group believing that members of minority groups threaten traditional values, such as self-reliance, the work ethic, obedience and discipline (Kinder and Sears, 1981). Traditional values are based on the assumption that people should be (and are) rewarded on their merits, which are determined by how hard and diligently they work. Symbolic racism arises when whites believe that policies aimed to reduce racial discrimination violate these traditional assumptions. For example, where a company introduces racial quotas, this is seen to give blacks an unfair advantage in the job market. Symbolic racism is rooted in the same mechanisms of socialization as stereotyping and has the same effect – prejudicial attitudes towards minority black members of the community.

B Explanations of sex discrimination

The explanation for the segregation of women in employment also reflects deep-seated, cultural values. Here, the explanation revolves around the historical divide between women as domestic carers and men as 'breadwinners', although equally important are the resilient attitudes which stereotype women as less career oriented than men, less assertive and less likely to exhibit 'strong' leadership.

1 The dual role of women

One of the most important reasons for women's continued dominance in the lower echelons of organizations is their family responsibility. While women have entered the labour force in increasing numbers, men (or for that matter robots) have not correspondingly taken up a share of the household work traditionally done by women. Mothers, rather than fathers, are still assumed to have primary responsibility for the care of the children and the home. This is illustrated by the work of Brannen and Moss (1988), who were able to construct a definition of what it means to be a 'good' mother or a 'good' father on the basis of an analysis of the values and ideas prevalent in society. They concluded that although there can never be a universal, objective definition, the dominant value in the 1980s (and it could be argued the 1990s) is of well-defined and differentiated mother and father roles. The 'good' mother is expected to give up employment in order to look after her children on a full-time basis, at least until they start school. The 'good' mother is expected not only to nurture her children but also to help them develop their full potential. In the event of a child failing to achieve, the mother is held to be responsible.

Conversely, the social construction of the 'good' father dictates that his main responsibility should be to provide financially for his wife and children. He is expected to be at the birth of his child, and maybe to take leave from work (very few firms in the UK actually make provision for paternity leave) to help in the first few days when the child is at home. He should also be involved in some physical aspects of child care, but the undertaking of general household duties is not expected of him.

There is a third and final construction identified by Brannen and Moss, which describes the 'good' worker. The 'good' worker works full-time, has a continuous record of employment until retirement, and does not allow domestic responsibilities to conflict with those at work. This definition of the 'good' worker clearly conflicts with the definition of the 'good' mother, while being totally compatible with that of the 'good' father. If a woman chooses to participate in employment when her children are very young, she is neglecting her children and, by definition, is not a 'good' mother. If she chooses to have time off to look after her children, she is neglecting her career, and is clearly not a 'true professional'.

Even where a woman has returned to paid employment, she will typically continue to hold the major responsibility for the home and family. This includes women in professional and managerial occupations who have been found to do a significantly greater proportion of household tasks than their spouses. For example, in families where the woman works full-time, while men participate slightly more in household tasks, this hardly means that the relationship can be described as egalitarian (Newell, 1993). It remains only a little less unequal. Indeed, Cannings (1991) concluded that the lower earnings of women managers could be directly attributed to their disproportionate responsibility for work in their family homes. For this reason, women who have been successful in their careers are much more likely than the equivalent men not to have a family (Coe, 1992).

There remains a pervading assumption that a woman should fit her career around her children and that although the male partner will help out, this is nevertheless the woman's role. Hence, her career will suffer. If, on the other hand, the woman does choose to pursue a career, she is likely to experience considerable stress in coping with the dual role: 'Compared to married male managers, married female managers were much more likely to experience higher pressures in respect of career and spouse/partner conflicts, career/home conflicts and career and marriage/child bearing conflicts' (Davidson, 1989). Women have been enticed back to employment for a variety of reasons, not in return for their domestic responsibility, but in addition to it. Even where men in dual career marriages believe that they should undertake an equal share of family commitments, social institutions, including the employment policies of the firms for which they work, do not provide sufficient moral or material support for such equality to occur.

2 Organizational barriers: stereotypes and attitudes

In our society women are typically assumed to be less assertive, less ambitious and less career-oriented than men. This stereotype reflects the tradition that for women the family takes precedence over a career. Even if an individual woman is totally career oriented, if the expectations of those involved in selection and promotion are that a woman will be less concerned with advancement and challenge, then she is unlikely to get selected for a job in middle or senior management. And the evidence, both anecdotal and collected by formal research, suggests that these are precisely the attitudes typically held by those in positions of power to select and promote (Alimo-Metcalfe, 1993). Schein (1989) summarizes this in the statement 'Think Manager equals Think Male'.

A survey by the British Institute of Management (Coe, 1992) of 1,500 women members and 800 male members confirmed these findings. Women in this survey perceived the existence of the 'men's club', and the associated 'all-boy network', as the greatest barrier to women in management. Prejudice of colleagues was the next most commonly cited barrier. Attitudinal barriers were seen as more of a problem than the tangible difficulties such as lack of child care (mainly because a majority of the female managers had opted to forego a family). Thus, one-third of the women felt that they did not receive adequate respect from their male superiors and 13 per cent felt that the attitude of their organization to women was negative. To some extent this was confirmed by the results from the men participating in the survey. Only one-third of the men 'strongly agreed' that 'women managers bring positive skills to the workplace', compared to 74 per cent of women who believed this.

In reality, the research which has been undertaken to identify gender differences in leadership or management style has tended to conclude that there is as much difference within women (or men) as a single group as between women and men as separate groups. However, more recently there has been some evidence that men are more likely to adopt a 'transactional' leadership style and women to adopt a 'transformational' style (Rosener, 1990; Vinnicombe, 1987). A transactional leadership style relies on the exchange of reward or punishment for performance and is based on formal position power. A transformational style relies on motivating people through encouragement and empowerment. Subordinates are inspired to feel good about themselves and the organization, and are motivated to perform well because of this. Ironically, it is precisely the latter type of leadership style which would appear to be a requirement for organizations in the 1990s, where values of co-operation and caring are seen to be as important for success as task orientation (Harrison, 1987). However, it is clear that to date the majority of organizations are based on assumptions of patriarchal power that devalues women and feminine qualities (Martin, 1990). So women continue to be undervalued and under-represented in positions of power within organizations.

Even when women have made it to the top, there remain subtle barriers to power. Ibarra (1992), for example, found that, although women in the advertising firm she studied were not denied access to informal networks, there remained obstacles. For example, she found that women developed two separate kinds of network. One network involved access to resources and advice, and mainly involved male co-workers. The other network was for friendship and social support, and mainly involved female co-workers. This second type of network was needed for the women in her sample because there were few women in positions of power and authority, which meant that the job network could not also provide the social support. For the men, friendship networks reinforced job ties. Women therefore divided their time between these two types of network which detracted from the time they could put into building important work links.

CONCLUSION

Despite nearly twenty years of Equal Opportunity legislation and a clear increase in the diversity of the workforce, this diversity is not reflected in the structures of power within organizations which remain dominated by white males. Thus, women remain horizontally and vertically segregated from men, dominating in the lower echelons of organizational structures, and in jobs which are based on nurturance and dependence ('women's work'). People from ethnic minorities are twice as likely to be out of work as whites, even when they are as well or better qualified. Those who work are more likely to be in low-paid, semi-skilled jobs and their chances of promotion are smaller than their white colleagues'. Thus, 30 per cent of London Underground workers are from ethnic minorities, but 97 per cent of the managers are white.

There can be no simple answer to the causes of prejudice and discrimination. Group conflicts over economic and political resources, individual personality needs, and tradition embedded in deep-seated cultural values must all be taken into account when attempting to analyse its roots. The three elements are not mutually distinct, but rather reinforce each other. Moreover, the strength of the resulting prejudice and discrimination in society helps to create the conditions which provide a superficial justification for the original attitudes in a cycle which becomes self-fulfilling. For example, prejudice reduces the chances of a black person getting a good education and job so that they become relegated to the jobs at the bottom of the occupational hierarchy (if they can find jobs at all). This in turn is used as evidence that the original prejudice was justified.

Given the deep-rooted nature of prejudice it is clearly going to be very difficult to reduce. Indeed, as suggested, certain actions taken to reduce discrimination may even help to sustain it. For example, encouraging positive discrimination, or even simply positive action, may be seen by some (white males) as unfair. This may increase the prejudice against blacks and/or women. However, in the long run, opening up such opportunities, and actually increasing the number of black people and women in positions of power and authority in all types of organizations, rather than just employing the 'tokens' which exist at present in most organizations, is likely to be the only real way in which the cycle of prejudice and discrimination can be broken.

Moreover, with the emergence of the global economy, it is argued that we need to go beyond affirmative action to affirming diversity. Instead of finding slots for women and minorities, and helping them adjust to the dominant white male style, companies need to acknowledge and embrace a range of styles. Rather than suppressing differences between people, companies will need to learn to value differences. 'Managing diversity' has become the buzzword of the 1990s. Workforce diversity refers to the reality of a workforce consisting of a broad mix of workers from different racial and ethnic backgrounds, of different ages and genders, and of different domestic and national cultures. These groups have different needs which must be accommodated within organizational structures if their full talents are to be utilized for the benefit of the organization. At present, these 'different' groups have to work much harder to succeed within organizations and many will fail.

Thus, the talents and abilities of many are being underutilized by organizations at the same time as they are professing that their human resources are their greatest asset. The waste of potential is great. Organizations that do not want to waste such potential must recreate structures and processes which cater for a diverse workforce, rather than simply reflect traditional white values and attitudes. Organizations must work to ensure that outdated stereotypical assumptions about women and ethnic minority members (as well as other minority groups) are not allowed to influence employment and promotion decisions. These issues will be addressed in Chapter 7.

7 The promotion of Equal Opportunities in employment

Managing diversity

INTRODUCTION

Equal Opportunities are about treating everyone fairly and equally, regardless of their background or lifestyle. A concern with Equal Opportunities is needed because of various prejudices which exist in society. These prejudices are normally directed at a minority group which suffers discrimination at the hands of a more powerful majority in relation to education and training, housing and employment.

Discrimination in employment is manifested in poorer pay and promotion prospects for those who manage to find jobs. At a more fundamental level, discrimination against minority group members means that fewer are offered jobs in the first place and so they experience a higher level of unemployment. Indeed, prejudice may filter a person out of the selection process at the very earliest stage. For example, a woman of childbearing age may be rejected at the application stage due to fears that she will have a child at some later stage which would mean extra maternity costs for the employer. Of course, this real reason for her rejection will be disguised with a number of acceptable alternative explanations. This particular problem may become even more exaggerated as new European laws demand improved maternity provision for British women, which the government has indicated will be directly passed on to the employer.

It is clear that the various groups identified at the beginning of Chapter 6 as being the subjects of discrimination are not discrete. A woman might be able-bodied or disabled, black or white, heterosexual or homosexual. However, for conceptual clarity it is often necessary to consider them independently in order to examine the various issues underlying the prejudice and discrimination. There has not been scope in this book to look at each of these areas of discrimination, so we have concentrated on sex discrimination and racial discrimination, looking at the manifestation of these discriminations in employment and some of the explanations for their existence. We now turn to consider why it is so important that organizations attempt to reduce discrimination in employment and how this can be achieved.

WHY EQUAL OPPORTUNITIES ARE SO IMPORTANT

The Ashridge Management Group (Hammond, 1992) identified a number of sound commercial reasons why equality of opportunity is inextricably linked to organizational competitiveness:

- Attracting and retaining the best people – becoming an 'employer of choice'.
- Better business orientation.
- Cost saving associated with Equal Opportunities policies.
- Valuing diversity.
- Belief in the individual.
- Improved creativity and flexibility.
- Improved return on investment.

Clearly, these factors are not discrete. For example, cost savings associated with Equal Opportunities policies are partly created by being able to attract and retain able employees. We can look at some of these factors in more detail.

1 Making full use of potential

Despite high levels of unemployment, there are still skills shortages in many industries, and employers find themselves competing not only for markets but also for skilled workers. To attract and retain the skills and experiences of the highest calibre workforce is a major employment challenge of the 1990s. Women and ethnic minority members (as well as other groups discriminated against) represent a largely underutilized resource in most organizations. Even when they form the majority of the workforce they tend to be concentrated in jobs of low status and low pay. This is socially and economically wasteful, and unprofitable in business terms. To exclude over 50 per cent of potential recruits to senior management positions means that companies are not making full use of employee potential and they are restricting the chance of finding the 'best *person* (not necessarily white man) for the job'.

2 Becoming internationally competitive

Trading across national borders is increasingly important for all types of business as the pressures of international competition intensify and borders become more open. In the UK this has been epitomized by the single European market which has lifted trade barriers between member countries of the European Community. If UK companies are to survive, they will need to penetrate this wider European (and world) market. If they fail to do this, they will find themselves shrinking as companies from other European countries penetrate the UK market. Promoting and developing business internationally depends on recruiting and selecting individuals who can achieve this international growth. Sometimes this will involve the selection of internal managers and professionals for overseas assignments (expatriates). However, increasingly companies are recruiting people from the countries in which they are developing their business in order to ensure that the company adopts a more truly international perspective (Bartlett and Ghoshal, 1989). This is not proving to be easy, because of both language and more general cultural differences (e.g. Shackleton and Newell, 1994). Nevertheless, the emphasis is on *managing diversity* as an important competitive advantage.

This concept – managing diversity – is an interesting one to consider, given that in the past organizations have proved to be so resistant to changing the make-up of their organizational personnel. That is, despite twenty years of Equal Opportunities legislation in the UK, organizations are still dominated, at least in the positions of power where important decisions are made, by white, indigenous males. Women, ethnic minority members and the disabled have all faced immense problems in penetrating the upper echelons of all types of organization, both public and private. However, the organization which is able to manage a diverse workforce will be at an important competitive advantage.

3   Responding to demographic changes

The 1990s were heralded as the decade which would reduce the dominance of white males. As well as the more intangible requirement for diversity, there was also the demographic imperative. That is, there has been, and is continuing to be, a dramatic reduction of 16 to 24-year-olds entering the labour market, from 200,000 new entrants each year in the 1980s to only 50,000 per annum in the 1990s. This has occurred because of a fall in the birth rate in the 1970s. The prediction was that this would result in a shortage of one million workers by the year 2000 unless companies turned to alternative, previously untapped, or at least underutilized, types of employee. Coleman and Salt (1992), for example, point out that the most recent national projections from 1990 to 2001 show an almost static male labour force at approximately 15.9 million. In contrast, females in the labour force are projected to rise by 700,000 to total 12.9 million by the end of the century.

To date, these demographic changes have had much less impact than anticipated (e.g. Herriot, 1992) because of the dramatic effect of the recession. In any case, doubts have been raised as to whether the increased utilization of this untapped resource will be in areas other than those in which they currently dominate, namely low-status, low-paid, low-interest jobs (Alimo-Metcalfe, 1993), despite the other advantages, discussed above, which can come from diversifying the workforce in the positions of power.

In order to understand such scepticism, we have considered the current labour market position of the two largest groups of dis-advantaged workers (women and racial minority members: Chapter 6) and assessed the barriers which are at present restricting their job opportunities. This understanding is a first step which is necessary if organizations actually wish to tap this pool of diversity fully. Organizations which make the effort to exploit fully the diversity which exists in the community will reap tremendous benefits. However, the barriers to doing this are great, residing not only in the organizations themselves but also in the values and beliefs of society at large.

CREATING AND IMPLEMENTING AN EQUAL OPPORTUNITIES POLICY

For all types of unfair discrimination, if Equal Opportunities are to become a reality organizations will need to take practical action to promote change. As Lady Howe, chair of the Opportunity 2000 Target Team (Opportunity 2000, 1993a), noted, 'passive support for equal opportunities is just not an option if we are to bring about real change'. The starting point for action is the development of an Equal Opportunities policy. The problem is that many organizations have a policy statement relating to Equal Opportunities and claim to be committed to Equal Opportunities. However, in reality, many organizations (perhaps the majority of organizations) do little more than publish a statement claiming 'we are an Equal Opportunities employer'. To actually promote change demands a high level of commitment from those at the top, together with a clear action plan, which specifies what the organization hopes to achieve from the policy, how it intends to implement the policy and how it will evaluate its achievements. There is not scope in this book to consider in detail the development and implementation of an Equal Opportunities policy, but we can identify some of the things an organization can introduce to promote good practice.

1 Policy statement

This is a brief statement of the organization's commitment to Equal Opportunities. Many organizations now have such a statement which they include on job advertisements, etc., but they do not back this up with any other action (see below). This will not be effective in promoting change, although it is a necessary first step. A typical statement might read:

> This organization recognizes that discrimination exists in society, but is committed to ensuring that no member of this organization (or potential member in the future) is treated less favourably because of their sex, marital status, race, disability or sexual orientation. It also guarantees that no group will be disadvantaged by a condition or requirement that is not deemed to be essential for a particular job.

Such a statement, if clearly backed by senior management, sends a message to all staff that the issue of Equal Opportunities is on the agenda. It demonstrates the commitment of senior management. All employees should be made aware of this statement but to maximize acceptance and ensure understanding of the implications, it needs to be backed up by training and development.

2 Equal Opportunities training and development

Ideally, all members of the organization should be involved in programmes of education and training in Equal Opportunities, but it is most essential for those staff involved in recruitment and staff evaluation (internal or external). This training will need to give employees space to confront their own negative assumptions and stereotypes, such as: black people are lazy; women are not suited to management jobs; women with small children are unreliable; old people are more difficult to train and are not as productive as young people; people with criminal convictions do not make reliable employees; people with disabilities are incompetent. It is also necessary to include details of what constitutes discriminatory practice. For example, details of and discussion of why certain questions should not be asked during an interview, such as: are you planning to get married?; have you got any children?; what child care arrangements have you made?; won't you find it difficult to cope with the demands of a young child and the demands of this job?; how likely is your husband to change jobs?; what does your husband do for a living? The point is that questions about the private life of an individual bear no relationship to his/her ability to do a job. They are asked because they relate to the stereotyped views held about groups of people and serve to reinforce prejudice and increase the likelihood of discrimination occurring.

Some companies have started to take the issue of Equal Opportunity training seriously, with positive results. For example, Boots the Chemist has initiated an Equal Opportunities awareness programme for all staff. In the time that this programme has run (between 1992 and 1993) the number of women returning to work after maternity leave increased from 29 to 49 per cent.

3 Positive action training

While it is not legal in this country (unlike in the USA) to discriminate positively in favour of a particular group (e.g. only allow blacks to apply for a particular job where they have been under-represented in the past), it is possible to introduce certain kinds of positive action (see Chapter 6). If women or minority group members, for example, are not being promoted to supervisory level because they lack a particular kind of skill, it is possible to provide training in these skills for those at this disadvantage. Individual members of these groups will then be able to compete more equally in promotion opportunities in the future. In order to have knowledge of where these 'blockages' are occurring, it is vital that the organization introduces comprehensive monitoring procedures to identify what is happening to different groups within the organization.

4 Monitoring

There are many methods which organizations can use to monitor what is happening in the organization, including statistical analysis of the workforce, attitude surveys, questionnaires, review of application forms and selection decisions, retention rates, and participation in training courses. The point is that unless some form of monitoring takes place it is impossible to know whether the Equal Opportunities policy is having any impact. This is why organizations involved in Opportunity 2000 are required to publish the results of their actions at regular intervals (see below). Statistical analysis of the workforce will enable the organization to identify where the bottlenecks are actually occurring – the so-called 'glass-ceiling' effect. This is the point in the organizational hierarchy at which the proportion of any, or all, of the disadvantaged groups under discussion becomes very small or non-existent. Action can then be taken to try and promote members of these groups beyond this level, for example introducing positive action training courses. The results can be monitored to assess how successful this training has been.

Attitude surveys will allow organizations to monitor the dominant beliefs of organizational members, and so identify prejudices. Training can then be geared to changing such attitudes. Later surveys can be used to monitor how much change, if any, has actually occurred. Such monitoring is thus fundamental to good practice, but it is also necessary in a defensive sense. If a person takes a complaint to an industrial tribunal for unfair discrimination, factual written evidence as provided by systematic monitoring procedures will be necessary to defend against the complaint.

The above are all fundamental to 'fair' practice, but there are many other things which an organization can do to promote equal opportunities. For example, it may be helpful to review recruitment literature to ensure that it does not promote certain kinds of images. For instance, portraying the boss as male and the secretary as female sends out very powerful messages which can help to perpetuate the gendered status quo. Another example of promoting equal opportunities is to ensure jobs are marketed and advertised to reach all groups in the community, for example by using ethnic minority publications. These activities go well beyond satisfying the requirements of the Equal Opportunities legislation, but are necessary to promote real organizational change. There is no quick fix to change and only those organizations that are truly committed to promoting equality will be successful. However, the benefits to both the organization and its employees can be tremendous.

A SPECIFIC CASE: GETTING WOMEN BACK TO WORK VERSUS GETTING WOMEN INTO POSITIONS OF RESPONSIBILITY

Having considered in general what an employing organization can do to promote equality of opportunities, the final part of this chapter will consider some specific measures which can be, and are being, used to redress the problem of the segregation of 'women's work'. I have concentrated on this area as it appears to be the one which organizations are currently taking most interest in, especially in view of the recent proposed change in maternity benefit arrangements, which would leave employers to pick up the extra costs of the improved benefit.

This issue is also related to the current political furore over the cost and availability of child care. Thus, the lowest level of participation in employment is that of women with pre-school children, with the rate in the UK being lower than in other European countries. Not unrelated is the fact that the UK also has one of the worst records for the provision of pre-school day care for young children (Cohen, 1988). The recent initiative 'Employers for Child Care', promoted by some of the largest UK companies, is an attempt to encourage the government to put more resources into nursery provision, perhaps in partnership with business.

We will consider the measures which some organizations are implementing to encourage more women to stay in employment after they have started a family. However, it is also necessary to examine how far such measures are actually going to change the position of women in the workforce. It could be that they will simply increase the numbers of women in the currently segregated, low-status female ghetto jobs.

Practical measures

There are many things which an organization can do to attract people (typically women) with child care or other domestic responsibilities back into paid employment. Many of the larger organizations in the UK are implementing some or all of these measures:

1   *Career break schemes*: allowing women (or men) to return to their job, or one at an equivalent level, within a specified period of time after going on maternity (or paternity) leave (usually 3–5 years). For example, Sainsburys has introduced a Career Bridge scheme which allows employees breaks from work for up to five years to look after children. The status and employment benefits of the employee are protected in this period.

2   *Child care assistance*: providing some form of help to cover the costs of child care. This might involve an allowance or the direct provision of the service, for example workplace crèches, holiday play schemes, after-school clubs. For example, Debenhams, the high street retailer, piloted Child Care Vouchers, which can be exchanged by the employee for child care of their choice, at its store in the Lakeside shopping centre in Essex. The store reported a 50 per cent rise in the retention of employees working peak trading hours after the initial year, compared with similar retailers in the shopping centre. A new innovation in this area is to provide parents with information about child care provision, rather than provide the service itself. For example, the Halifax building society started to use a company called Childcare Solutions in 1992. The Halifax pays a fee to Childcare Solutions (just over £2.00 per staff member per year) and then any Halifax employee looking for child care can telephone Childcare Solutions free of charge and speak to a qualified and experienced child care expert who has access to a database of childminders, nurseries and out-of-school schemes.

3   *Job sharing*: allowing one job to be shared by two people so that they can both accommodate their child care responsibilities.

4   *Term time only contracts*: allowing parents with children to work on a full-time basis, but only in term time. Boots the Chemist, for example, has introduced this option.

5   *Home-working*: enabling employees to work from home so that they can develop maximum job flexibility around their child care responsibilities. A survey by the Institute of Management (1993)

found that 11 per cent of large employers were using teleworking and 22 per cent were using employed home-workers. By 1997 more than 40 per cent of the organizations expected to have had an increase in both these forms of working arrangement.

6   *Part-time work*: providing jobs where the person works only a limited number of hours during the week, usually less than twenty hours. For example, Sainsburys appointed a senior deputy store manager to work only on a Sunday. When the store started to trade on Sundays, this employee was attracted to return to work, taking up a senior position, but on a part-time basis which was beneficial for both employee and employer. A survey of one hundred blue-chip companies (Boyer, 1993) found that 70 per cent were employing part-time managers and most reported that the arrangement had often increased the managers' productivity and commitment. However, the majority of part-time jobs continue to be located at the bottom of organizational hierarchies (see below).

WHO BENEFITS FROM JOB FLEXIBILITY?

All of the above are examples of ways in which organizations can increase the flexibility of work. *Flexible working* enables women (and/or men) to combine parental responsibilities with a job. Hewitt (1993) depicts the scenario of two happy parents, each working three-quarters of a full-time job, each spending time with their children, employed by two happy employers, each enjoying the improved productivity, lower recruitment costs and higher retention rates their 'flexible' workforce brings them. Hewitt argues that this scenario could become a reality if models of flexibility are adopted which aim to meet the needs of both employer (for reduced unit costs or improved return on capital equipment) and employee (for a better balance between work and home). She gives the example of British Airways, who wanted to reduce labour costs in 1993 as a result of the recession. Instead of embarking on an expensive and unpopular redundancy scheme, the company offered the option of part-time employment to employees in several job categories. There was no shortage of volunteers.

Research from the Institute of Management (1993) suggests that many more organizations are set to introduce flexible working amongst their staff. Three-quarters of the British employers surveyed expected to have introduced flexible working by 1997, with many of these also predicting an increase in contracting out. Job flexibility can help a person marry the responsibilities of a family with those of paid employment – hence they have been called 'family friendly policies'. Such arrangements can therefore help women (and/or men) to accommodate the dual roles of mother (and/or father) and worker which were examined in Chapter 6 as major barriers to women's career progress. It is possible to make a strong business case for the introduction of such measures. For example, the potential cost of having to replace a junior manager earning £15,000 a year totals £6,688. In comparison, the annual employer subsidy for a workplace nursery for forty children costs £62,359 or just over £1,500 per child. Similarly, the cost of increased sick leave and absenteeism of a working mother has to be costed out and balanced against the price of administering job sharing and flexible hours schemes (Opportunity 2000, 1993).

There are some notable examples of the successful introduction of flexible working practices which have met both the employers' and employees' needs. For example, Listawood Magnetics, a company designing magnetic games and puzzles, adopts a very positive attitude to staff requests for time off for family reasons, whether this be to go to watch the children on sports day or to look after a sick member of the family. The firm also allows employees to work evening shifts during school half-term holidays if their children are at home. The founder of this fast-growing company believes that allowing employees such flexibility can have a tremendous commercial advantage for the employer in terms of commitment and calibre of staff. As an example, Listawood won a large order for promotional magnets but came up against a problem when an outside packaging house cut the deadline for the order from six weeks to one weekend. When the workforce (forty full-timers and twenty outworkers) heard of the problem, they came up with a schedule which allowed the order to be filled with continuous staffing over the weekend. In this company the flexibility for employees is genuinely geared to their domestic needs, as well as providing competitive advantage for the company.

Unfortunately, not all flexible working schemes are similarly motivated. By far the most popular form of flexibility is the introduction of part-time work. The vast majority of part-time workers are women (95 per cent). While this can enable more flexibility and so help the employee to accommodate family respons- ibilities, it is highly questionable whether this has been the under- lying rationale for the introduction of such jobs. Part-time jobs are typically those of very low status and responsibility, with limited, if any, prospects for advancement. They are not covered by much of the UK employment law (although such workers are covered under the European Social Chapter, which the UK government is resisting) and so make the employee highly vulnerable to redundancy. They thus provide the organization with a cheap source of expendable labour, and have been introduced for this reason rather than because they promote equal opportunities for women.

Furthermore, while many of the above job schemes are open to men as well as women, in reality it is women whom they are aimed at and indeed who are utilizing them where they exist. In this sense, it could be argued that such organizational arrangements might, in the long term, not be in the best interests of women themselves. As Cockburn (1991) points out, such 'mother's privileges' are a mixed blessing as they enable women to sustain a career after motherhood but confirm them as the domestic sex. Men, then, do not perceive the need to change their own career schedules when they become fathers as the organizational arrangements are already well established for their partners.

Friedan (1981) pointed out that while women have been pulled into the public domain of work, men have not been enticed into the private realm. The resulting lopsided division of familial responsibil- ity leads to the condition Friedan termed the 'superwoman syn- drome'. Women attempt to excel at both the traditional sex-role of housewife and the role of paid labourer, and men want, and indeed expect, their partners to carry the domestic burden. Yet when it comes to work, the fact that their female colleague is leaving work at 5.00pm to pick up the children is considered to be her choice, and because she is letting her domestic life affect her work it is seen to be her fault that she is hitting the glass ceiling (Kelly, 1991). She is simply viewed as not preparing to make sacrifices for her career. This construction of reality shifts the blame for women's difficulties in the workplace on to women themselves, rather than recognizing the socially institutionalized and individually internalized stereotypes that underpin these 'choices'. Men continue to expect the women to run the home and look after the child care arrangements, to take time off when the children are sick, during school holidays and on teacher training days. Yet when she is not devoting herself 100 per cent to her job precisely because of this, she is to blame.

In the light of this, Equal Opportunities policies introduced by organizations are going to have limited effect for the majority of women. Generally, such policies have as their goal the opening up of access to all jobs within an organization by the introduction of fair recruitment, appraisal and promotion practices, supplemented by training courses that will enable women to compete with men on an equal basis. In 'progressive' organizations this is also combined with organizational arrangements such as extended maternity leave, flexible working and job sharing. Yet none of this confronts the issue of the difference between men and women (and specifically mothers and fathers) in their domestic roles. And, as seen, in some ways it helps to reconfirm the woman as the primary manager of the home. What needs to be confronted is the gendered domestic economy, as without change here Equal Opportunities policies are, for the majority of women, simply enabling them to be exploited in dead-end jobs which are low paid and which have few, if any, promotion prospects. This requires a fundamental change of attitudes among men and women.

CONFRONTING STEREOTYPES AND PREJUDICES

Changing attitudes and prejudices is much more difficult than introducing flexible working practices but in the long term such change will be necessary if women are going to make a more significant contribution to organizations. The Institute of Management Survey (Coe, 1992) made a number of suggestions for beginning to tackle this issue.

1 The management career

It is vital that all employees receive career counselling. This is important because promotion to senior positions often depends on having been through particular jobs and departments. It has often been the case that women are ineligible for promotion because they have been side-lined to administrative or support functions which do not have a route through to senior positions.

It is also important, however, for an organization to review the recruitment and selection criteria for *all* management posts to identify how far they assume a traditional male career pattern or conjure up a picture of a male manager. For example, it may be necessary to consider development and succession policies with a view to removing all age limits and other unnecessary criteria. This will ensure that women who have had a career break are eligible for all management training and development schemes.The Royal Bank of Scotland has recently started to 'profile' jobs and individuals to try to ensure that subjectivity is taken out of recruitment and selection decisions.

Another possible way to facilitate more active career preparation by women is to introduce a mentoring system. Mentoring can provide employers with a low cost but effective way of developing staff, while mentors, in the process of training and coaching other people, often find themselves re-evaluating and improving their own working methods. Mentoring was recently initiated as a pilot scheme at Staffordshire University, with thirty-two mentors and mentees being involved. The university was able to identify some success from the system within a few months.

2 The design of managers' jobs

The report recommends that managers' jobs are reviewed to see what scope there is for job share, part-time work or the introduction of flexible hours. In the past, there has been a belief that a manager's job must be full-time, yet a few organizations have introduced job share or part-time work at senior levels and found it can work very successfully (e.g. some local authorities). It could even be argued that organizations are benefiting from job share by getting two competent managers for the price of one (Boyer, 1993).

It may also be possible to introduce home-working in certain managerial or professional jobs. Certainly, new information technologies make the prospect of this much more likely, although the number of organizations that have introduced home-working remains very small.

3 Organization culture

The first step is for an organization to recognize that prejudice exists in every organization. One way to identify the barriers within the particular organization is to carry out a survey of the women within it and ask them about the problems they face. This can lead to a review of meetings, decision-making processes and general culture.

One specific factor which women thought impeded their management careers was non-participation in male networks (the boys' club). While it is difficult to prohibit this informal networking activity, it is possible for women to start to counteract the advantages from such activity by developing their own clubs, such as the Bloomsbury Club which has opened in London. The Bloomsbury Club opened specifically to offer women the same networking opportunities private clubs have traditionally offered to men.

While these recommendations are admirable, they still do not confront the issue of the domestic division of labour. Nor do they really make tangible suggestions about how to change organizational culture to reduce the prejudices and discrimination working against women, and from all we know about organizational culture change, it is clear that this will be a very difficult result to achieve (Pettigrew, 1985). So, while organizations have a lot to gain by harnessing the talents of the currently underutilized female (and black and disabled, etc.) pool of labour, it is clear that this will not be easy to achieve, even in the medium term. This should not stop organizations from trying and there are some exemplary examples of what can be achieved if the organization has the political will to invest the effort and resources needed.

OPPORTUNITY 2000

One example of positive action in the UK is the Opportunity 2000 initiative launched in 1991 and supported by the Prime Minister, John Major. The mission of the campaign is to increase the quality and quantity of women's participation in the labour market by the year 2000. The Opportunity 2000 Target Team was set up by Business in the Community and the campaign is based on the belief that British business is not taking full advantage of the economic potential of women in the workforce. The campaign aims to encourage its members to pay greater attention to the economic worth of women in employment, and to recognize the enormous contribution that women have made and continue to make at work. They urge that to keep women at low grades represents an economic waste of half the workforce. The philosophy of many of the campaign's members is that female staff development and skills training should contribute towards a company's general development, growth and future success.

Sixty companies were involved at the launch of the campaign, each of these having demonstrated its commitment towards improving the opportunities for women at work by eliminating the sexist barriers which have traditionally oppressed women and belittled their attempts to gain equal rights in the work place. Each member organization is required to set measurable goals and targets in order to achieve improvements in the employment rates of women, especially in higher grades. Moreover, each member organization is required to publish its progress at regular intervals.

Success of Opportunity 2000

By the end of 1993, two years after the launch of Opportunity 2000, a review of progress suggested that the campaign was making an impact, despite the fact that this period coincided with the continued economic recession. Membership had risen from sixty companies to over two hundred, representing over 25 per cent of the workforce. The second year review by the Opportunity 2000 Target Team involved 70 per cent of its membership and highlighted significant increases in the proportion of members offering women friendly policies. Specifically:

1   *Job share*: 82 per cent of members reported they offered job share to some staff, compared to 54 per cent in the previous year.
2   *Equal pay*: 49 per cent had carried out reviews to ensure staff received equal pay for work of equal value, compared to 31 per cent in the previous year.
3   *Maternity packages*: 60 per cent offered maternity packages which are above the statutory minimum, compared to 46 per cent in the previous year.
4   *Paternity leave*: 68 per cent offered paternity leave, compared to 54 per cent in the previous year.
5   *Common terms and conditions*: 81 per cent offered common terms and conditions to all staff against 59 per cent in the previous year.

Another study conducted by Incomes Data Services (1993) also found evidence that the campaign was working when it studied six campaign member organizations. The Opportunity 2000 programme can help member companies achieve their targets and goals in a number of ways:

1   *Interorganizational networks*: member companies have the opportunity to share experiences and so to learn from the initiatives of other member organizations.
2   *Local workshops and seminars*: these are designed specifically to respond to the needs of campaign members and can help to establish regional networks. Line managers are also invited to attend good practice visits.
3   *Knowledge diffusion*: all member organizations are provided with an action pack of materials based on leading edge research carried out by Ashridge Management Research Group. Member companies regularly receive relevant information, including bi-monthly factsheets on topical issues, quarterly case studies of good practice and annual progress reports.

The literature on the diffusion of innovation would suggest that Opportunity 2000 has had some success because it has stimulated the interorganizational communication channels which are necessary to facilitate the diffusion of new ideas about best practice (Newell et al., 1993). In this case the innovation is the idea that organizations cannot afford to waste the potential of the women in their workforce. It is clear that those companies involved do recognize that investment in people is a key issue for business survival in the increasingly competitive international markets. These companies, not coincidentally, also represent some of the most successful British businesses.

CONCLUSION

To meet the increasingly intense commercial challenges of the 1990s, it is vital that an organization works to build a heterogeneous workforce, including women, blacks, disabled, etc., at all levels. Commitment to Opportunity 2000 is a practical campaign which an organization can join to help combat one type of discrimination – that against women. Many of the ideas of good practice diffused through the Opportunity 2000 campaign can, and should, be directed at other sources of discrimination. For example, setting goals and making action plans are equally appropriate to combating racial discrimination. The organization that takes these issues seriously and works to overcome the long history of white male dominance will provide an environment in which all employees will have the potential to develop their careers as fully as possible. At the same time, the organization, by making full use of its human resources, is more likely to be successful in an increasingly competitive market. But there is no 'quick-fix' solution and commitment to action over time from all levels of the organization will be needed.

Unfortunately, many organizations continue to pay lip service to such ideas. To promote real change requires a change in attitudes and values about the roles and value of men and women, blacks and whites, abled and disabled, etc., in society. Few organizations take on board these issues. Rather (and perhaps inevitably), they modify structures and practices which accommodate rather than confront the traditional attitudes and values. For example, it was argued that flexible working arrangements, at least as they are currently focused (i.e. almost exclusively on women), simply help to perpetuate the status quo by referencing women as the domestic carer. We cannot expect deep-seated prejudices to disappear overnight, but to ensure the full contribution of all groups through fundamental attitude change should be the long-term goal.

Part III
The organization and society

8 Business ethics

The impact of the organization on the wider community

INTRODUCTION

The earlier chapters in this book have concentrated on how a work organization can affect those who work within it. This effect can be either positive or negative and we have considered ways of reducing the negative impact and increasing the positive. In this final part we turn to consider how the organization can affect those outside its boundaries – consumers of its products, people who live in the local community and, at times, even the national or international communities.

The fact that organizations can have a dramatic, and at times devastating, effect on the wider community has led to a concern with what has been termed the social responsibility of organizations. But what is 'social responsibility'? Jones (1980) defined social responsibility as inferring that corporations have an obligation to constituent groups in society other than stockholders and beyond that prescribed by law or union contract. Following this definition, Matthews (1988) devised a scale relating to social responsibility which grades issues by the seriousness of their impact on society.

Tier one issues

Tier one issues are the most serious in that they cause the greatest harm to the greatest number of people. Tier one issues would include the manufacture of unsafe products or drugs, the pollution of air or water beyond that allowable, disregard for worker health and safety. It could be argued that these are not issues of social responsibility as they go beyond the definition of Jones in that they break the law. However, this may not always be the case. For example, a company may legally be able to market a drug in a Third World country which it would not be able to market in the UK because of stricter safety testing regulations in the UK. But the question is whether the company is acting responsibly in marketing a drug which it recognizes has not been fully tested.

Tier two issues

Tier two issues are those that are of intermediate importance and can affect a large number of people. Examples include monopolies and issues of anti-trust, affirmative action issues, bribery/payoffs and false advertising.

Tier three issues

Tier three issues are less likely to be life-threatening. However, they are relevant to any discussion of the problems of social responsibility. Examples include lack of involvement in community affairs and few or no charitable donations.

What all these issues have in common is that they are concerned with the impact on others of an organization's behaviour. Matthews (1988) identified this awareness of the effect of one's actions and behaviours on others as being the 'very heart' of social responsibility. Social responsibility can be taken further to infer that business has some responsibility to actually get involved in alleviating social problems, as it often contributes to them. It is this last point which is the most debatable and, as we will see, some people argue that rather than seeing these issues as being on a continuum from serious to less serious, there is a clear distinction which needs to be made between social and moral responsibility (see below).

The discussion of the social and moral responsibility of organizations has been debated under the general heading of business ethics, which has only really become a topic of concern, at least in the academic world, in the 1980s and 1990s.

ETHICAL DILEMMAS

The problem is that issues of social responsibility do not involve black and white decision choices. Ethical issues most often arise when there is some kind of dilemma. It is not possible to manufacture a totally safe car, but what standard of safety should be considered ethical? Clearly, the Ford Pinto (see below) was not seen to reach this standard but this does not help in pinpointing where the standard should be. Similarly, there are few drugs which have no harmful side effects. Thus, while a drug might help thousands of people who would otherwise suffer, it may make a certain percentage more ill or even die. Thus, decisions have to be made about what is an acceptable level of death or injury. While there can never be a right answer to this dilemma, the ethical 'answer' to it would be that the decisions which are made keep human costs paramount in the decision-making process, with economic costs kept to a minimum.

A good example of where economic costs were given priority over human costs can be seen in the manufacture and marketing by Ford of the Pinto car. In the Ford Pinto case the decision to market can be described as unethical because it was the economic factors which were treated as paramount and the human factors which were treated as a secondary consideration. In the late 1970s the Ford motor company designed, manufactured and marketed the Pinto car. Yet it was known within the company that there was a major design fault in the car – the petrol tank was likely to explode if there was a collision from the rear. The cost of correcting the defect would have substantially reduced market prospects. The company decided to go ahead and launch the car, after calculating the costs of civil damages if an accident did occur. That is, Ford executives calculated that it was more cost efficient to manufacture the Pinto with the cheaper, but unsafe, petrol tank, and pay costs to individuals or families for injuries and deaths caused because of the defect, rather than develop a safer, but more expensive tank.

A serious accident eventually did occur in which a number of people were killed. Now while there is possibly no such thing as a 'safe product', and the search for perfect safety (were that in any case achievable) would price most products out of the reach of ordinary people, the Ford company demonstrated by its actions a clear lack of concern for the potential safety of its customers in the overriding pursuit of profit. To the executives concerned the decision was based on a simple cost-benefit analysis – of the probable costs of civil action against the costs of correcting the fault.

EVALUATION OF ETHICAL DILEMMAS

Despite the fact that ethical dilemmas do not allow right/wrong answers, scholars interested in them have attempted to produce concepts that can help evaluate conduct which arises from such dilemmas. There are two competing approaches for the evaluation of conduct which exist in ethical theory: teleological and deontological moral reasoning. The Ford example would be considered unethical using either approach.

1   *Deontological reasoning*: such reasoning follows Kant in suggesting that morality consists of doing one's duty according to principles established a priori by the mind. So if it is wrong to tell lies then any incidence of lying is ethically bad.
2   *Teleological reasoning*: such reasoning follows John Stuart Mill's maxim that ethics consists of doing things that promote the greatest good for the greatest number, that is, acting on the basis of utilitarianism. So it is not necessarily wrong to tell lies if a lie will actually produce more good than telling the truth would ('a white lie'!). For example, a doctor may not be totally honest about the amount of suffering experienced by an accident victim, if she believes that the family of the victim would not be able to cope with the truth.

Teleological principles are based on outcomes, rather than the actions that lead to those outcomes. Deontological reasoning is concerned with the actions rather than the consequences – behaviour must conform to moral rules of fairness, irrespective of outcomes. So those taking a deontological perspective would have condemned trade with South Africa when it was ruled by a system of apartheid because it was an unjust regime and it was not morally right to trade with such a partner. Those taking a utilitarian perspective (teleological reasoning) might have condemned apartheid in South Africa and yet nevertheless have condoned trade with it because to ban trade would have made everyone worse off, with black people possibly suffering most of all. Trade would thus promote utilitarian ends of improved welfare for the majority of blacks.

In terms of the Ford example, the actions of the company could be condemned from both a utilitarian and a deontological perspective. From a utilitarian perspective, it is clear that the company did not consider the consequences of its actions on its customers, at least from a well-being perspective. Rather, the consequences were considered in purely monetary terms (how much the compensation would be) and from the perspective of the company only. From a deontological perspective, customers' rights were not considered in the decision to go ahead. This could only have happened if Ford had given customers the information at the time of purchase that the car was unsafe. Even this might not be ethical since if an individual customer had decided to go ahead and buy and take the risk, they were in turn putting at risk other road users who might get caught up in an accident. In terms of justice, it should be pointed out that in this instance Ford's calculations misfired, since the corporation was eventually prosecuted for the criminal offence of 'reckless homicide', rather than for civil damages. Although the Ford corporation was eventually acquitted, the case is notable because it was the first example of a corporation being charged with unlawful homicide under products liability legislation (Cullen et al., 1987). This, then, is a clear example of unethical business behaviour.

In reality, both deontological and teleological principles need to be taken into account in assessing decisions made in the face of ethical dilemmas. Velasquez et al. (1982) produced an integrative model to analyse how ethical decisions are made, which suggests that behaviour must satisfy the following criteria to be considered ethical:

1 *Criterion of utilitarian outcomes*: the behaviour results in optimizing the satisfaction of people inside and outside the organization. In other words, the decision produces the greatest good for the greatest number of people. This is very clearly based on teleological reasoning.
2 *Criterion of individual rights*: the behaviour respects the rights of all affected parties, so that it respects human rights of free speech, free consent, freedom of conscience, privacy and due process.
3 *Criterion of distributive justice*: the behaviour respects the rules of justice in that it treats people equitably and fairly rather than arbitrarily. The second and third criteria are clearly based on deontological reasoning.

Their model, however, recognizes that at times these criteria might conflict or indeed, that a behaviour may be unable to pass any of these criteria and yet still be considered ethical. They include a fourth criterion to accommodate this:

4   *Criterion of overwhelming factors*: this factor enables decisions to be regarded as ethical even when, for example: a behaviour results in some good and some bad being done; a behaviour uses questionable means to achieve a positive end; or a person's behaviour is based on inaccurate or incomplete information.

To some extent the fourth factor in this model undermines the first three criteria as guides to the analysis of ethical behaviour. The first three factors appear to indicate that there are criteria which can be specified which will enable us to assess whether or not any given example of behaviour is ethical. The fourth factor indicates that there will always be instances where these criteria are not enough. What the model therefore does is emphasize the complexity of business ethics.

ETHICS AND THE LAW

One point to note is that in the Ford Pinto case the corporation was prosecuted for breaking the law. The issue is whether corporations can be said to be acting ethically simply if they do not break the law. One exponent of this view is Milton Friedman. Friedman (1962) argues that business personnel have no moral responsibility to society at large. The job of managers is to make as much money as possible for their shareholders. Managers are, like any other worker, employees of the owners of the enterprise – the shareholders – and are directly responsible to them. The main aim of shareholders is to maximize their wealth and managers must pursue that objective exclusively. Friedman argues that if corporations pursue social responsibilities, their performance will begin to be judged by non-economic criteria. Eventually, the importance of economic measures of performance will decline, which will, in turn, erode economic efficiency so that ultimately society will lose. Furthermore, Friedman believes that Western democracies have adequate governmental machinery to achieve social aims. If corporations begin to take over this social responsibility, governments, and the whole system of accountability through democracy, will be undermined.

This line of argument sees the fundamental aim of business as being to provide cheap and reliable products for the consumer through competition. The more successful it is in this enterprise, the less 'fat' there will be for other activities such as charitable donations to worthy causes, for example a gift of books to a local school. It is only large monopolies which are able to support such worthy causes, but this is precisely because they are inefficient and make excess profits at the expense of the consumer.

When a corporation chooses to invest in some social project, this inevitably entails a selective attitude towards the potential bene-ficiaries of its generosity, at the same time as it sacrifices profitability. For example, Coca-Cola decided to invest in an extensive welfare system for those of its employees who were working in rather poor conditions in Florida. This group of employees benefited from this project. However, Coca-Cola had to pay for the project out of its profits so that it could not afford to offer as many employment opportunities as it would have done if it had not chosen to invest in this particular 'good cause'. Thus, it could be argued that while this was morally 'good' from the point of view of current employees, it was morally 'bad' from the point of view of those who otherwise might have been offered a job but instead had to remain unemployed (Manne, 1966).

Friedman thus concludes that, given that such social projects inevitably involve selective attention, the morality is dubious. Moreover, a company that engages in such projects is almost certainly doomed to failure because of the nature of competition in a capitalist economy. The excessive use of profits for social projects will reduce those profits with a consequent reduction in share values for the company. This, in turn, will make a takeover by less socially conscious individuals very likely.

SOCIAL VERSUS MORAL RESPONSIBILITY

The implication of this type of argument is that it is necessary to distinguish between social and moral responsibility. Companies ought to conform to basic moral constraints, whether or not these are legally defined, such as the production and marketing of unsafe products (tier one issues) or using bribes to secure a sale (tier two issues). However, this is very different from demanding that companies take on social responsibility projects, such as investment in areas of high unemployment (tier three issues). It is argued by some that the latter are supererogatory duties about which there will be no agreement as to those that are most important, and which inevitably detract from the main obligation of the organization.

This emphasis on moral rather than social responsibility may appear straightforward, but the problem comes in defining morality, since some of the more interesting business scandals have not involved explicit law-breaking, either criminal or civil. A good example of this involves problems concerning the environmental impact of business activity. While environmental standards that organizations must conform to have now been more clearly laid down, those lobbying from the green movement would condemn virtually every organization for not having done enough to reduce its impact on the environment. The problem for a particular company is that were it to invest in meeting some non-enforceable standard, there is no guarantee that its competitors would do so. Given that meeting the standard will involve costs, this will put the company at a competitive disadvantage. While there might be some PR advantage for the claim that the company's products are more environmentally friendly, this will not always offset the extra costs involved.

Moreover, companies that get on the 'green bandwagon' are not inevitably going to be successful even if they can contain costs. Consumers will not buy products, however environmentally friendly, if they are inferior. This was demonstrated most clearly in the huge peak and trough of consumer spending on green domestic cleaning products such as washing powder and toilet cleaner. Consumers were keen to buy such products and sales soared. However, when consumers found that the cleaning power of these environmentally friendly products was vastly inferior, sales dropped dramatically. Nevertheless, what this market analysis demonstrates is the consumer desire for green products as long as they are actually effective.

The problem is that if each company views the earth as a common and free good to be exploited without restraint, the sum of their activities produces bad outcomes for everyone. Pollution is inevitable and not inherently bad; it is only an excess of it that causes the problem. But the person creating the excess can never be identified, so the business community as a whole is blamed. However, such pollution cannot be seen as the outcome of the inevitable search for higher profits, since in communist countries the environmental records are even worse. Thus, there is a debate between those who advocate stronger regulatory mechanisms to control pollution and those who argue that the market can correct itself. The latter argue that as people do not like living in badly polluted cities, they will punish corporations who pollute their environments. In this way significant pressures can be brought to bear on recalcitrant managements, as is demonstrated by the evidence that major corporations are responding to this pressure. Legislation, some suggest, would undermine the delicate trade-offs between productivity and environmental protection that a free society has to make.

INDIVIDUAL RESPONSIBILITY VERSUS STATE INTERVENTION

Problems of immoral business behaviour often revolve around the issue of personal autonomy and responsibility for consumers, as against excessive paternalistic protection from state intervention. The most clear example of this revolves around the cigarette industry and especially its activities in advertising. On the one hand, some would take the position that it is simply immoral to allow the sale of a potentially life-threatening substance. This would be an extreme deontological standpoint. Yet an outright ban can also be interpreted as morally wrong since it deprives the individual of the freedom and responsibility to make his own decisions. Thus, the moral issue is seen to revolve around the advertising of cigarettes, rather than the morality of actually producing them.

Most of this advertising activity is focused on attracting young people to start smoking by highlighting the pleasurable sensations associated with smoking and ignoring, or even refuting, the life-threatening aspects of the activity. It is interesting to note that many governments (including the British government) have chosen not to intervene and ban cigarette advertising. While this is undoubtedly partly due to the tax revenue from tobacco sales, there is also the problem of excessive paternalism. There is a dilemma between the imperative of personal responsibility for action and the desire to protect people from their own folly.

Another example of the morality of the production and marketing of 'unsafe' products concerns the sale of a product which is not inherently unsafe at all – the marketing of powdered baby milk to mothers in Third World countries. Here the problem occurred because of the misuse of the product by some mothers, rather than because the product itself was harmful. In some cases problems occurred because mothers could not afford to purchase baby milk power once the free samples they had been given were used up. However, by this time their own breast milk had dried up. Fatalities also occurred because some mothers overdiluted the formula and/or used contaminated (unboiled) water to mix with the powder. This was due to both the poor economic conditions in which people were living and a lack of information. The World Health Organization identified these problems and issued warnings to the companies marketing baby milk to these countries. Nestlé was singled out for criticism because it continued to market the product even after these warnings and strong advice not to do so. There was a public outcry against Nestlé which included boycotting the company's products.

In defence of its actions, Nestlé argued both that the benefits outweighed the costs and that they could not be held responsible for the misuse of their product since there was no attempt to deceive the consumer in its marketing or advertising. This defence is thus made from a utilitarian perspective. However, if the arguments are taken further, Nestlé can be found wanting on both counts. First, in terms of the argument of benefits outweighing costs, it can be considered morally weak to suggest that gains to the majority, however great, override harm caused to a minority, however small. Second, in terms of information, while it is true that Nestlé did not deliberately deceive, it was clear that there were disparities between various sets of consumers. Certain groups were given less information and this put some at a distinct, and possibly fatal, disadvantage.

The actual criticism against Nestlé, however, came from a deontological perspective. It was argued that Nestlé had violated the rights of mothers in the Third World by continuing to market the product in the face of mounting evidence of the problems it was causing. This is more difficult to defend as it is not clear that Nestlé actually violated any individual's rights, as the notion of individual rights usually includes some notion of individual choice and autonomy. Nestlé does appear to have acted unethically, pursuing its drive for profits while ignoring other considerations. The corporation did not break any laws but, from a utilitarian perspective, it failed to take into account the adverse impact that its product was having on a significant minority of its consumers.

SOCIAL RESPONSIBILITY

Thus, many ethicists, while accepting Friedman's (1962) first premise, that corporations behave morally when they make efficient use of scarce resources, strongly reject the second, that business morality consists in simply obeying the law. Although ethicists see a relationship between the law and morality, they do not see them as identical. Moreover, many ethicists go further and reject the view that it is only moral responsibility which is important. Rather, they endorse the view that organizations should assume a social as well as a moral responsibility. There are a number of arguments put forward as to why:

1 *Society expectations*: the argument here is simple – society expects business to assume social responsibilities and since the corporation operates under a franchise from society (sanctioned by society to achieve objectives set for it by society), the corporation must respond or society will take away that franchise by not buying its products or coming forward as employees.

2 *Self-interest*: it is in the long-term self-interest of business to assume social responsibilities. This is based on the idea that people who have a good environment, education and more opportunities make better employees and customers. Solving social problems can thus help to increase opportunities for individuals, which in turn will benefit corporations.

3 *Resistance to regulation*: when business assumes social responsibilities, it reduces the pressure to increase legal regulation. This will ultimately reduce costs, because regulation is expensive, reduce flexibility and freedom in decision-making, and reduce corporate power in favour of government power.

4 *Stakeholder rights*: more fundamentally, there is an increasing number of people who reject the premise that shareholders' rights are all important. Rather, they argue for the adoption of a stake-holder model where the manager's job is to find a balance between the interests of all those who have a 'stake' in the organization – employees, customers, shareholders and the wider community.

Proponents of this view also argue that those opposing social responsibility overstate the trend and ultimate magnitude of such responsibility. To engage voluntarily in a few social projects is not inevitably going to mean that the economic imperative is overridden. If a corporation is not profitable in the long term, there is no way that it can fulfil any responsibilities to society. Short-term profits *may* be compromised, but this will not be that significant and, more importantly, in the long term it might well lead to an improved profit position as some of the benefits of the social projects come to fruition, for example by providing a better educated workforce from which to select.

CONCLUSIONS

The social and moral responsibilities of business organizations are increasingly important issues as it becomes clear that many business decisions have been taken without proper regard for their impact on the wider community. This chapter has considered the difficulties of actually analysing the issue of business responsibility since, except in clear cases where the law is flouted, most decisions can be looked at as being right and wrong from different perspectives. There is the dilemma as to whether we should simply look at the means or whether the means can sometimes justify the ends. There is also the dilemma as to whether companies have a social as well as a moral responsibility – not just making decisions according to legal and moral guidelines but also attempting to 'put something back' into society in terms of gifts which help to solve problems in the community.

While there is no straightforward answer to the social and moral responsibility issues considered in this chapter, it is becoming clearer that today's organizations and their managers face increased account-ability for their decisions. We, the customers, increasingly expect higher social and moral standards from organizations, as reflected in the penalties imposed upon companies who have been judged to have failed to meet these standards. For example, in the USA two senior executives were recently sent to jail because they had been involved in covering up the fact that an apple juice for infants, sold as 100 per cent pure fruit juice, was actually a blend of chemical ingredients.

It is also clear that companies which take their social responsibil-ity seriously can be highly successful. Perhaps the best known example of this in the UK has been Anita Roddick's success with the Body Shop. The Body Shop is known for its innovative 'natural' cosmetics and a commitment to the environment. This is demonstrated, for example, by its use of biodegradable products and refillable containers, and the fact that it does not use animals to test its products. The firm's business strategy is based on Roddick's own social activism, which promotes environmental consciousness by supporting causes such as Greenpeace, Save the Whales and the Stop the Burning (of the rainforest) Campaign. The Body Shop has an Environmental Projects department whose job is to monitor compliance with its environmental principles. The success of this approach is demonstrated by the phenomenal growth of the Body Shop empire, which is expected to be a $1 billion enterprise by 1995. Clearly, Roddick's own business acumen has had much to do with the success, but it is also clear that customers have been attracted by the 'green' label of Body Shop products.

While there are other examples of companies and whole industries (e.g. the adoption of catalytic converters in cars) taking on board their social and moral responsibilities, it is also evident that many business decisions are made without regard for their wider consequences. The important point about this, however, is that it is individuals who make these decisions, not some dehumanized organization. In order to understand this we turn, in the next chapter, to consider the psychological factors which drive ordinary humans to make those seemingly callous decisions which appear to disregard normal, acceptable standards of moral and social responsibility.

9 *Individual decisions and ethical behaviour*

INTRODUCTION

In the last chapter we considered the social and moral responsibility of organizations from a macro-perspective. What this demonstrates is that companies have very different responses to ethical dilemmas. To contrast two cases, Firestone (tyre manufacturer) and Perrier (bottled water), vividly illustrates why companies urgently need to consider the issue of business ethics. Firestone eventually made the decision to recall 10 million of its 500 series radial tyres in October 1978, but only after pressure from the US National Highway Traffic Safety Administration, which in turn had only acted after receiving 14,000 customer complaints. In the time between recognition of the problem and recall of the product, apart from the customer complaints, there had been at least twenty-nine fatal traffic accidents and hundreds of property damage accidents involving cars using Firestone 500 tyres. Throughout this period Firestone had continued to deny, against public anxiety, that there was anything wrong with the product. Analysts estimated that the bad publicity had cost Firestone 3 per cent of its 25 per cent share of the multimillion US tyre market. In contrast, when Perrier found traces of benzene in its bottled water in February 1990, it instantly recalled all its bottles worldwide. While this resulted in significant cost to the company, Perrier recognized that this short-term cost was insignificant compared to the potential loss of customer faith in the company.

Taking social and moral responsibility issues seriously, therefore, makes economic sense. However, from the perspective of this book, what is most important is to consider why immoral and socially irresponsible behaviour continues to occur within organizations and how it can be prevented. The first point to note is that it is not organizations but individuals who make the decisions which result in a negative impact on others. Thus, we can consider the factors which impact on the individual and influence the way in which he makes decisions within organizational contexts.

MORAL MATURITY

Maturity in adults is associated with advanced levels of moral development. Kohlberg (1973), for example, suggests that people progress through three levels of moral development, each divided into two stages. At the first, *preconventional* level individuals defer to socially defined conceptions of right and wrong. These are identified in terms of the punishments or rewards likely to follow as consequences of actions. In other words, morality is defined through a self-interested orientation. At the second level, *conventional* morality, actions are evaluated in terms of maintaining a good image in the eyes of other people, with the emphasis therefore on self-respect. At the third level, *postconventional* morality, actions are guided by self-chosen ethical principles which value, for example, justice, dignity and equality. The principles are upheld at this level to avoid self-condemnation – it does not matter if others do not think what I did was wrong, only that I think this.

Research has shown that people's level of moral maturity can differ between situations, but that most operate at level two rather than level three (e.g. Nisan and Kohlberg, 1982). Moreover, much unethical behaviour in organizations can be seen to stem from a level one, self-interest orientation, because of the heavy costs of ignoring the consequences for self if operating at a higher level (see below). However, if organizations are truly going to become more socially and morally responsible, this can only be achieved if the individuals making decisions are operating at a postconventional level. This will depend on the organization putting resources into education and development to foster this level of moral maturity in its managers. However, individuals will only operate at this level of maturity if they are not penalized for doing so. Organizations will therefore also need to foster a climate in which ethical morality is part of the culture. As we will see, these conditions are not met in many organizations.

INDIVIDUAL RESPONSIBILITY

Korn (1989) asked business executives what they thought would be needed of the corporate leader in the year 2000. Interestingly, a concern for ethical behaviour was mentioned as one of the most important attributes. Furthermore, there are examples of executives of major companies who do actually reflect this concern in their business behaviour. For example, the Corning Glass company philosophy is that total quality equals total ethics. The company bases its decisions on what it calls a 'transnational ethical system' which means that decisions are made which consider: does the intended action do the most good for the greatest number of people?; does the intended action meet standards of justice for the individual? However, as we will see, there are many pressures on individual corporate members which operate to deflect normal moral responsibility concerns. It is helpful to look at this by considering two scenarios which any individual may face in their career:

1   Sophie is a laboratory technician working for a large pharmaceutical company which is running an experiment using rats to test a new drug. She finds that a tiny percentage of the rats are dying following the drug injection. Her boss tells her to replace the dead rats and not to record those that die. What should she do?
2   Jamie has recently been appointed as a middle manager in a chemical company. He finds out that toxic waste from the chemical process is being illegally disposed of in a local river. He informs his senior manager who tells him to ignore it as 'everyone else does it'. What should he do?

The reality is that in many such instances Sophie and Jamie would do exactly what the boss has told them to do, and because of their actions an adverse impact on others results – people die through taking the new drug and rivers are polluted through the dumping of toxic waste. Sophie and Jamie may well try to rationalize their behaviour so that it appears to have been justified. Gellerman (1986), for example, identifies a number of common rationalizations used to justify unethical behaviour including pretending that the behaviour was not really unethical or illegal; excusing the behaviour by reflecting that it is really in the organization's or your best interests; or assuming that the behaviour is okay because no one could ever find out about it. However, it is also important to recognize that Sophie and Jamie are likely to feel very uncomfortable with their actions and are unlikely to feel very positive about their organizations. They operate at a preconventional level of moral reasoning, not because they cannot operate at a higher level of moral reasoning, but because to do otherwise would jeopardize not just their career prospects, but probably their very jobs (i.e. their livelihood). Thus, in companies where unethical and illegal behaviours are encouraged the problems of low employee morale and commitment are likely to be prevalent.

LEARNING AND ETHICAL BEHAVIOUR

So, given that Sophie and Jamie did not feel happy with what they were doing, why did they do it? Edwin Sutherland (1949, 1961) maintained that criminal behaviour is learned just like any other behaviour. His book, *White Collar Crime*, was a seminal piece bringing the problem into perspective. Sutherland did not himself specify how this learning actually took place, but the learning theories developed in psychology have been used to analyse this learning process (Burgess and Akers, 1966; Akers, 1985).

Burgess and Akers (1966) begin by stating that criminal behaviour is learned according to the principles of operant conditioning. Operant conditioning states that behaviour is a function of its past and present environmental consequences. These consequences act as reinforcers, with positive reinforcers *increasing* the occurrence of the behaviour that preceded it and negative reinforcers *reducing* the occurrence of the behaviour that preceded it. Positive reinforcers include praise, monetary rewards and promotions. Negative reinforcers include being told off, demotion and being excluded from a team or group. Thus, if unethical behaviour is positively reinforced, through praise and promotion, while ethical behaviour is condemned and leads to demotion and reprimand, then the individual is likely to behave unethically, even though he knows that his behaviour is wrong. In the two examples given above to behave ethically would have meant going against what the person had been told to do by his/her boss. If in the past not doing what they have been told to do has led to negative reinforcement, they are likely to avoid this in the current situation and so behave unethically, perhaps against their conscience, but in accordance with their bosses' commands.

At times the communication from the boss may contain messages condemning and condoning unethical behaviour at the same time. For example, being told not to engage in illegal behaviour but to meet a production deadline, 'no matter what it takes'. If meeting the production deadline is only possible if some important safety test is not carried out, this will pose a dilemma for the individual. What she does in this situation will depend on what has happened in previous, similar situations. On the one hand, if in the past missing a production deadline in order to ensure the necessary safety tests have been done has been commended, or at least if there have been no negative sanctions, then the person is likely to carry out the tests and miss the deadline. On the other hand, if missing deadlines has in the past led to very negative sanctions, such as demotion, the person is likely to miss out the tests. Otherwise she would be jeopardizing her career prospects.

Organizational culture

While learning theory might be a very simple explanation it does help us to begin to understand why inside an organization an individual engages in unethical behaviour which they would not have considered doing outside this context. It suggests that the important factor to consider is the *culture* of the organization. In some organizations it is unethical behaviour which is rewarded with promotions and pay rises, and in these organizations individuals are likely to find it hard to resist acting unethically, at least not unless it is at the expense of their career prospects. A classic example of such an organization was demonstrated in the Challenger Shuttle disaster in 1986. One of the causes of the explosion of the shuttle on take-off was found to have been a seal problem in the attachment of the booster rockets to the shuttle.

The seal joining segments were designed and made by the Morton Thiokol corporation. During the Presidential Commission enquiry which followed the tragedy two of the Morton Thiokol engineers testified that this problem had been known well in advance of the launch of the shuttle. They told the enquiry that they had tried to convince their senior managers that the launch should not go ahead because they knew that there was a high probability that the seals would fail in very cold weather. These problems had been taken to a meeting with NASA officials, but NASA had put pressure on Morton Thiokol to 'prove' the problem. It had been difficult to conclusively prove that the seals would fail, and so Morton Thiokol senior managers had bowed to NASA pressure and agreed to the launch. Thus, rather than have safety at the top of the agenda, which would have led to an emphasis on proving that the launch should go ahead, the emphasis had been on proving that the launch should not go ahead.

What is especially interesting about this case is the fate of the two engineers who had 'blown the whistle' on their company. Both were moved to new jobs and effectively demoted. This is a clear example of punishment acting to reinforce unethical behaviour in this company. Other research suggests that this is not an uncommon fate for 'whistle-blowers' (see below). In other organizations ethical behaviour is promoted and rewarded, and in these organizations it is ethical behaviour which will lead to career progress.

CONFORMITY AND GROUPTHINK

It is not only the fact that we want to try to advance rather than restrict our career opportunities which leads us to follow the example and commands of both peers and superiors in our organization. It is also a more general psychological need to conform to group norms so that we are accepted and liked by those we work with. If we are ostracized, or in some other way not allowed to become a full member of our work group because we do not conform to the norms or standards of what is considered acceptable behaviour by the group, whether this behaviour is ethical or unethical, then this is very uncomfortable. It is easier for us to ignore our own scruples and go along with the group even though we may believe that what we are doing is wrong. Whyte (1956) pointed out long ago the pitfalls of the 'organization man' – the person willing to go along and conform with the group, no matter what, to ensure acceptance and a trouble-free time.

Indeed, the Space Shuttle Challenger disaster has been analysed as an example of groupthink (Morehead et al., 1991). The concept of groupthink was first developed by Janis (1983) to explain why disastrous military and political decisions had been made by groups of intelligent individuals. Those making the decisions were, in hindsight, seen to have ignored vital evidence which should have been taken into account and which would have led to a different decision. This is similar to the shuttle disaster, in which the evidence that the seal joints might fail was ignored (see above). Thus, groupthink refers to 'a mode of thinking that people engage in when they are deeply involved in a cohesive in-group, when the members' striving for unanimity overrides their motivation to realistically appraise alternative courses of action' (Janis, 1972: 8).

Groupthink occurs when members of a decision-making group become so concerned about not disrupting what appears to be a consensus among the rest of the group that they fail to make known their own reservations and alternatives. The problem arises because members in very cohesive groups often have more confidence in the group's decision than in their own doubts about what action is being decided. As a result, they may suspend their own critical thinking in favour of conforming to the group. The group insulates itself from potentially useful outside information, especially if this challenges the group's decision. The result of this process is that the group's decision may be completely uninformed, irrational or even immoral (Morehead and Montanari, 1986).

INCREASING ETHICAL BEHAVIOUR

The last section of this chapter will address ways of improving the morality of business decisions. What is quite clear is that there is a growing public concern about the many examples of organizations behaving in ways which have had an adverse impact on the wider community. There are two solutions to these problems. The first is to increase governmental regulation so that top executives of organizations are held accountable for the actions of those in their organizations. The second solution is for corporations themselves to increase their self-regulation. This would involve companies fostering a corporate culture in which it would be 'unthinkable' to commit crimes on behalf of the organization.

It is very clear that organizations vary in the ethical climates they establish for their members. What is important is what top managers *do*, and the culture they establish and reinforce. This will determine the way lower-level personnel act and the way the organization as a whole acts when ethical dilemmas are faced. There are examples of organizations where an ethical climate has been fostered such that actions are based on considerations of doing the right thing, regardless of cost. For example, Johnson and Johnson immediately acted to withdraw one of their drugs from the marketplace when there was a slight hint that the product might be contaminated with Tylenol poison. They acted from a base of social responsibility. In such companies, when the ethical climate is clear and positive, individual employees can act with confidence when presented with an ethical dilemma, knowing that they will be supported by top management. In other organizations concerns for operating efficiency may outweigh social considerations when similarly difficult decisions are faced.

Organizations which take responsibility issues seriously will often establish an ethical code (see below) which can sensitize employees to the ethical dimension of their work. However, there will always be ethical dilemmas which cannot be resolved by appeal to such guidelines. Furthermore, as Donaldson (1989) observed, codes can sometimes be used as an institutional defence in which personal judgement is suspended. It will therefore be necessary for an organization to put resources into education and development programmes which allow individuals to develop higher levels of moral reasoning (Maclagan, 1990) so that they can progress away from conformity towards more independence of mind, and questioning of organizational goals and values (i.e. postconventional morality). However, this clearly poses a threat to the organization which in the past has tended to put profit before other concerns.

Thus, the reason why many doubt the ability of corporations themselves to improve their behaviour is because this will involve major organizational change. The propensity to unethical, or ethical, behaviour within an organization is deeply embedded within that organization's culture. It is part of the value system of the organization which is accepted by all and which newcomers soon learn. If everybody 'knows' that meeting production deadlines is paramount, then the likelihood of an individual questioning that piece of 'knowledge' is extremely low. Furthermore, it is sustained or reinforced by the systems of rewards and punishments such that it is the unscrupulous production manager, who does meet deadlines regardless of whether this flouts the rules (or even the law), who gets promoted, rather than the manager who misses deadlines because she is concerned with ensuring all tests have been done properly. Thus, in order for a corporation which has previously tolerated, if not openly condoned, unethical behaviour to change and promote ethical considerations, the whole organization culture will need to be changed. Yet there is a huge literature which attests to the difficulties, if not the impossibility, of organizations changing their cultures (Pettigrew, 1985).

WHISTLE-BLOWING

As an example of the kind of change needed we can consider the case of 'whistle-blowing'. Research on this subject has increased considerably recently (e.g. Jensen, 1987; Matthews, 1987). Whistle-blowing refers to situations when an individual 'blows the whistle' about some activity which he observes in the organization he works for, which he considers to be corrupt, illegal, fraudulent or harmful (Nader et al., 1972). While from the perspective of society the whistle-blower is often treated as a moral hero, within the organization he is typically treated as a traitor. This is because the individual has rejected the group norms and as such has been disloyal to the group. He is therefore seen to have acted deviantly. For example, if a group norm has grown up that it is 'OK' to make 'minor' modifications to the results of a drug-testing experiment in order to complete the project on time, an individual who objects to this illegal practice will be seen as a deviant. If he then goes and 'blows the whistle', whether internally or externally, he will be considered to have acted disloyally to his work group. The consequence for whistle-blowers is that they will be treated as any deviant is treated by his group – ostracized and regarded as a troublemaker. Yet from the point of view of the wider community, such individuals have acted extremely positively in bringing to attention the possibility of unsafe drugs.

Despite this fact, research has shown that whistle-blowers are typically treated within their organization as 'villains' and, instead of being commended for their concern, are punished. For example, Soeken (1987), in a study of 233 whistle-blowers, found that 84 per cent had been fired as a result of their actions. The example of the two Morton Thiokol engineers is typical. However, if a company wants to encourage increased social responsibility and ethical behaviour among its employees, one step towards achieving this would be to encourage whistle-blowing, at least internally. This can be achieved by establishing a clear ethical code of practice which is seen to be endorsed by those at the very top of the organization and communicated to all. Further, it is important to have a clear channel of communication which is open to employees with concerns. It is no good suggesting that the employee turns to her supervisor, as it is often this person who is reinforcing the unethical behaviour. Rather, it is important to set up an ethics committee to which employees with concerns about illegal or unethical activity can turn. This committee should have the power to act on the information received, while keeping confidential the source of the information if this is necessary to avoid retaliation against the individual.

Setting up such codes and committees is a first stage. What is more important is that actions follow, such that unethical or illegal behaviour is seen to be punished and ethical and legal behaviour rewarded. Clearly, to change such deeply embedded practices and beliefs will take time, but the organization that makes the effort is likely to be rewarded in the long term with improved commitment from internal employees as well as an improved impact on the wider community.

PUBLIC CONCERN AT WORK

In response to the problems faced by those who know that something is going wrong at work but do not know how to handle it, a new organization was launched in the UK in October 1993 – Public Concern at Work. The rationale for this organization is that it is employees who are the first people to realize that something is wrong. Public Concern at Work provides free advice to employees who have a concern about their work, whether this be a ferry sailing in an unsafe condition, abuse in a children's home, a design defect in a new product, the dumping of toxic waste or fraud. In the first month of the launch of this organization they had over eighty requests for advice. The main dilemma facing those ringing for help was whether to raise their concern about malpractice in the workplace or keep quiet. Public Concern at Work gives professional and independent advice to people facing this dilemma. The advice is free, strictly confidential and without obligation. This allows any employee who has a worry to discuss how best to raise a concern without breaching any duty of confidence or loyalty they may owe their employer.

Public Concern at Work acknowledges that the culture in many workplaces appears to be that employees' concerns should be handled in an adversarial way or not at all. However, it helps worried employees identify the most likely route to allow them to express their concerns inside the organization whilst minimizing the risks of reprisal. Initial feedback from clients who had used Public Concern at Work showed that they were very satisfied with the service. Clearly, this organization is meeting a need, but this is precisely because most organizations do not have cultures which are conducive to dealing with employees who have moral or ethical concerns about what is being done in their workplace.

MAKING YOUR OWN ETHICAL DECISIONS

This chapter has emphasized that it is individuals who make decisions which are at times morally and socially irresponsible, and has considered the pressures which can help to explain why this happens. An important point to bear in mind is that almost every individual will be faced with some kind of ethical dilemma during their career – and that includes you. While the climate of the group and organization will influence what you do, ultimately it is the individual who must take responsibility for the decision which he makes. Given this, Schermerhorn (1989) provides a seven-step checklist for resolving ethical dilemmas. He suggests that when faced with the kind of dilemma posed earlier for Sophie and Jamie it is necessary to:

1   Recognize and clarify the dilemma.
2   Get all the possible facts.
3   List your options – all of them.
4   Test each option by asking: 'Is it legal? Is it right? Is it beneficial?'
5   Make your decision.
6   Double check your decision by asking: 'How would I feel if my family found out about this? How would I feel if my decision was printed in the local newspaper?'
7   Take action.

The acid test for considering the morality of the decision is clearly step six. However, acknowledging this is not going to make it any easier for an individual to make an ethical decision in an organization which puts profits before its moral and social responsibility, and in such an organization it is highly likely that the individual that does 'do the right thing' is likely to suffer in career terms, if he does not actually lose his job. It is only when the organizational climate actually fosters and actively encourages moral and social responsibility that such an individual-focused orientation will become acceptable. On a more positive note, there are indications that such organizational climates are increasingly prominent in successful organizations, although there probably remain a larger number of organizations which do not foster such a climate.

CONCLUSION

Although there may be short-term gains from acting unethically, it is in the long-term interest of the corporation and its managers to foster a legal and ethical culture (Matthews, 1988). There are four main reasons for this. First, because if the corporation is generally regarded as law-abiding and ethical, this will add to the morale and psychological well-being of those who are employed by the corporation. Conversely, an organization with a reputation for unethical behaviour will contribute to lowering the self-esteem and morale of employees. Chapter 5 has already demonstrated why the development of healthy employees is so important for business success in the 1990s.

Second, because in the long term the bad publicity attracted by a company's 'wrongdoings' will have an adverse impact on its future prospects. All the examples of unethical behaviour by corporations given in this chapter and the last resulted in very bad publicity for them – Ford, Nestlé, Morton Thiokol, etc. As worldwide competition becomes ever more intense, such adverse publicity is likely to be increasingly harmful to a company.

Third, there is an element of self-interest involved as the past decade has seen a dramatic growth in instances of criminal charges being taken out against individual executives and directors, as well as against the corporate entity. Thus, a senior executive can be prosecuted for the wrongdoings of a junior employee, even if she was unaware that the individual was doing anything wrong. One of the earliest examples of this was in 1943 when a man called Dotterweich, the chief executive of a drugs company, was held criminally responsible for the shipping of adulterated and misbranded drugs. It was not a defence that he had no knowledge of the adulteration or misbranding. He was held to be legally responsible for the acts of his subordinates. In recent years there have been more examples of senior executives being held responsible for the acts of their subordinates, even though they had no knowledge that they were acting wrongly: for example, as happened after the *Herald of Free Enterprise* ferry disaster.

Finally, it is argued that it is in the long-term interests of corporations to 'clean up their act' because, if they do not, growing pressure from consumer groups will ensure that governments increase statutory regulations on the behaviour of companies. This will reduce the freedom of companies and so, to avoid such restriction, it will be beneficial for them to increase their self-regulation. However, there are widely divergent views as to the ability of companies to increase self-regulation so that they adhere to legal and ethical concepts in their corporate organization and operations.

All decisions, at all levels within a company, need to be infused by a concern for social and moral responsibility. Moreover, although companies need to be more responsible and include in their decision-making process a thorough review of the possible impact of the decisions they make on the wider community, corporations will always make blunders. Taking responsibility after a decision is as important as building responsibility into the decision-making process. The failure to do so is equally disastrous. The most recent example was the Hoover fiasco over free flights to the USA or Europe for all customers spending over £100 on Hoover products. While initially this was clearly a marketing error of judgement (to put it mildly), the response by the company dramatically exacerbated the problem. This was epitomized by the comment from one senior Hoover executive that the customers were being rather foolish in expecting something for nothing. Eventually, Hoover admitted that there was a problem and tried to honour its promise. However, from a public relations perspective, the damage had already been done. An understanding of how and why such disasters occur is the first step towards change.

This chapter has considered the causes of unethical behaviour from a social-psychological perspective. This makes it clear that behaving unethically is a learned behaviour which, in some organizations, has become the culturally accepted norm. Individuals often behave unethically because there are strong pressures on them to do so, rather than because they are dishonest or immoral individuals. While this helps us to understand why 'good' people appear to behave 'badly' in a work setting, it also suggests that it will be extremely difficult for some companies to change and take more responsibility for the outcomes of company acts on the wider community. Change will involve a fundamental shift in organizational culture, and a commitment to training and education to develop postconventional levels of moral thinking among employees. In the long term at least, companies which do not take ethical considerations seriously are likely to suffer as consumers 'vote with their feet', and avoid their products and services, as happened for example with the consumer boycott of Nestlé products. Thus, the chapter concluded by looking at actions a company can take to give business ethics a central place on the agenda.

Conclusion

Implementing a policy of good human relations which gives priority to demonstrating a commitment to *all* employees is not an expensive luxury. Rather, it is an essential ingredient of business success in the 1990s and beyond. Yet many companies have ignored this as demonstrated by a study carried out at Warwick University (reported in the *Financial Times*, February 1989). Interviews were conducted with the personnel managers and senior executives of 175 establishments owned by large companies. They concluded that most big companies lacked an employee relations policy. But if companies do not demonstrate commitment to their employees, how can they expect workers to show commitment to the company?

It is sometimes argued that because companies need to be so much more flexible in the 1990s, to be able to respond to their dynamic environment, it is actually better not to generate too much employee commitment, at least among the majority of the workforce. A small core of employees are seen as the mainstay of the organization and are 'cared for' (Handy, 1989). This hub (core) is privileged over the rest of the workforce. For example, they are:

1 Given a contract which emphasizes *security*, as with the Rover New Deal.
2 Recruited on the basis of *potential competence*, not a narrow range of skills.
3 Offered continuous *learning opportunities* throughout their career.
4 Given *challenging jobs* which stimulate the development of skills.
5 Given responsibility and *autonomy* in the job so that they have opportunities for real empowerment.

6   Provided with a high level of *flexible benefits* which can be modified to suit their changed circumstances as they grow older.
7   Encouraged to develop *networks* with suppliers, professional bodies, customers, etc., so that they have a full understanding of developments in the environment from which they are encouraged to develop innovations.
8   Provided with opportunities to engage in *career planning* so that they become self-guided professionals.

The rest of the workforce (the periphery) are given few if any of these benefits. They are viewed as expendable and are given short-term contracts which will be renewed 'at the pleasure of the company'. This core–periphery strategy appears to be intensifying in the sense that the core is getting smaller and the periphery much larger. For example, a declared strategy of one of the largest computer companies is to have 70 per cent of its workforce on contracts by the turn of the century. For all the reasons outlined in this book, I would predict that such a strategy is, in the long term, going to be unsuccessful, at least if contract staff are not given access to the 'privileges' of the core. What is needed is a dedicated, highly skilled and responsible workforce at all levels of the organization (Sief, 1990). This can only be achieved if there is a two-way commitment such that employees can grow and develop at the same time as they ensure the products or services they are responsible for meet the competitive standards of quality, flexibility, innovation and responsibility (as outlined in the Introduction).

Contract workers might receive a good salary because they are on contracts, although this is only likely for those at the professional end of the contract market, but as Akio Morita, co-founder of Sony, wrote, 'people do not work just for money' and if you are trying to motivate them 'money is not the most effective tool. To motivate people you must bring them into the family, and treat them like respected members of it.'

The best 'people' strategy is therefore to treat all employees with respect and trust and provide them with work environments which offer them the opportunity to develop skills and competencies relevant not just to their current job, but to jobs which will need to be done in the future, even if in a different company. Ensuring employability (Kanter, 1993) for all employees is the key to success because it both ensures the development of future skills that will be needed by the company, and demonstrates commitment to the employee, which is required if the company wants the employee to demonstrate reciprocal commitment to the success of the company.

Such a strategy has been made possible by the advancement of technology. Machines will increasingly take over the mundane and repetitive elements of the job. However, rather than making people less important in organizational settings, this will actually make them more important. Information technology is restructuring the work situation and leading to an emphasis on a totally new set of human competencies based on abstract thought, explicit inference and procedural reasoning. Zuboff (1986) refers to these as 'intellective skills'. Thus, workers are now provided with information-text about what is happening in the production or service process, rather than seeing or feeling what is happening. They must then use this information to infer the situation, deduce the outcome of possible interventions and then make decisions. In order to be able to do this workers need to have a theoretical conception of the total process.

In the past such theoretical knowledge has been the exclusive domain of managers and engineers, and in many organizations this group (the core) maintains that exclusive right. The workers (the periphery) are not given the opportunity to develop and use intellective skills. Rather they are at the mercy of the computer, knowing simply which button to press when a certain thing happens, without understanding why they are doing it. However, given that a programmed response is never going to be appropriate for all situations, this builds in an inflexibility to the system and so the system works suboptimally. Intellective skills must be fostered in all workers within an organization so that, in making decisions, they can fully exploit the information available. The distinction between the managers as the privileged core and the workers as the periphery needs to be eradicated so that all employees are empowered to use their unique human intellective skills. While this is not going to be easy, it provides the key to business success.

The core thus becomes all the employees in the organization who will be working together in multi-disciplinary, multi-cultural teams. The removal of barriers between those with and without power in the organization is the surest way to remove the prejudice and discrimination which remains in most organizations. Managing diversity will be the norm rather than the exception.

All this may seem idealistic and there are clearly many institutional barriers. But the beginnings of change are apparent in many organizations. Those that change fastest will reap tremendous benefits from a healthy, diverse workforce whose members have been empowered to develop and use their skills and competencies for the benefit of both themselves and the organization.

References

INTRODUCTION

Bolwijn, P.T. and Kumpe, T. (1990) 'Manufacturing in the 1990s: productivity, flexibility and innovation', *Long Range Planning*, 23, 44–57.

Braverman, H. (1974) *Labor and Monopoly Capital*, New York: Monthly Review Press.

Hackman, R. (1990) *Groups that Work (and those that don't)*, San Francisco: Jossey-Bass.

Rogers, E. (1962) *Diffusion of Innovations*, New York: Free Press.

Schlesinger, L. and Heskett, J. (1991) 'The service-driven service company', *Harvard Business Review*, September–October, 71–81.

Zuboff, S. (1986) *In the Age of the Smart Machine: The Future of Work and Power*, Heinemann Professional Publishing.

CHAPTER 1

Argyris, C. (1957) *Personality and Organisation*, New York: Harper and Row.

Braverman, H. (1974) *Labor and Monopoly Capital*, New York: Monthly Review Press.

Fayol, H. (1949) *General and Industrial Management*, London: Pitman.

Friedmann, G. (1955) *Industrial Society*, Glencoe, IL: Free Press.

Gilbreth, F.B. (1908) *Field Systems*, New York: Myron C. Clark.

Herriot, P. (1992) *The Career Management Challenge: Balancing Individual and Organisational Needs*, London: Sage.

McGregor, D. (1960) *The Human Side of the Enterprise*, New York: McGraw-Hill.

Mayo, E. (1949) *Hawthorne and the Western Electric Company: The Social Problems of an Industrial Civilisation*, London: Routledge.

Myers, C.S. (1924) *Industrial Psychology in Great Britain*, London: Cape.

Naoi, A. and Schoder, C. (1985) 'Occupational conditions and psychological functioning in Japan', *American Journal of Sociology*, 90, 4, 729–752.

Peters, T.J. and Waterman, R.H. (1982) *In Search of Excellence: Lessons from America's Best-run Companies*, New York: Harper and Row.

Roethlisberger, F.J. and Dickson, W.J. (1939) *Management and the Worker*, Massachusetts: Harvard University Press.

Rose, M. (1975) *Industrial Behaviour: Theoretical Developments since Taylor*, London: Penguin.

Taylor, F.W. (1911) *Principles of Scientific Management*, New York: Harper.

Weber, M. (1947) *The Theory of Social and Economic Organisation*, Chicago: Free Press.

Whitehead, T.N. (1938) *The Industrial Worker*, Oxford: Oxford University Press.

Zuboff, S. (1986) *In the Age of the Smart Machine: The Future of Work and Power*, London: Heinemann Professional Publishing.

CHAPTER 2

Bandura, A. (1977) 'Self-efficacy: toward a unifying theory of behavioural change', *Psychological Review*, 84, 191–215.

Cooper, C. (1986) 'Job distress: recent research and the emerging role of the clinical occupational psychologist', *Bulletin of the British Psychological Society*, 39, 325–331.

Cooper, C. and Marshall, J. (1976) 'Occupational sources of stress: a review of the literature relating coronary heart disease and mental health', *Journal of Occupational Psychology*, 49, 11–28.

Davidson, M. (1989) 'Women managers and stress: profiles of vulnerable individuals', *Clinical Psychology Forum*, 22, 32–34.

Davidson, M. and Cooper, C. (1983) *Stress and the Woman Manager*, London: Martin Robertson.

Duffy, E. (1962) *Activation and Behaviour*, New York: Wiley.

Eysenck, M.W. (1982) *Attention and Arousal: Cognition and Performance*, New York: Springer-Verlag.

Fried, Y. (1988) 'The future of physiological assessments in work situations', in C. Cooper and R. Payne (eds) *Causes, Coping and Consequences of Stress at Work*, Chichester: John Wiley.

Hockey, G.R., Gaillard, A.W. and Coles, M.G. (1986) *Energetics and Human Information Processing*, Dordrecht, The Netherlands: Martinus Nijhoff.

Hull, J.G., Van Treuren, R.R. and Virnelli, S. (1987) 'Hardiness and health: a critique and alternative approach', *Journal of Personality and Social Psychology*, 53, 518–530.

Jahoda, M. (1982) *Employment and Unemployment: A Social-psychological Analysis*, Cambridge: Cambridge University Press.

Kearns, J. (1986) *Stress at Work: The Challenge of Change*, BUPA series *The Management of Health – Stress and the City*, London: BUPA.

Kirmeyer, S.L. and Biggers, K. (1988) 'Environmental demand and demand engendering behaviour: an observational analysis of the Type A behaviour pattern', *Journal of Personality and Social Psychology*, 54, 997–1005.

Kobasa, S.C. (1979) 'Stressful life events, personality and health: an inquiry into hardiness', *Journal of Personality and Social Psychology*, 37, 1–11.

Lacey, J.I. (1967) 'Somatic response patterning and stress: some revisions of activation theory', in M.H. Appley and R. Trumbell (eds) *Psychological Stress: Issues in Research*, New York: Appleton-Century-Crofts.

Leiter, M.P. and Maslach, C. (1988) 'The impact of interpersonal environment on burnout and organizational commitment', *Journal of Organizational Behaviour*, 9, 4, 297–308.

Leiter, M.P. and Meechan, K.A. (1986) 'Role structure and burnout in the field of human services', *Journal of Applied Behavioural Sciences*, 22, 47–52.

Levine, P. (1986) 'Stress', in M. Coles, E. Donchine and S. Porges (eds) *Psychophysiology: Systems, Processes and Applications*, New York: Guilford Press.

Merton, R.K. (1957) 'The role set: problems in sociological theory', *British Journal of Sociology*, 8, 106–120.

Oullette-Kobasa, S.C. and Pucetti, M.C. (1983) 'Personality and social resources in stress resistance', *Journal of Personality and Social Psychology*, 45, 839–850.

Payne, R. and Fletcher, B. (1983) 'Job demands, supports, constraints as predictors of psychological strain among school teachers', *Journal of Vocational Behaviour*, 22, 136–147.

Schachter, J. (1957) 'Pain, fear and anger in hypertensives and normatensives', *Psychosomatic Medicine*, 19, 17–29.

Scheier, M.F. and Carver, C.S. (1985) 'Optimism, coping and health: assessment and implications of generalised outcome expectancies', *Health Psychology*, 4, 219–247.

Scheier, M.F., Weintraub, J.K. and Carver, C.S. (1986) 'Coping with stress: divergent strategies of optimists and pessimists', *Journal of Personality and Social Psychology*, 51, 1257–1264.

Shaw, J.B. and Riskind, J.H. (1983) 'Predicting job stress using data from the Position Analysis Questionnaire', *Journal of Applied Psychology*, 68, 253–261.

CHAPTER 3

Cooper, C. and Payne, R. (1978) *Stress at Work*, Chichester: John Wiley.

Curtis, J.D. and Detert, R.A. (1981) *How to Relax: A Holistic Approach to Stress Management*, Palo Alto: Mayfield.

Greenberg, J. (1983) *Comprehensive Stress Management*, Dubuque, IA: Wm. C. Brown Publishers.

Jacobson, E. (1938) *Progressive Relaxation*, Chicago: University of Chicago Press.

Kohn, J.P. (1981) 'Stress modification using progressive relaxation muscle relaxation', *Professional Safety*, 26, 15–19.

MacLeod, A.G. (1985) 'EAPs and blue collar work', in C.L. Cooper and M.J. Smith (eds) *Job Stress and Blue Collar Work*, Chichester: John Wiley.

Murphy, L.R. (1983) 'A comparison of relaxation methods for reducing stress in nursing personnel', *Human Factors*, 25, 431–440.

Murphy, L.R. (1984) 'Occupational stress management: a review and appraisal', *Journal of Occupational Psychology*, 57, 1–15.

Rice, P.L. (1987) *Stress and Health: Principles and Practice for Coping and Wellness*, Monterey, CA: Brooks/Cole.

Rogers, C. (1961) *On Becoming a Person*, Boston: Houghton Mifflin.

Shapiro, D.H. and Giber, D. (1978) 'Meditation and psychotherapeutic effects', *Archives of General Psychiatry*, 35, 294–302.

Wallace, R.K. and Benson, H. (1972) 'The physiology of meditation', *Scientific American*, 226, 84–90.

Wrich, J. (1980) *The Employee Assistance Program: Updated for the 1980's*, Minnesota: Hazelden Educational Foundation.

Wrich, J. (1984) *The Employee Assistance Program*, Minnesota: Hazelden Educational Foundation.

CHAPTER 4

Allied Dunbar (1992) *National Fitness Survey: A Summary*, London: Sports Council and Health Education Authority.

Baun, W.B. and Bernacki, E.J. (1988) 'Who are corporate exercisers and what motivates them?', in R. Dishman (ed.) *Exercise Adherence: Its Impact on Public Health*, Champaign, IL: Human Kinetics Books.

Baun, W.B., Bernacki, E.J. and Tsai, S.P. (1986) 'A preliminary investigation: effect of a corporate fitness program on absenteeism and health care cost', *Journal of Occupational Medicine*, 28, 18–22.

Bernacki, E.J. and Baun, W.B. (1984) 'The relationship of job performance to exercise adherence in a corporate fitness program', *Journal of Occupational Medicine*, 26, 529–531.

Biddle, S. and Mutrie, N. (1991) *Psychology of Physical Activity and Exercise*, London: Springer-Verlag.

Blair, S.N., Jacobs, D.R. and Powell, K.E. (1985) 'Relationships between exercise or physical activity and other health behaviours', *Public Health Reports*, 100, 172–180.

Blair, S.N., Piserchia, P., Wilbur, C. and Crowder, J. (1986) 'A public health intervention for work-site health promotion', *Journal of the American Medical Association*, 255, 921–926.

Brennan, A.J. (1982) 'Work site health promotion', *Health Education Quarterly* (special supplement), 9, 1–91.

Breslow, L., Fielding, J., Herman, A. and Wilbur, C. (1990) 'Worksite health promotion: its evolution and the Johnson and Johnson experience', *Preventive Medicine*, 19, 13–21.

Brown, J.D. (1991) 'Staying fit and staying well: physical fitness as a moderator of life stress', *Journal of Personality and Social Psychology*, 60, 555–561.

Bruning, N.S. and Frew, D.R. (1985) 'The impact of various stress management training strategies: a longitudinal experiment', in R.B. Robinson and J.A. Pearce (eds) *Academy of Management Proceedings*, San Diego, CA: Academy of Management.

Charlesworth, E.A., Williams, B.J. and Baer, P.E. (1984) 'Stress management at the worksite for hypertension', *Psychosomatic Medicine*, 46, 387–397.

Coe, T. (1992) *The Key to the Men's Club: Opening Doors to Women in Management*, Institute of Management Report, Corby: Institute of Management.

Colgan, F. and Tomlinson, F. (1991) 'Women in publishing: jobs or careers?', *Personnel Review*, 20, 5, 16–26.

Deyo, R.A. (1983) 'Conservative therapy for low back pain: distinguishing useful from useless therapy', *Journal of the American Medical Association*, 250, 1057–1062.

Fletcher, C. (1991) 'Candidates' reactions to assessment centres and their outcomes: a longitudinal study', *Journal of Occupational Psychology*, 64, 117–127.

Fletcher, C. and Williams, R. (1985) *Performance Appraisal and Career Development*, London: Hutchinson.

Gebhardt, D. and Crump, C. (1990) 'Employee fitness and well-being programs in the workplace', *American Psychologist*, 45, 262–272.

Haskell, W.L. (1984) 'Cardiovascular benefits and risks of exercise: the scientific evidence', in R.H. Strauss (ed.) *Sports Medicine*, Philadelphia: W.B. Saunders.

Herriot, P. (1984) *Down from the Ivory Tower*, Chichester: John Wiley.

Herriot, P. (1992) *The Career Management Challenge: Balancing Individual and Organisational Needs*, London: Sage.

Holzbach, R., Piserchia, P. and McFadden, D. (1990) 'Effect of a comprehensive health promotion program on employee attitudes: a study of worksite health promotion program and absenteeism', *Journal of Occupational Medicine*, 32, 973–978.

Hughes, J.R. (1984) 'Psychological effects of habitual aerobic exercise: a critical review', *Preventive Medicine*, 13, 66–78.

Jones, R., Bly, J. and Richardson, J. (1990) 'A study of worksite health promotion program and absenteeism', *Journal of Occupational Medicine*, 29, 572–575.

Keys, A. (1984) 'Serum cholesterol response to dietary cholesterol', *American Journal of Clinical Nutrition*, 40, 351–359.

Krolner, B. and Taft, B. (1983) 'Vertebral bone loss: an unheeded side effect of therapeutic bed rest', *Clinical Science*, 64, 537–540.

London, M. and Stumpf, S.A. (1982) *Managing Careers*, Reading: Addison Wesley.

McNulty, S., Jeffrys, D., Singer, G. and Singer, L. (1984) 'Use of hormone analysis in the assessment of the efficacy of stress management training in police recruits', *Journal of Police Science and Administration*, 12, 130–132.

Morgan, P.P., Shepard, R.J., Finucane, R., Schimmelfing, L. and Jazmaji, V.

(1984) 'Health beliefs and exercise habits in an employee fitness programme', *Canadian Journal of Applied Sport Sciences*, 9, 87–93.

Murphy, L.R. (1988) 'Workplace interventions for stress reduction and prevention', in C.L. Cooper and R. Payne (eds) *Causes, Coping and Consequences of Stress at Work*, Chichester: John Wiley.

Newell, S. (1993) 'The superwoman syndrome: gender differences in attitudes towards equal opportunitities at work and towards domestic responsibilities at home', *Work, Employment and Society*, 7, 275–289.

Newell, S. and Shackleton, V. (1993) 'The use (and abuse) of psychometric tests in British industry and commerce', *Human Resource Management Journal*, 4, 14–23.

Nicholson, N. and Arnold, J. (1989) 'Graduate early experience in a multinational corporation', *Personnel Review*, 18, 3–14.

Paffenbarger, R.S., Wing, A.L., Hyde, R.T. and Jung, D.L. (1983) 'Physical activity and incidence of hypertension in college alumni', *American Journal of Epidemiology*, 117, 245–257.

Parsons, D. and Hutt, R. (1981) *The Mobility of Young Graduates*, Brighton: Institute of Manpower Studies.

Pelletier, K. (1991) 'A review and analysis of the health and cost-effective outcome studies of comprehensive health promotion and disease prevention programs', *American Journal of Health Promotion*, 5, 311–315.

Pleck, J. (1985) *Working Wives/Working Husbands*, Beverly Hills, CA: Sage.

Premark, S.L. and Wanous, J.P. (1985) 'A meta-analysis of realistic job preview experience', *Journal of Applied Psychology*, 70, 706–719.

Robertson, I., Illes, P., Gratton, L. and Sharpley, D. (1991) 'The impact of personnel selection and assessment methods on candidates', *Human Relations*, 44, 963–982.

Rosenbaum, J.M. (1984) *Career Mobility in a Corporate Hierarchy*, New York: Academic Press.

Shackleton, V. and Newell, S. (1994) 'European management selection methods: a comparison of five countries', *International Journal of Selection and Assessment*, 2, 91–102.

Shekelle, R., Lepper, M., Liu, S., Maliza, C., Raynor, W., Rossof, A., Paul, O., Shryock, A. and Stamler, J. (1981) 'Dietary vitamin A and risk of cancer in the Western Electric study', *Lancet*, 2, 1185–1190.

Shepard, R.J. (1986) *Fitness and Health in Industry*, Basel: Karger.

Siscovick, D.S., LaPorte, R.E. and Newman, J.M. (1985) 'The disease specific benefits of physical activity and exercise', *Public Health Reports*, 100, 180–188.

Song, T.K., Shepard, R.J. and Cox, M. (1982) 'Absenteeism, employee turnover and sustained exercise participation', *Journal of Sports Medicine and Fitness*, 22, 392–399.

Storey, W.D. (ed.) (1979) *A Guide for Career Development Inquiry*, ASTD Research Series Paper No. 2, Madison, WI: American Society for Training and Development.

Wanous, J.P. (1977) 'Organisational entry: newcomers moving from outside to inside', *Psychological Bulletin*, 84, 601–618.

Willet, W.C. and MacMahon, B. (1984) 'Diet and cancer – an overview', *New England Journal of Medicine*, 310, 633–638, 697–703.

Williams, R.S. (1982) *Career Management and Career Planning*, London: HMSO.

Wolfe, W., Slack, T. and Rose-Hearn, T. (1993) 'Factors influencing the adoption and maintenance of Canadian, facility-based health promotion programmes', *American Journal of Health Promotion*, 7, 189–198.

CHAPTER 5

Argyris, C. (1964) *Integrating the Individual and the Organisation*, New York: Wiley.

Bandura, A. (1977) 'Self-efficacy: towards a unifying theory of behavioural change', *Psychological Review*, 84, 191–215.

Bandura, A. and Cervone, D. (1983) 'Self-evaluative and self-efficacy mechanisms governing the motivational effects of goal systems', *Journal of Personality and Social Psychology*, 45, 1017–1028.

Bower, D. (1994) 'Rover's return', paper presented at the British Psychological Society, Occupational Conference, Birmingham.

Clark, P.A. and Staunton, N. (1989) *Innovation in Technology and Organisation*, London: Routledge.

Eisenberg, P. and Lazarsfeld, P.F. (1938) 'The psychological effects of unemployment', *Psychological Bulletin*, 35, 358–390.

Fryer, D.M. and Payne, R.L. (1984) 'Proactivity in unemployment: findings and implications', *Leisure Studies*, 3, 273–295.

Goldthorpe, J.H., Lockwood, D., Bechhofer, F. and Platt, J. (1968) *The Affluent Worker: Industrial Attitudes and Behaviour*, Cambridge: Cambridge University Press.

Gore, S. (1978) 'The effect of social support in moderating the health consequences of unemployment', *Journal of Health and Social Behaviour*, 19, 157–165.

Handy, C. (1989) *The Age of Unreason*, London: Business Books.

Herriot, P. (1992) *The Career Management Challenge: Balancing Individual and Organisational Needs*, London: Sage.

Herzberg, F. (1966) *Work and the Nature of Man*, Cleveland: World Publishing.

Jahoda, M. (1958) *Current Concepts of Positive Mental Health*, New York: Basic Books.

Jahoda, M. (1982) *Employment and Unemployment: A Social-psychological Analysis*, Cambridge: Cambridge University Press.

Kanter, R.M. (1993) *Men and Women of the Corporation: With a Major New Afterword by the Author*, New York: Basic Books.

Koopman, A. (1991) *Transcultural Management: How to Unlock Global Resources*, Oxford: Basil Blackwell.

Locke, E.A. (1968) 'Toward a theory of task motivation and incentives', *Organisational Behaviour and Human Performance*, 3, 157–189.

Maslow, A.H. (1954) *Motivation and Personality*, New York: Harper and Row.

Peters, T.J. and Waterman, R.H. (1982) *In Search of Excellence: Lessons from America's Best-run Companies*, New York: Harper and Row.

Rotter, J.B. (1966) 'Generalized expectancies for internal versus external control of reinforcement', *Psychological Monographs*, 80, 1–28.

Vroom, V.H. (1964) *Work and Motivation*, New York: Wiley.

Warr, P. (1987) *Work, Unemployment and Mental Health*, Oxford: Oxford University Press.

Zuboff, S. (1986) *In the Age of the Smart Machine: The Future of Work and Power*, London: Heinemann Professional Publishing.

CHAPTER 6

Adorno, T.W., Frenkel-Brunswick, E., Levinson, D.J. and Sanford, R.N. (1950) *The Authoritarian Personality*, New York: Harper and Row.

Alimo-Metcalfe, B. (1993) 'Women in management: organisational socialisation and assessment practices that prevent career advancement', *International Journal of Selection and Assessment*, 1, 68–83.

Bass, B.M. (1955) 'Authoritariansim or acquiescence', *Journal of Abnormal and Social Psychology*, November, 616–623.

Beck, J. and Steel, M. (1989) *Beyond the Great Divide: Introducing Inequality into the Company*, London: Pitman.

Brannen, J. and Moss, P. (1988) *New Mothers at Work*, London: Unwin Hyman.

Brown, C. (1984) *Black and White Britain: The Third PSI Survey*, Aldershot: Gower.

Brown, C. and Gay, P. (1985) *Racial Discrimination 17 Years after the Act*, Policy Studies No. 646, London: Policy Studies Institute.

Campbell, E.Q. (1961) 'Moral discomfort and racial segregation – An examination of the Myrdal Hypothesis', *Social Forces*, 39, 228–234.

Cannings, K. (1991) 'An interdisciplinary approach to analysing the managerial gender gap', *Human Relations*, 44, 679–696.

Coe, T. (1992) *The Key to the Men's Club: Opening the Doors to Women Management*, Corby: Institute of Management.

Daniel, W.W. (1967) *Racial Discrimination*, London: Political and Economic Planning/Research Services.

Davidson, M. (1989) 'Women managers and stress: profiles of vulnerable individuals', *Clinical Psychology Forum*, 22, 32–34.

Dex, S. (1987) *Women's Occupational Mobility: A Lifetime Perspective*, London: Macmillan.

Dollard, J., Miller, N. and Doob, L. (1939) *Frustration and Aggression*, New Haven: Yale University Press.

Hakim, C. (1981) 'Job segregation: trends in the 1970s', *Department of Employment Gazette*, 12, 521–529.

Harrison, R. (1987) *Organisation Culture and Quality of Service: A Strategy for Releasing Love in the Workplace*, London: Association for Management Education and Development.

Hirsh, W. and Jackson, C. (1990) *Women into Management: Issues*

Influencing the Entry of Women into Managerial Jobs, IMS Report No. 158, University of Sussex: Institute of Manpower Studies.

Hubbuck, J. and Carter, S. (1980) *Half a Chance? A Report on Job Discrimination Against Young Blacks in Nottingham*, London: Commission for Racial Equality.

Ibarra, H. (1992) 'Homophily and differential returns: sex differences in network structure and access in an advertising firm', *Administrative Science Quarterly*, 37, 422–447.

Katz, D. and Braly, K. (1933) 'Racial stereotypes of 100 college students', *Journal of Abnormal and Social Psychology*, October–December, 280–290.

Kinder, D.R. and Sears, D.O. (1981) 'Prejudice and politics: symbolic racism versus racial threats to the good life', *Journal of Personality and Social Psychology*, 40, 414–431.

Krug, R.E. (1961) 'An analysis of the F-Scale', *Journal of Social Psychology*, April, 285–291.

La Piere, R. (1934) 'Attitudes versus actions', *Social Forces*, 13, 230–237.

Martin, J. (1990) 'Re-reading Weber: searching for feminist alternatives to bureaucracy', paper presented at the annual meeting of the Academy of Management, San Francisco.

Newell, S. (1993) 'The superwoman syndrome: gender differences in attitudes towards equal opportunities at work and towards domestic responsibilities at home', *Work, Employment and Society*, 7, 275–289.

Podmore, D. and Spencer, A. (1982) 'Women lawyers in England: the experience of inequality', *Work and Occupations*, 9, 337–361.

Ray, J. (1980) 'Authoritarianism in California 30 years later – with some cross-cultural comparisons', *Journal of Social Psychology*, June, 9–17.

Rosener, J. (1990) 'Ways women lead', *Harvard Business Review*, Nov.–Dec., 195–213.

Schein, V.E. (1989) 'Sex-role stereotypes and requisite management characteristics among female managers', *Journal of Applied Psychology*, 60, 340–344.

Shipley, P. (1990) 'Personnel management and working women in the 1990's: beyond paternalism', *Personnel Review*, 19, 3–12.

Vinnicombe, S. (1987) 'What exactly are the differences in male and female working styles?', *Women in Management Review*, 3, 13–21.

Word, C.O., Zanna, M.P. and Cooper, J. (1974) 'The nonverbal mediation of self-fulfilling prophecies in inter-racial interactions', *Journal of Experimental Social Psychology*, March, 109–120.

CHAPTER 7

Alimo-Metcalfe, B. (1993) 'Women in management: organisational socialisation and assessment practices that prevent career advancement', *International Journal of Selection and Assessment*, 1, 68–83.

Bartlett, C.A. and Ghoshal, S. (1989) *Managing Across Borders*, London: Hutchinson.

Boyer, I. (1993) *Flexible Working for Managers*, London: Chartered Institute of Management Accountants.

Cockburn, C. (1991) *In the Way of Women: Men's Resistance to Sex Equality in Organisations*, London: Macmillan.

Coe, T. (1992) *The Key to the Men's Club: Opening Doors to Women in Management*, Corby: Institute of Management.

Cohen, B. (1988) *Caring for Children: Services and Policies for Childcare and Equal Opportunities in the UK*, report for the European Commission's Childcare Network, London: Family Policy Studies Centre.

Coleman, D. and Salt, J. (1992) *The British Population: Patterns, Trends and Processes*, Oxford: Oxford University Press.

Friedan, B. (1981) *The Second Stage*, New York: Summit.

Hammond, V. (1992) 'Opportunity 2000: a culture change approach to equal opportunity', *Women in Management Review*, 7, 3–10.

Herriot, P. (1992) *The Career Management Challenge*, London: Sage.

Hewitt, P. (1993) *Flexible Working: Asset or Cost?*, London: Policy Studies Institute.

Incomes Data Services (1993) *Opportunity 2000*, Study No. 535, London: Incomes Data Services.

Institute of Management (1993) *The Survey of Long-term Employment Strategies*, London: Institute of Management.

Kelly, R.M. (1991) *The Gendered Economy: Women, Careers and Success*, London: Sage.

Newell, S. (1993) 'The superwoman syndrome: gender differences in attitudes towards equal opportunities at work and towards domestic responsibilities at home', *Work, Employment and Society*, 7, 275–289.

Newell, S., Swan, J. and Clark, P. (1993) 'The importance of user design in the adoption of new information technologies', *International Journal of Operations and Production Management*, 13, 4–22.

Opportunity 2000 (1993) *Corporate Culture and Caring*, London: Opportunity 2000 and the IPM.

Opportunity 2000 (1993a) 'Opportunity 2000 is making a difference, reports Lady Howe', *Opportunity 2000 Newsletter*, Winter.

Pettigrew, A. (1985) *The Awakening Giant: Continuity and Change in ICI*, Oxford: Blackwell.

Shackleton, V. and Newell, S. (1994) 'European management selection methods: a comparison of five countries', *International Journal of Selection and Assessment*, 2, 91–102.

CHAPTER 8

Cullen, F.T., Maakestad, W.J. and Cavender, G. (1987) *Corporate Crime under Attack: The Ford Pinto Case and Beyond*, Cincinnati: Anderson.

Friedman, M. (1962) *Capitalism and Freedom*, Chicago: University of Chicago Press.

Jones, T.M. (1980) 'Corporate social responsibility revisited, redefined', *California Management Review*, 22, 59–67.

Manne, H. (1966) *Insider Trading and the Stock Market*, New York: Free Press.

Matthews, M.C. (1988) *Strategic Intervention in Organisations*, California: Sage.

Velasquez, M., Moberg, D.J. and Cavanagh, G.F. (1982) 'Organisational statesmanship and dirty politics: ethical guidelines for the organisational politician', *Organisational Dynamics*, 11, 65–79.

CHAPTER 9

Akers, R.L. (1985) *Deviant Behaviour: A Social Learning Approach*, Belmont, CA: Wadsworth.

Burgess, R.L. and Akers, R.L. (1966) 'A differential association-reinforcement theory of criminal behaviour', *Social Problems*, 14, 128–147.

Donaldson, J. (1989) *Key Issues in Business Ethics*, London: Academic Press.

Gellerman, S.W. (1986) 'Why "good" managers make bad ethical choices', *Harvard Business Review*, 64, 85–90.

Janis, I. (1972) *Victims of Groupthink*, Boston: Houghton Mifflin.

Janis, I. (1983) *Groupthink* (2nd ed., revised), Boston: Houghton Mifflin.

Jensen, J.V. (1987) 'Ethical tension points in whistle-blowing', *Journal of Business Ethics*, 6, 321–328.

Kohlberg, L. (1973) 'Continuities in childhood and adult moral development revisited', in P.B. Baltes and K.W. Schaie (eds) *Life Span Developmental Psychology: Personality and Socialisation*, New York: Academic Press.

Korn, L.B. (1989) 'How the next CEO will be different', *Fortune*, 119, 157–158.

Maclagan, P. (1990) 'Moral behaviour in organisations: the contribution of management education and development', *British Journal of Management*, 1, 1, 17–26.

Matthews, M.C. (1987) 'Whistle-blowing: acts of courage are often discouraged', *Business and Society Review*, 63, Fall, 40–44.

Matthews, M.C. (1988) *Strategic Intervention in Organisations*, California: Sage.

Morehead, G. and Montanari, J.R. (1986) 'An empirical investigation of the groupthink phenomena', *Human Relations*, 39, 399–410.

Morehead, G., Ference, R. and Neck, C.P. (1991) 'Group decision fiascoes continue: Space Shuttle Challenger and a revised groupthink framework', *Human Relations*, 44, 6, 539–550.

Nader, R., Petkas, P. and Blackwell, K. (1972) *Whistle-blowing: The Report on the Conference on Professional Responsibility*, New York: Grossman.

Nisan, M. and Kohlberg, L. (1982) 'Universality and variation in moral judgement: a longitudinal and cross-sectional study in Turkey', *Child Development*, 53, 865–876.

Pettigrew, A. (1985) *The Awakening Giant: Continuity and Change in ICI*, Oxford: Blackwell.

Schermerhorn, J.R. (1989) *Management for Productivity*, New York: John Wiley.

Soeken, D.R. (1987) 'Whistle-blowers face retaliation, dismissal, study shows', *Ethikos*, Sept.–Oct., 4–9.

Sutherland, E.H. (1949, 1961) *White Collar Crime*, New York: Holt, Rinehart and Winston.

Whyte, W. (1956) *The Organisation Man*, New York: Simon and Schuster.

CONCLUSION

Handy, C. (1989) *The Age of Unreason*, London: Business Books.

Kanter, R.M. (1993) *Men and Women of the Corporation: With a Major New Afterword by the Author*, New York: Basic Books.

Sief, M. (1990) *Management the Marks and Spencer Way*, Glasgow: Fontana.

Zuboff, S. (1986) *In the Age of the Smart Machine: The Future of Work and Power*, Heinemann Professional Publishing.

— *Index*

absenteeism 37, 60, 78, 154
accountability 5, 176, 189–90
adaptability 115, *see also* flexibility
Adorno, T.W. 133
advertising 5, 166, 173
Advisory, Conciliation and Advisory
    Service (ACAS) 124
affective well-being 91
affirmative action 166
Akers, R.L. 181
alcohol problems 60–1
Alimo-Metcalfe, B. 140, 147
Allied Dunbar 71, 72
anti-trust 166
apartheid 168
Argyris, C. 29, 30–1, 94
Arnold, J. 79
Ashridge Management Group 145,
    160
aspiration 96–8
assessment centres 84
attribution theory 95–6
authoritarian personality 133–4
authority, managers' 7, 31
autogenic training 57
autonomy 94, 192

Bandura, A. 39, 92–3
Bartlett, C.A. 146
Bass, B.M. 133
Baun, W.B. 72, 75, 76
Beck, J. 128
behaviour: causes of 95–6; ethical

181–6; Type A 51–2
Benson, H. 57
Bernacki, E.J. 72, 75, 76
Biddle, S. 71
Big Hans 21
Biggers, K. 52
biofeedback 77, 78
Blair, S.N. 71, 72
blood pressure 58, 70, 77, 78
Bloomsbury Club 158
BMW 114
Body Shop 176–7
Bolwijn, P.T. 2, 4
Boots the Chemist 149, 152
Bournville 19
Bower, D. 110
boycotting products 5, 174, 191
Boyer, I. 153, 157
Braly, K. 137
Brannen, J. 138–9
Braverman, H. 2, 33
'breadwinner wage' 9
Brennan, A.J. 76
Breslow, L. 72
bribery 166, 171
Britain *see* United Kingdom
British Aerospace 114
British Airways 153
British Institute of Management 140
brittle-bone disease 71
Brown, C. 127–8
Brown, J.D. 69
Bruning, N.S. 77

bureaucracy 22–3, 35–6
Burgess, R.L. 181
Business in the Community 158

Cadbury 19, 70
Campbell, E.Q. 131–2
Canada Life Assurance 73–4, 75
Cannings, K. 139
canteens 70
career: break schemes 152; ceiling 48;
    counselling 83–4, 156;
    development 80–1, 119, 144,
    156–7; early 87–8; expectations
    85, 86–7; management 156–7;
    middle years 88; planning and
    development 79–89, 193;
    planning by individuals 82–5,
    193; prospects 48–9; workshops
    83
Career Bridge scheme 152
Carter, S. 127
Carver, C.S. 52
chain of command 44
Challenger Shuttle disaster 182–3
challenging jobs 192
Charlesworth, E.A. 77
child care: assistance 152; availability
    151–2
Child Care Vouchers 152
Childcare Solutions 152
Civil Service 123
Clark, P.A. 115
class and prejudice 131–2
Coca-Cola 171
Cockburn, C. 155
Coe, T. 85, 139, 140, 156
cognitive therapy 58–60, 77, 78
Cohen, B. 151
Coleman, D. 147
Colgan, F. 87
Commission for Racial Equality
    (CRE) 125
commitment, employee 6, 82, 110
Community Relations Council 127
competence 6, 92–3, 192
competitiveness, international 1, 2,
    146
computers 3, 33, 194

conformity 183–4
contract: employment 113; short-term
    193; term time only 152; workers
    114, 193
control: locus of 95; managerial 31;
    opportunity for 104, 111;
    organizational 3
Cooper, C. 40, 42, 50, 58
core workers 192–3
Corning Glass 180
coronary heart disease (CHD) 40, 70
corporate fitness programmes 72–6
cost reductions 2
counselling 62–5, 66; career 83–4
criminal behaviour 181–2, 190
crisis counselling 83–4
Crump, C. 72
Cullen, F.T. 169
culture, organization 157–8
Curtis, J.D. 57

Daniel, W.W. 126
Davidson, M. 45, 50, 140
Debenhams 152
decision-making: ethical 188–9;
    impact on community 190;
    participation in 50, 55
demands, occupational 43
democracy 49
demographic changes 147
Denning, Lord 124
Depression (1930s) 99
Detert, R.A. 57
development centres 82, 84–5
Dex, S. 129
Deyo, R.A. 71
diabetes 71
Dickens, C. 18
Dickson, W.J. 28, 29
diet *see* nutrition
discrimination: cultural factors 136–8;
    direct and indirect 122–3, 124;
    explanations of 130–41;
    organizational structures 9;
    positive 123, 149; racial 130–8;
    sex 138–41; Sex Discrimination
    Act 122–3; unfair 119–20
Discussion Groups 113

diversity: managing 9, 142–3, 144–61; intolerance of 119–20
Dollard, J. 135
Donaldson, J. 185
Dotterweich 189
drug: marketing 166, 189; problems 60–1
Duffy, E. 38

Eisenberg, P. 100
Ellis, A. 58
employability 115
employee relations policy 192
employers: good and bad 8–10; nineteenth-century 18–19
Employers for Child Care 151
employment *see* work
Employment Act (1989) 123
Employment Assistance Programmes (EAPs) 60–1, 65–6
Employment Gazette 129
empowerment 3, 6, 34
environmental: clarity 105, 112; features contributing to mental health 107–9
Equal Opportunities: importance 145–7; legislation 12, 121–6, 146; monitoring 150–1; policy 147–51; policy statement 148; positive action training 149–50; promotion in employment 144–61; training and development 149
Equal Opportunities Commission (EOC) 122, 124–5
equal pay 121–2, 159
Equal Pay Act (1970) 121
Equal Pay (Amendment) Regulations (1983) 121–2
ethical behaviour and individual decisions 178–91
ethical dilemmas 167–8, 184–5; evaluation of 168–70; resolving 188–9
ethics and the law 170–2
ethnic minorities 6, 9, 11–12, 124, 126–8, 145–7
ethnocentrism 130

European Commission 121
European Community (EC) 121, 146
European Court of Justice 124
European Social Chapter 50, 155
exercise 70–1; corporate fitness programmes 73–6
expectancy 93
expectations 93–4; career 85, 86–7; society 175
experiments, Hawthorne studies 25–8
Eysenck, M.W. 38

F Test 133
family friendly policies 154
family life: flexible working practices 153–6; home-work interface stress 7, 50–1, 85; women's dual role 138–40
fatalism 100
Fayol, H. 20
Firestone 178
First World War 21, 23
fitness: corporate programmes 72–6; physical 69
Fletcher, B. 41
Fletcher, C. 80, 82, 85
flexi-time 9, 49
flexibility 3–4, 54, 114
flexible: benefits 193 working practices 153–6
Ford Pinto 167–8, 169, 170, 189
freedom 49
Frew, D.R. 77
Fried, Y. 39
Friedan, B. 155
Friedman, M. 170–1, 175
Friedmann, G. 24
frustration and prejudice 135–6
Fryer, D.M. 103

Gay, P. 127–8
Gebhardt, D. 72
Gellerman, S.W. 180
General Electric Company (GEC) 19
General Foods Corporation 74
Genuine Occupational Qualification (GOQ) 123

Germany, works councils 49
Ghoshal, S. 146
Giber, D. 57
Gilbreth, F.B. 20
glass ceiling 155
goals 94; externally generated 105, 112
Goldthorpe, J.H. 113
Gore, S. 101, 103
green products 172–3
Greenberg, J. 57
Greenpeace 176
groupthink 183–4

Hackman, R. 4
Hakim, C. 128
Halford, A. 125
Halifax building society 152
Hammond, V. 145
Handy, C. 114, 192
hardiness 52
Harrison, R. 141
Harvard Business School 25
Haskell, W.L. 70
Hawthorne studies 19, 23, 24–9, 62
health: care costs 72; mental *see* mental health; promotion programmes 68–9
Herald of Free Enterprise disaster 190
Herriot, P. 34, 79, 80–1, 110, 147
Herzberg, F. 96, 97
Heskett, J. 3
Hewitt, P. 153
hierarchies: management 48–9; organizational 6–7, 111; Rover 111; segregation 9, 129, 141–2
Hirsh, W. 129
Hockey, G.R. 38
Holzbach, R. 72
home-work interface 50–1
home working 152–3
Honda 111
Hoover free flights fiasco 190
hostility, intergroup 130–2
hours of work 9
Howe, Lady 148
Hubbuck, J. 127

Hughes, J.R. 71
Hull, J.G. 52
Human Factor group 23, 24
human growth and development 30–2
Human Relations approach 29–32; employee satisfaction 32, 35; Hawthorne effect 26; human growth and development 30–1; Theory X/Theory Y 29–30
Hutt, R. 86

Ibarra, H. 141
IBM 114
In Search of Excellence 31
incentives 28
Incomes Data Services 159
individual: decisions and ethical behaviour 178–91; differences 51–3; organization and 11; personality and prejudice 132–6; responsibility 173–4, 180–1
Industrial Fatigue Research Board (IFRB) 23
industrial psychology *see* psychology
Industrial Revolution 8, 18
informating 33–4
information technology (IT) 33–5, 194
innovation 4–5, 115, 160
Institute of Management 152, 153, 156
instrumentality 93–4
integrated functioning 98–9
interpersonal contact, opportunity for 106, 113
interviews, Hawthorne studies 26–7

Jackson, C. 129
Jacobson, E. 57
Jahoda, M. 49, 98, 101–3, 108
Janis, I. 183–4
Japanese companies 31–2, 111
Jensen, J.V. 186
job sharing 152, 159
Johnson and Johnson 184–5
Jones, R. 72
Jones, T.M. 165, 166

Kant, I. 168
Kanter, R.M. 91, 115, 193
Katz, D. 137
Kearns, J. 37
Kelly, R.M. 155
Keys, A. 70
Kinder, D.R. 138
Kirmeyer, S.L. 52
Kobasa, S.C. 52
Kohlberg, L. 179
Kohn, J.P. 57
Koopman, A. 110
Korn, L.B. 180
Krolner, B. 71
Krug, R.E. 133
Kumpe, T. 2, 4

La Piere, R. 134
Labour Force surveys 129
Lacey, J.I. 38
law suits 5
Lazarsfeld, P.F. 100
leadership styles 141
'lean' organization 111
learning opportunities 192
leisure age 18
Leiter, M.P. 47
Lever Brothers 19
Levine, P. 39
Listawood Magnetics 154
Locke, E.A. 94
locus of control 95
London, M. 79
London Underground 142
Low Pay Unit 122

McGregor, D. 29–30, 31
Maclagan, P. 185
MacLeod, A.G. 61
MacMahon, B. 70
McNulty, S. 77
Major, J. 158
management: accountability 5, 176,
    189–90; authoritarian 7, 31;
    career 156–7; female managers
    50, 139–41; job design 157;
    leadership styles 141;

participative 31–2; role 194;
    scientific 20–2, 29; stress factors
    42–53
Manne, H. 171
Marshall, J. 42
Martin, J. 141
Maslach, C. 47
Maslow, A.H. 31, 63, 96–7, 105–6
maternity provision 144, 159
matrix organizations 44
Matthews, M.C. 165, 166, 186, 189
Mayo, E. 23, 25, 29
meditation 56, 57
Meechan, K.A. 47
Meldrew, V. 89
menopause, male 48
mental health: components of 91–9;
    impact of unemployment 99–101
mentoring 157
Merton, R.K. 44
Midvale Steel Company 20
Mill, J.S. 168
minority groups see ethnic minorities
money: availability of 106, 112; equal
    pay 121–2, 159; Equal Pay
    legislation 121–2; motivation
    193
monopolies 166
Montanari, J.R. 184
moral: development levels 179;
    maturity 179; responsibility 5–6,
    165–6, 171–3, 176–7, 190
Morehead, G. 183, 184
Morgan, P.P. 74
Morita, Akio 193
Morton Thiokol 182–3, 184, 189
Moss, P. 138–9
motivation 90–1, 193; expectancy
    theory 93; goal theory 94; need
    theories 96–8
motivators 97
Murphy, L.R. 58, 77, 78
Mutrie, N. 71
Myers, C.S. 23, 24
Myers, P. 125

Nader, R. 186
Naoi, A. 32

National Health Service 19, 73
National Institute of Industrial
      Psychology 23
need(s): employee 32–3; hierarchy
      96–6
Nestlé 174, 189, 191
networks 141, 193
Newell, S. 84, 85, 88, 139, 146, 156,
      160
Nicholson, N. 79
Nisan, M. 179
nursery, workplace 154
nutrition 69–70

obesity-related diseases 71
occupational demands 43
Opportunity 2000 148, 150, 154,
      158–60
optimism 52–3, 100
organization culture 157–8
Organizational Behaviour 26, 35
organizational structures: chain of
      command 44; discrimination in
      9; matrix 44; stress factors
      49–50; stress reduction
      initiatives 55, 65–7
organizations in the 1990s 2–6
Oullette-Kobasa, S.C. 47, 52
output rates: Hawthorne studies 25–8;
      Scientific Management 20–2
overheads, reducing 2

Paffenbarger, R.S. 70
Parsons, D. 86
part-time work 128, 153, 154–5
participation in decision-making 50,
      55
paternalism 8
paternity packages 159
pay structures 121–2, *see also* equal
      pay
Payne, R. 41, 58
Payne, R.L., 103
peer group forces 27–8
Pelletier, K. 68
people potential 6–8, 192
Perrier 178
Personal Development Files 112

personality and prejudice 132–6
pessimism 52–3, 100
Peters, T.J. 31, 110
Pettigrew, A. 158
Pleck, J. 88
Podmore, D. 129
police forces 125, 129–30
Policy Studies Institute (PSI) 127
Political and Economic Planning
      (PEP) 126, 127
pollution 5, 12–13, 165–6, 172–3
Port Sunlight 19
Position Analysis Questionnaire 43
positive action training 149–50
positive discrimination 123, 149
Post Office 64–5
potential, use of 145–6
prejudice, racial 130–8; authoritarian
      personality 133–4; cultural
      factors 136–8; frustration and
      135–6
Premark, S.L. 87
progressive relaxation 57
psychology, industrial 23–4
psychometric approach 80, 81
Public Concern at Work 187–8
publicity, adverse 189
Pucetti, S.C. 47, 52

Quaker families 19
quality 2–3
Quality Action Teams 112, 113
Quality of Work Life (QWL) 34–5

Race Relations Acts 124, 127–8
racial: minorities 6, 9, 11–12, 124,
      126–8, 145–7; prejudice 130–8
racism, symbolic 137–8
rational-emotional therapy 58–60, 65
Ray, J. 133
recession 5, 18, 29, 47, 48, 153
Records of Achievement 112
recruitment *see* selection
redundancy 47
regulation: resistance to 175; self-
      190; statutory 190
relationship(s): at work 46–8;
      intergroup hostility 130–2;

networks 193; opportunity for interpersonal contact 106, 113; supportive 64–5; women's networks 141
relaxation training 56–8, 65, 77, 78
reputation, company 5
responsibility: individual 173–4; in work situation 31; social and moral 5–6, 165–6, 171–3, 176–7, 190
responsiveness, proactive 115
retirement 86, 89
Rice, P.L. 57
Riskind, J.H. 43
Robertson, I. 82
Roddick, A. 176–7
Roethlisberger, F.J. 28, 29
Rogers, C. 63–4
Rogers, E. 5
role: ambiguity 45; conflict 43–6; overload 45–6; underload 46
Rose, M. 29
Rosenbaum, J.M. 79
Rosener, J. 141
Rotter, J.B. 95
Rover 110–14; New Deal 113, 192
Rover Employee Assisted Learning Programme (REAL) 111
Rover Learning Business (RLB) 111
Rowntree 19
Royal Bank of Scotland 157

safety issues 5, 165–6, 167–8, 173
Sainsburys 153
Salt, J. 147
satisfaction: theories 97; work and 29–35
Save the Whales 176
Schachter, J. 39
Scheier, M.F. 52, 53
Schein, V.E. 140
Schermerhorn, J.R. 188
Schlesinger, L. 3
Schoder, C. 32
Scientific Management (Taylorism) 20–2, 24, 29, 32
Sears, D.O. 138

security: job 48, 192; physical 106, 113
segregation, vertical and horizontal 9, 129, 141–2
selection and career development 80–1, 119, 144, 156–7
self-concept 63–4
self development 81–2
self-efficacy beliefs 39–40, 92–3
self-esteem 82
self-interest 175, 189
self-regulation 190
sex discrimination 138–41
Sex Discrimination Act (1975) 122–3
Shackleton, V. 84, 146
Shapiro, D.H. 57
Shaw, J.B. 43
Shekelle, R. 70
Shephard, R.J. 73, 75
Shipley, P. 129
shock 100
Shuttle disaster 182–3
Sief, M. 193
Siscovick, D.S. 71
skills: development 6; opportunity for use 6, 105, 111; shortages 5, 145
slavery 131
smoking 173
social: position 107, 113; responsibility 5–6, 165–6, 171–3, 176–7, 190
society: expectations 175; organization and 12–13
Soeken, D.R. 186
Song, T.K. 73
Sony 193; Walkman 4
South Africa 168
Spencer, A. 129
staff reductions 2
Staffordshire University 157
status incongruity 48–9
Staunton, N. 115
Steel, M. 128
stereotypes 136–8, 140–1, 156–8
Stop the Burning Campaign 176
Storey, W.D. 81
stress: arousal 37–9; career development 85–9; exercise

benefits 71; factors 37, 42–53; helping individuals to cope with 55–67; increasing individual resilience to 68–89; job factors associated with 41–2 (Figure 1); management training 77–9; occupational demands 43; overload 7; physiological responses 37–9; psychological responses 39–40; reduction initiatives 56–67; waste of talent 7; work 40–2; work-related causes 42–53
structures, organizational 44
Stumpf, S.A. 79
superwoman syndrome 155
supportive relationship 64–5
Sutherland, E. 181

Taft, B. 71
Taylor, F.W. 19, 20–2, 23, 33, 114
teams, multi-disciplinary 4, 194
teleworking 153
term time only contracts 152
terms and conditions, common 159
textualization 34
Theories X and Y 29–30
Tomlinson, F. 87
Total Quality Improvement (TQI) programme 112
transnational ethical system 180
tribunals, industrial 124
'trip wires' 4
Type A behaviour pattern 51–2

unemployment: fear of 48; impact on mental health 99–101; meaning of work 101–4
United Airlines 61
United Kingdom (UK): career ladder 87; career planning 82; cigarette advertising 173; drug marketing 166; ethnic discrimination 126–8; exercise and fitness 71; Human Factor research 23–4; nineteenth century employers 19; positive discrimination 123, 149; pre-school day care 151; racial discrimination and prejudice 126–8, 132; single European market 146; stress absenteeism 37; Treaty of Rome 121
United States of America (USA): career planning 82; corporate fitness programmes 72, 74–5; management accountability 5; National Highway Traffic Safety Administration 178; positive discrimination 123, 149; racial segregation 132; shuttle disaster 182–3; slavery 131; *see also* Hawthorne, Taylor
utilitarian perspective 168–9, 174

valence 93
variety 105, 112
Velasquez, M. 169
Vinnicombe, S. 141
vitamin model of work 104–9
Vroom, V.H. 93

Wallace, R.K. 56
Wanous, J.P. 87
Warr, P. 81, 86, 91, 92, 98, 104, 107–9
Warwick University 192
Waterman, R.H. 31, 110
Weber, M. 22, 35
well-being, affective 91
Western Electric Company 25, 62
whistle-blowing 186–7
White Collar Crime 181
Whitehead, T.N. 28
Whyte, W. 183
Willet, W.C. 70
Williams, R. 80, 85
Williams, R.S. 82
Wolfe, W. 68
women: child care availability 151–2; discrimination against 11–12, 138–41, 145–6; dual role 138–40; employment 128–30, 151–2; Equal Opportunities legislation 121–6; Equal Pay legislation 121–2; home-work interface stress 50, 85; importance of equal

opportunities 145–7;
independence/dependence 98;
managers 50, 85, 139–41;
maternity provision 144, 159;
networks 141; position in
organizational hierarchy 6, 9; sex
discrimination 138–41; Sex
Discrimination Act 122–3;
stereotypes and attitudes 140–1;
unemployment experiences 103
Word, C.O. 137
work: concept of 17–18; contract 114;
ethic 18; meaning of 101–4;
nineteenth-century 18–19; output
rate 25–8; relationships 46–8;
satisfaction 29–35; stress 40–2;
vitamin model 104–9
workaholic 98
works councils 49–50
workshops: career 83; Rover 113
World Health Organization 174
World Wars *see* First, Second
Wrich, J. 61

yoga 56

Zuboff, S. 7, 33–4, 115, 194